underbelly

Merry Christmas 2010
Dan

More special because
you are here

Love you heaps

Jo

The authors

John Silvester has been a crime reporter in Melbourne since 1978.

He has co-authored many crime books with Andrew Rule, including the *Underbelly* series, *Leadbelly* and *Tough: 101 Australian Gangsters*. In 2007 he was the Graham Perkin Journalist of the Year and Victorian Law Foundation Journalist of the Year.

In 2009 he and Rule co-hosted the compelling and slightly disturbing ABC documentary *Dead Famous*.

He is currently senior crime reporter for *The Age* and is an excellent driver. He is described as a spooky eccentric by people who do not know him.

Andrew Rule is a Walkley award-winning reporter who has worked in newspapers, television and radio since 1975. He wrote *Cuckoo*, the inside story of the 'Mr Stinky' case and has co-written, edited and published too many crime books, including the *Underbelly* series.

Twice Australian journalist of the year, he is a senior writer and deputy editor for *The Age* and a failed racehorse owner.

The authors' work has been adapted into the top-rating *Underbelly* television series.

underbelly

THE GOLDEN MILE

JOHN SILVESTER AND ANDREW RULE

SLY Ink..

Published by Floradale Productions Ltd and Sly Ink Pty Ltd
January 2010

Distributed wholesale by The Scribo Group www.scribo.com.au

Underbelly: The Golden Mile
The events that inspired the Screentime series for the Nine
Network.
ISBN: 978 0 9806971 0 0

Typesetting, layout and design: R.T.J. Klinkhamer
Cover photograph and design: Harry Rekas, harry@large.ac
Image selection and styling: Danie Sprague

. . . .

Corruption is like
a ball of snow:
once set a-rolling,
it must increase.

CHARLES CALEB COLTON, *LACON* **(1825)**

CONTENTS

. . . .

The real king of the Cross
is cash: money sucked from
the pockets and pay packets
of the many who fuel
the black economy of
sex and drugs, then
redistributed to a rich
and powerful few.

1

THE CASH, THE BASH
AND THE GASH

In Sin City the fix was in -
in the boxing ring and betting
ring, at police headquarters
and Parliament House. This was
Australia's underbelly.
And it didn't get any tougher
than the strip they called
the Golden Mile.

IT'S a wonder Christopher Dale Flannery lasted as long as he did. By the time George Freeman found the nerve and the manpower to kill him, the mad dog from Melbourne had already survived a few close shaves.

Not all were as public as the one in January 1985, when he copped bullet wounds in one hand and one ear courtesy of two men in a green car who opened fire near the house he shared with Kath and the kids in Turrella.

Flannery, crazy brave, had jumped a fence and called to Kath to grab him a rifle. It's not easy hitting a hit man once he's been spooked, so the would-be assassins left the scene.

They knew there would be another day.

Not long before, Flannery had fluked another lucky escape – one he might not even have known about.

It was an incident that shows how red hot some Sydney police were running in the 1980s and 1990s. It also confirms the theory that killer cops got rid of Flannery on Freeman's behalf – and that when they did get him, it was not their first attempt.

The story, revealed by an eyewitness to the events described below, goes like this ...

A delegation of bent cops – Sydney's deadliest – made a flying visit south of the border because they'd heard Flannery was visiting his old haunts around Brunswick in inner Melbourne. Kill him back in his hometown, the theory went, and the hit could be blamed on almost anyone, with no blowback north of the Murray. It was a good theory but a dud plan.

The would-be hit squad of rogue detectives made their temporary headquarters at the shady Port Melbourne pub run by the notorious former VFA footballer Fred Cook, a full-forward whose prolific scoring on the field was overshadowed by all the scoring he did off it.

Drugs and sex were Cook's principal vices, which led him to keep bad company. The sort of company that comes with strings attached. So when the Sydney crew arrived late at night and woke Cook and his wife of the moment – he's had a few, between jail stretches – he had to oblige their demands for a full range of the adult entertainment the pub provided.

This ranged from the barely legal – topless barmaids –

to strippers and hookers who weren't fussy about the company they kept, as long as cash and drugs were in the deal.

Not that the coppers would pay for anything, of course. Their motto was 'Crime doesn't pay – and neither do we'. The bill for the girls and the grog was picked up by arch criminal – and police informer – Dennis 'Mr Death' Allen, who kept cash, guns and drugs at the pub as well as at various addresses among the sixteen houses he owned across the river in Richmond.

Just 'looking after' the mysterious visitors that night cost Allen five grand, Cook reckoned later. Allen's willingness to pick up the tab and show the Sydney cops a good time was an interesting connection given Allen's longstanding relationship with a couple of Melbourne cops, one being the corrupt Paul Higgins.

At some stage that night, two of the Sydney cops went to Brunswick. Their information was that Flannery would be at or near a certain address. It seemed too good a chance to miss – but they missed. Whether by dumb luck or intuition or a tip-off, Flannery didn't front that night, and the Sydney guns went back to Port Melbourne with no extra blood on their hands and consoled themselves by partying the night away. No expense spared – because they weren't paying.

Fate, of course, in the form of George Freeman, would catch up with Flannery back in Sydney. And the dogs were barking that a couple of the same bent cops that visited Melbourne that night were among the last to see him alive.

That's how it went in the 1980s. For a while there, gangster money could buy police easier than it could fix a boxing match. Anybody that didn't know that could ask Barry Michael.

BARRY 'Boy' Michael was good-looking for a fighter until the night Alphonse Gangitano bit a hole in his cheek and smashed his nose flat with a glass ashtray while hoodlums held him down.

Michael was maybe the toughest white lightweight boxer of his time and confident with it. But he should have known better than to sit down with his back to the traffic in a nightclub where the gangsters hung out.

One consolation for him, later, was that Gangitano needed a crew of goons to do the damage. The other was that no one shot him, which was his first thought when they turned on him.

Michael had fought hundreds of rounds in the ring in half a dozen countries and had punched his way out of street fights and pub brawls. He'd survived three of the great ring 'wars' of Australian boxing in the 1980s. But that night was the nearest he came to death – and disfigurement.

He didn't see the trouble coming. Truth was, it had been festering ever since the night he won the International Boxing Federation (IBF) junior-lightweight title from Lester Ellis two years earlier, in 1985.

The bashing was revenge, a sickeningly violent postscript to one of the greatest (and most brutal) title fights in Australian sports history. Michael had won it when the Carlton crew wanted him to lose and they were bad losers.

Michael – too old and supposedly too heavy to make the weight safely – had pulled off an audacious heist to lift Ellis's new world title in one of the last fifteen-round fights ever held.

Age and cunning, in the form of 30-year-old Michael, had upset public sentiment – and the betting – by weathering and then wearing down the murderous attack of the champion, who was ten years younger.

Barry Michael was one of the most intelligent pro boxers in the business – not just cool under fire but cocky with it. He talked to Ellis right through the fifteen rounds, goading him into wasting his energy so the younger man would try to hurt him instead of boxing clever.

It was risky – a version of Ali's legendary 'rope-a-dope' strategy to undermine the stronger and younger George Foreman in Zaire. Michael took the biggest shots in Ellis's armoury and, ignoring his broken nose and the blood on the canvas and all over the referee's shirt, somehow persuaded Ellis none of it really hurt him.

'That all you can do, Lester?' he said in one clinch. 'That wouldn't hurt my sister.'

The crowd of 10,000 had booed Michael – the old villain of the piece – and cheered the young 'Master Blaster' from Sunshine. Most bet accordingly – including unhappy gangsters in the Gangitano camp, closely connected with promoting the fight.

Michael had called Gangitano weeks earlier to tell him he'd made the weight limit at his training camp without losing the strength to go fifteen rounds, and advised him not to bet against him.

It was the truth but maybe it had sounded to Gangitano like pre-fight tactics to rattle the Ellis camp. In the event, Gangitano's people had ignored the tip and bet heavily on Ellis. The Carlton crew had big plans for the kid and none of them involved Michael, who was aligned with the painters and dockers through veteran fight trainer Leo Berry and waterfront identity 'Spider' Holman.

But the fight unfolded according to Michael's plan – not Gangitano's. With each fighter aligned to opposing underworld camps, the unexpected result would inevitably cause tension. Pride and money were at stake. Gangitano had lost both, and it would fester.

The ideal outcome for the Carlton crew was that Ellis would get away with a crowd-pleasing win to beef up his record – and prospects of more title fights, big gate money and the chance of sponsorships and television rights that come with a championship belt.

Betting on certainties is as close as most gangsters get to a religion but cheeky Barry Michael, born Barry Swettenham, had torn up the script.

Losing money and face was a poisonous mixture but Gangitano hid it fairly well until the night Jeff Fenech beat Tony Miller in early 1987. After the fight Michael had agreed to meet Gangitano at Lazar's nightclub, a big bluestone pile on King Street, heart of the nightclub strip. By the time Michael and his mate and wife got there, it was hours after midnight, a time when only bad things happen. The wannabe 'Godfather' was waiting with his crew.

They shook hands and discussed their grievances: Michael wanted money and Gangitano a re-match to promote. Michael, sitting on a couch with Gangitano, had his back to the other gangsters. Suddenly, his wife screamed a warning: they had king hit Barry's friend Simon and knocked him out.

Michael snapped his head around and saw the bouncers carrying Simon out. 'I thought I was off,' he would tell the authors later, meaning he expected to be shot. He turned to Gangitano and yelled, 'You rat, you set me up.'

Gangitano grabbed him and bit his face. Michael gouged the big man's eyes, trying to make him let go. The hoods all grabbed him, and he went down in a blur of savage punches, kicks and bites.

The bouncers were wary because they knew the gangsters were armed but they stopped the beating turning into murder, yelling, 'He's had enough!'. When they dragged the boxer out of the crush, his nose was under his left eye, his cheek was torn open and he was gouting blood.

But he could still think. 'Take me to St Vincents,' he said, 'and let them think they've had a win.' It was a smart move. He knew he would be safe from a follow-up attack in hospital.

Later, a bouncer told Michael he'd kicked a pistol away from one of the hoods. He will never know if they'd planned to kill him – or whether Gangitano was clawing back some face to boost his reputation as a standover man.

Big Al would find out a decade later, after doing it again in another King Street bar, that his psycho routine could be fatal. The legal fallout from that bar room bashing led to his execution by his ally Jason Moran – making Gangitano an early casualty in what would become known as the Gangland War. That war, of course, would be fought in a glare of publicity that reached a crescendo when Moran and a mate were gunned down at a junior football game in 2003.

But in the time between Barry Michael's bashing and Gangitano's murder in 1998, there had been plenty going on, too – it's just that most of it wasn't making it to the front page or the evening news. And it wasn't all in Melbourne.

When it came to money, the biggest rackets were in Sydney, where the lines between the underworld and the everyday world were more blurred. In Sin City the fix was in – not just in the boxing ring and betting ring but at police headquarters and Parliament House.

This was Australia's underbelly. And it didn't get any tougher than in Kings Cross, on the strip they called the Golden Mile.

THE cops who work the Cross have always taken a perverse pride in their beat. For years, Kings Cross detectives have had their own tie and cufflink motif – a crude hybrid of a syringe, dagger and pistol under the letters 'KX'.

It looks like something knocked up by one of the several tattooists whose parlours do a roaring trade just up the street from the police station.

One thing is sure, if a local tattoo parlour did it, the price would be right. They know how to look after the law at the Cross. It's been that way since the heyday of the razor gangs, sly groggers, two-up schools and SP bookmakers who flourished there between the world wars.

A good place for a cop to get a cold drink or a hot steak in the 1980s and 1990s was the Bourbon and Beefsteak, known as the 'Bourbon' and still a Kings Cross landmark. The three-storey white wedding cake of a building is part of the scenery, like the giant Coca Cola sign sitting above the intersection of Darlinghurst Road and William Street, the hardened arteries in the heart of the Cross.

The Coca Cola sign, the Bourbon, the Texas Tavern and other garish Americana reflect the Cross's history as

8

the place US soldiers flocked to spend their pay on R & R leave. Half a lifetime after the Vietnam War ended, the legacy of R & R lives on in the Cross's free-for-all street market in sex and drugs.

The Bourbon might have been redecorated since the fall of Saigon but the decor was never the secret of its drawing power. Sydney criminal lawyer Charles Waterstreet says its main appeal 'in the old days' was that it was one of few places that stayed open all night.

'That was what it had going for it. It was all red, with mood lighting and smoky, a sort of Land's End full of people who had kicked on from somewhere else,' says Waterstreet.

People have flocked to the Cross after dark for decades, like moths to a lamp. Some visit for a few hours. Others return too often or stay too long for their own good. Some die there.

Dirty money has always been milked from the Cross, from the oldest profession and its near relatives. Faces and names change but the rackets don't.

Once, Abe Saffron was called 'King of the Cross' for good reason. There have been pretenders since, like the Bayehs and the Ibrahims, but the real king is cash: money sucked from the pockets and pay packets of the many who fuel the black economy of sex and drugs, then redistributed to a rich and powerful few.

Cash greases the wheels of corruption and for too long it reached the highest levels in Sydney. It flows uphill, seeping up from the streets to reach premiers, police chiefs and public servants, prosecutors and judges.

None of this could have flourished without people in high places turning a blind eye to police who were conniving, complicit or compromised by bribery, blackmail and protection.

Bent cops profited from protecting rackets in the streets where they were supposed to uphold the law. Others felt powerless to do anything about it.

They could tell themselves it didn't matter – that police were above the law, that the street people were below it and that what the rest of society didn't know wouldn't hurt it.

But they were wrong. Crime and corruption can touch anyone.

SHE was a judge's daughter but that didn't matter on the street. At the Cross, she was just another piece of meat in a market where everything had a price, in cash or powder.

As a teenager, she would stuff her private school uniform in a bag, pull on jeans and tee shirt and hang out in Darlinghurst Road.

It wasn't enough for her to play the tourist, to rubberneck at the needy, the greedy and the desperate in the Golden Mile, to smoke cigarettes and sip cappuccinos in dingy cafes before going home to dawdle through her homework.

This one had the self-destructive gene, the deadly blend of boredom, loneliness and thrill-seeking that the human vultures smell. The street hookers could have warned her to stay away but that wouldn't have stopped her. By the time she left school she'd met people in the clubs who got her into drugs because they 'liked' her. Soon she was shooting up heroin.

Even before she was really hooked on the gear she was hooked on the sick thrill of it, the guilty secret of chasing, of being a member of the fraternity of users.

When she ran out of ways to stretch her pocket money – to beg, borrow and steal from family and friends – she started hooking to support her habit: blowing gutter crawlers in cars and back streets, shucking up her mini-skirt to score money for the next hit. She worked mostly from a car park behind a service station.

Ask Chris Murphy, the standout criminal lawyer, about the Cross and this is the story he tells. He doesn't dredge up war stories about all the gangsters he's known over the years, although he easily could. He knows most of them and has acted for plenty. He's good at it.

Instead, he talks about the judge's daughter because he knew her and her father and because her story is the real story of the Cross: underneath the night-time glitz it's about as romantic as a road crash and just as dangerous.

For Murphy, hers was a tragedy that sums up the fatal attraction of the street life. He tells how he arranged for the girl to go to a friend's island off the Queensland coast to get her away from the scene, to dry out and start again, far from the sordid seductiveness of the street's predators and scavengers.

'But when it came to it, she wouldn't go,' he says. 'Two days later she was back there, in her high heels. The heroin was too good. The life just too exciting. Everything else too boring by comparison. That's why they can't give it up until it's too late.'

If Murphy knows what happened to the judge's daughter later, he doesn't give it away. But if she ended up dead, or wrecked, she would be only one of hundreds of victims washed up on the Golden Mile, addicted to the thing that will kill or crush them.

Just another story from the naked city. There were plenty more – but not many happy endings.

EVEN other bad men didn't like Jimmy Locchi. Some crooks called him the 'Loch Ness monster' – not because he was tough but because he was a nasty piece of work. 'Slimy and grubby, a bully and a big noter,' was how a former policeman describes him.

A contemporary of the infamous crim Neddie Smith, Locchi ran street prostitutes in Kings Cross and paid the women in heroin. This was convenient, as he was also a heroin dealer. He was also a sadistic rapist.

'He would abduct women and gang bang them in motels,' says the former policeman. Abduction and rape was his idea of entertainment. In business he was predictably ruthless – and surprisingly innovative.

He set up a system that became known around the Cross in the 1980s as 'Locchi's window'. It wasn't always the same window – sometimes he had two going at once – but the same trick.

He would rent a run-down ground floor apartment from a compliant landlord, fit bars on the windows and door and a buzzer intercom system so anyone at the building's entrance could talk to the flat's occupants without seeing them.

A buyer would ring the buzzer, order drugs, go to the barred window, poke the money in and get the drugs out the same way. It was highly secure, centralised marketing – and it made it hard for undercover police (or marauding criminals doing a 'run through') to get into the flat or identify the people handling the heroin. The iron bars made raids slow, and meant there was enough time for the occupants to get rid of evidence.

Locchi recruited a roster of clapped-out hookers, preferably addicts, to staff the place, earning more cash in relative safety and comfort than they could on the street. Many would work for a regular 'taste' of heroin and were willing to hide the drug inside their bodies, making them difficult to search. And they were easy for him to stand over, too frightened to steal money or drugs.

The success of 'Locchi's window' of course, relied partly on Kings Cross police keeping a polite distance. In that time and place, that was almost a foregone conclusion. Even honest cops talked about 'managing' crime rather than the impossible dream of wiping it out. The upshot was that neither the local police nor the drug squad seemed concerned that Locchi was selling drugs in a street behind the Coca Cola sign, close to the then brand new police station.

This apparent immunity infuriated a task force operating independently of the Kings Cross network. This was Operation Hobby, run by the New South Wales Crime Commission. Their idea was to catch crooks, a novelty in a district where crime had been franchised for decades.

The Hobby investigators set up in a flat about 100 metres from Locchi's window. The idea was to film undercover buyers to gather enough evidence to make arrests.

But there was a problem: a tree in the footpath obscured the view of the window. They either had to move position, which was nearly impossible, or move the tree. A detective called Mick Kennedy volunteered to move the tree. He had a chainsaw and a utility. At dawn one summer morning he swapped number plates on the utility in case someone noted the registration and reported him, parked around the corner and approached the tree with the chainsaw.

It had been a warm night and the street was crawling with people, so there was no chance of doing the deed unseen. So he decided to be as public as possible.

There were plenty of eccentric, drugged or deranged people wandering Kings Cross, ignored or avoided by other pedestrians. He pretended to be one of them.

'I behaved like a mad bloke and had an argument with the tree,' Kennedy recalls. 'I shook my fist at the tree and said "I'll show you!" then grabbed the chainsaw and cut it down.'

Being Kings Cross, everyone minded their own business. Not even keen Greens argue with lunatics with chainsaws.

The operation was a success. The investigators were able to film an undercover operative buying drugs at the window, then break into the fortified apartment.

Inside, they found retired prostitutes handling the heroin for Locchi. One was willing to testify against him after being reassured that he would get a hefty jail sentence.

'He pays well but he's dangerous,' she told the detectives.

She explained why she and others hated the man who supplied her with money and drugs. He carried a cordless electric drill so when he caught a prostitute who owed him money he would drill her knee – or her skull – as a warning.

It was DIY, Kings Cross style. But in the end, a chainsaw beats a cordless drill.

2

TEFLON JOHN, THE NEW KING

```
'He'll end up wearing the
bracelets or a bullet.'
```

TO hear John Housain Ibrahim tell it, he's never lost a fight. That's a good thing around Kings Cross because anyone who loses fights there doesn't get much back up. 'Loyalty' in the Golden Mile is for winners only – and there's usually a price tag attached.

Ibrahim learned to fight early in life – but he also learned something even more valuable. That is, when not to fight.

An example that seems to have slipped his mind is when a tough Melbourne gunman (and ex-boxer) called Tony Brizzi came calling on a club the young Ibrahim was running in Kings Cross in the early 1990s. Brizzi was the 'muscle' for one Bill A., who wanted to negotiate taking over the club. As soon as they stepped into the room with Ibrahim, Brizzi pistol-whipped him and told him to quit the club, because Bill was taking it. Even Bill was surprised by this. Ibrahim said he was going to complain about the hostile takeover bid to his friend, a senior police officer he named.

Brizzi knocked him down again for impertinence, took his wallet and emptied the till. He said he was disgusted with both of them for even considering bringing police into a man-on-man confrontation.

But before he left he warned Ibrahim: 'You come near me and I'll kill you. I'm from Melbourne and we don't shoot below the knee caps.'

Ibrahim got the message. Brizzi would eventually die of lupus but he never lost a minute's sleep over flogging someone he called a 'little Arab upstart'.

Ibrahim, the second child of poor Lebanese Muslim immigrants from the port city of Tripoli, was never going to have it easy. And he was never going to stand by while others took the lion's share of the world's riches. But whereas too many of his contemporaries – including his older brother 'Sam' – relied only on violence to get their way, John had other tricks as well.

He has not only punched but charmed, beguiled and traded his way to the top of Sydney's nightclub scene. As an entrepreneur he is a little like a riverboat gambler – behind the poker player's calm gaze and ready joke is the lingering suggestion he is quick on the draw when the chips are down. In fact, Ibrahim has negligible convictions for violence or anything else, but implied menace is a tool of his trade. Whatever that trade is, exactly. All that can be said with certainty is that it must be highly profitable.

In an underworld full of Armani-clad gorillas fuelled by drugs, ego and stupidity in equal measure, Ibrahim stands out because of his tenacity and ability to roll with the punches, qualities that have helped him survive a quarter-century in a notoriously rough game.

He can also lay claim to being, perhaps, the subject of the most surveillance and monitoring in the history of Australia. He claims that more than a thousand intelligence reports have been written about him by nearly every law-enforcement body in the country. But at the same time he denies the picture painted of him by law enforcement and the media, describing his reputation as a criminal overlord as hyperbole, myth and rumour-mongering.

Undisputed, however, is that the nightclub entrepreneur and property developer has been involved with some of the highest-profile crime figures in Australia. In the Cross, that goes with the territory.

He was once a driver and errand boy for the Kings Cross drug baron turned convict, Bill Bayeh, and is often seen with the sons of Sydney's infamous illegal bookmaking and race-fixing king, the late and mostly unlamented George Freeman. Ibrahim often says he was a bodyguard and driver for Freeman senior – although, given he was barely out of his teens when Freeman died of an asthma attack in 1990, that claim might be one of his trademark exaggerations.

Like many before him, the narcissistic Ibrahim is not one to let facts stand in the way of a good story – especially one that adds to the mystique that helps him stay at the top of the pile in a dangerously fickle business. Besides, the more mud he can throw in the pool, the harder it is for others to see the bottom. But he is at pains to ensure that his reputation as a businessman is kept separate from his brothers' penchant for crime.

The official line runs like this. John Ibrahim is a night-club promoter, entrepreneur and 'consultant' who works with seventeen (some say more) clubs in Kings Cross and Darlinghurst, and owns multimillion-dollar properties in Sydney's eastern suburbs.

According to his lawyer, Stephen Alexander, Ibrahim's reputation as a 'criminal mastermind' is undeserved – the result of rumour and innuendo.

John always says, "Either I'm the smartest criminal out there, or I just run a legitimate business and people want to fantasise",' Alexander told the *Sydney Morning Herald's* ace crime reporter Dylan Welch in January 2009.

'Go back to the many hundreds of police intelligence reports that do not even substantiate one iota of any allegation. All you've got is an illogical quantum leap. Everyone tries to assume that it's XYZ ... but [where's the] evidence?'

The hundreds of police reports, intelligence briefs and secret strike forces are nothing more than the proof of a police obsession with him, he said. 'At the end of the day it's just rumour and innuendo, because if you don't have a colourful character to have a go at, well, it's not going to be the Cross.'

But police don't buy his line and, in these enlightened days, they say that the kings of the Cross can no longer buy them, which makes a change after the corruption entrenched there for most of the 20th century.

In February 2009 the latest 'Ibrahim unit' was launched, named Strike Force Bellwood. Officially, its job is to 'to investigate alleged criminal activity involving a Middle Eastern criminal group.' But the twenty-odd detectives staffing the strike force know exactly what their job is – to bring down the Ibrahim family – especially John.

'The accused is a major organised-crime figure, the subject of 546 police intelligence reports in relation to his involvement in drugs, organised crime and associations with outlaw motorcycle gangs,' states a police allegation contained in court documents tendered during a 2005 trial.

'He has previously been investigated for intimidation, extortion and organised crime. He was also the subject of a similar investigation by the Wood Police Royal Commission.'

To be fair, Ibrahim's official criminal record hardly exists. The only crime he has ever been convicted of was assault for hitting another teenager when he was fifteen. As an adult he has been charged with manslaughter and witness tampering, but both charges were thrown out of court before trial.

Another indicator of Ibrahim's success is the large sums of money that seem to emerge in unexpected places. In mid-2009 around $3 million cash was found in the kitchen roof of a house belonging to John's sister, Maha Sayour. While the late crime boss Lennie McPherson boasted that his undeclared nightclub earnings gave him the title 'Mr 10 Per Cent', Ibrahim has been known to call himself 'Mr 50 Per Cent'. That's progress.

But fame has come with a price, and by 2009 Ibrahim

and his family were taking hit after hit in the media and on the streets. His lawyer, Stephen Alexander, has said that while John loves his brothers, he isn't involved in their criminal acts. But 2009 was a year of living dangerously for the Ibrahims and saw the nightclub king inevitably linked with the sins of his brothers.

Whether he deserved it or not, he got a reputation as a gangster because his brothers have never been able to balance the tightrope between legitimacy and their inclination to associate with controversial alleged crime figures.

In October 2004 Ibrahim was secretly taped by an associate, Roy Malouf, at the urging of police investigating John's youngest brother, Mick. While the resultant charge – witness tampering – was dismissed in the Supreme Court, it revealed John's view of 'family business'.

'I've never done any crime. I don't have a criminal record,' he railed to Malouf. 'It's all my fucking – my brothers' fuck-up. They think they are all working for me. [Police] think my brothers, Sam and Michael, work for me. Work that one out. And I know they're fucking lunatics. I can't control them.'

Evidence of John's lack of control over his brothers was provided in abundance by the events of June to September 2009. On 5 June, John's younger brother Fadi, 35, was shot five times as he sat in a Lamborghini outside his multi-million dollar home in Sydney's exclusive northern suburbs. He survived, but lost most of his stomach.

When police investigated the shooting, several suspects emerged. But inquiries were hampered by the refusal of Fadi and his brothers, including John, to be interviewed.

As Fadi lay in the intensive care unit of the Royal North Shore hospital, John's lawyer, the tireless Alexander, turned up to make a brief statement.

'My client's sole concern is for the welfare of his beloved brother Fadi,' Alexander said. 'My client wishes to dispel any speculation that there will be retaliation by, or on behalf of, the Ibrahim family ... My client has absolute faith in the police investigation and is confident that the police will bring the perpetrators to justice.'

Unfortunately, it seemed Fadi did not agree with his brother's pacifist views. In late September 2009 officers from the Middle Eastern Organised Crime Squad suddenly arrested Fadi, the youngest Ibrahim brother Mick and three other men allegedly plotting to kill a man they suspected of being behind shooting Fadi – and putting blood and bullet holes in a perfectly good Lamborghini.

It is hard to get the smell of blood out of the upholstery and some believe it can cause rust.

In an exclusive interview, this time not with Dylan Welch, John Ibrahim confided to the media that he was sick of media and police scrutiny and wanted to slip back into the shadows to run his businesses.

Ibrahim also said he had lost $50,000 in a friendly bet with his young mates, George Freeman's pretty-boy sons Adam and David.

In the interview, 'a relaxed and at times jovial' Ibrahim candidly admitted he hated the attention.

'Dressed in a black, military-style jacket and a dark, low-cut T-shirt, a smiling Ibrahim' told *The Sunday Telegraph* reporter: "I don't need it ... I need to keep a bit of a shadow on me at the moment".'

The reporter was speaking to him at the launch of a Kings Cross club called Lady Lux, where he'd made a rare public appearance without Tongan Sam.

The club had reportedly undergone an $800,000 makeover funded by Ibrahim's 'proteges' the Freeman brothers. 'Ibrahim has been a father figure to both since their dad died in 1990 and was happy to help relaunch the club,' the paper said.

'Although Ibrahim spoke freely and posed for pictures with the Freeman brothers and their mother Georgina, he was guarded about the ongoing war that has engulfed his family.

'He stuck to his line that it had brought unwanted attention.

'He said he was making a concerted effort to stay out of the spotlight for the good of the family and, presumably, his business interests. Smiling, Ibrahim said he didn't like the publicity but accepted it was beyond his control. He said: "I don't even need to say anything and you guys will put me in the paper."

'He also laughed at reports during the week that he would write an autobiography.

' "Today was the first I've heard about it," he said in reference to the media reporting of the claim. "But I've had calls and offers from four book publishers today. And *60 Minutes* called."

'He smiled again and offered no response when asked if he had accepted any of the offers.'

It was all part of Ibrahim's public relations offensive. He told the *Sydney Morning Herald*: 'I didn't shoot my way to the top, I charmed my way there.'

In public, he relies on his charisma, his apparent humorous disregard for the world around him, and his ability to attract beautiful women. He's been doing it for years.

When *Daily Telegraph* journalist Kate de Brito interviewed him several months after his appearance at the Wood Royal Commission in 1995, she clearly found him engaging.

'Tanned, fit and small in stature, John has full lips, sleepy eyes and a subtly engaging persona. When he speaks, people listen,' she gushed. A well-known Lothario around Sydney's nightclubs, John has escorted a steady stream of beautiful young blondes. He is rumoured to have a live-in hairdresser to maintain his styled and streaked hair, and his gleaming white teeth and gym-toned physique appearance testifies his love of self.

He has also featured heavily in the social pages of Sydney papers.

Not content with being a backroom businessman, he has, since 2008, been photographed with Paris Hilton, her oil-heir boyfriend Brandon Davis, a recent 'Miss Mexico', Georgio Armani, and the showbiz sisters Cheyne and Tahnya Tozzi.

Those close to Ibrahim say he has spent two years doing his best to 'whitewash' his past; to reinvent himself as a legitimate, if not respectable, businessman.

He has always had an extraordinary self-regard, which is not unusual in gangster circles. But he is more articulate than most – or gets good help – as can be seen in a quote he gave, aged just 21, to a book called *People of the Cross*:

'Society conditions you from the minute you go to school to be a good citizen, work and keep quiet. You live out your life, pay all your debts to the government, and you really haven't enjoyed any of it. It's the people who don't listen to that, the ones that break away, who let their minds grow, who end up getting somewhere. I still live in about four different worlds, but I think my time is still coming.'

Maybe it still is. But, as an observer of the Sydney underworld scene told the authors off the record: 'He'll end up wearing the bracelets or a bullet.'

AS the second of the Ibrahim children, John was the first of them born in Australia, shortly after his parents, Wahib and Wahiba, moved from Lebanon in the late 1960s. The eldest of the six children, the former bikie Hassan 'Sam', was born in Tripoli five years earlier.

When the children were young, Wahib was largely absent from the family home in Merrylands, near Parramatta in Sydney's west, and Wahiba, a traditional Muslim woman, had little to do with the boys' life outside home.

An absent father and timid mother left Johnny, as he was known for the first two decades of his life, the freedom to hang around with Sam – as a teenager already developing a reputation as muscle-for-hire at strip clubs and night spots – and Sam's friends.

In *People of the Cross*, John described his beginnings with the Sydney nightclub scene, when the then sixteeen-year-old Sam started working as a bouncer at a Parramatta strip club.

'He thought it was magic,' John wrote. 'I just followed in his footsteps, learning martial arts from the age of nine until I was fifteen. My brother and I aren't exactly bouncer material – we're not tall – so learning how to defend myself was definitely a plus.

' ... When I was fourteen I used to have my own little group I moved with and we'd always end up in the Cross, even though we lived out west near Parramatta. We'd come up here at least five nights a week for the bright lights and night life. We liked to think that we were Sam's back-up. He used to think of us as little pains in the arse.'

But John and Sam were hugely different people, even back then. Sam was a heavy puncher rather than a heavy thinker and would hit first and ask questions later, if ever. But John had the intelligence to realise that at least a bit of learning would go a long way.

'Most days I'd go to school. I used to avoid it as much as possible – roll up late all the time. School wasn't for me. It's just buying time 'til you're mature enough to get out and work. All I needed was to learn how to read and write and multiply. I'd come to the Cross and they'd teach me something completely different. I had a few teachers that hated me with a passion. They'd constantly throw me out of the classroom because I couldn't agree with anything they said. The principal made the best sort of prediction. He said I had three options – I'd be a very wealthy man, or I'd be in gaol, or dead.'

John left school the moment he got his School Certificate at the age of fifteen. He took a job as a bricklayer but chucked it in within six months.

While he still lived at home, his life seemed to be re-volving around Kings Cross more and more. That was un-doubtedly because, while John was still at school, Sam had begun to work for the Bayeh brothers, Bill and Louie.

In the 1980 and 1990s the Bayehs, Bill in particular, were big players in the Cross. During the Wood Royal Commiss-ion, Bill Bayeh was exposed as a major heroin and cocaine dealer. He was charged in 1996 and later sentenced to a long prison sentence.

But in the late 1980s, Bayeh was at the top of his game, and when Sam started working for him, the Ibrahim broth-ers were drawn into the heart of Sydney's organised drug distribution scene.

Sam was later to describe his role in the Cross at the time as an enforcer for drug dealers like Bayeh. He said he had known the Bayehs since he was a child.

'My job was if there was any trouble in there, someone was causing trouble, the boys were to call me. I would have to come in and stop the trouble,' Sam told the Royal Com-mission. He did not specify what 'trouble; was but it was unlikely to be helping old ladies cross the street.

It was through the Bayeh association that John became involved in the illicit networks at the Cross. In his book, he described how if he and his friends were ever short of money, they would go there.

'My brother's boss (Bayeh) would slip me a fifty or a hundred, give me a pat on the head and tell me to go and do whatever I wanted.' While Bayeh's 'charity' might seem generous, it paid off a year later, when John's loyalty saw him almost killed while protecting the older man.

Bayeh was on the Darlinghurst Road strip, on his own, and was being harassed by two men. John, then a month shy of his sixteenth birthday, came to his rescue and received life-threatening stab wounds as a result. It was this near-death experience that set John on a path that today sees him hailed as the latest King of the Cross.

Ibrahim recalls the incident like this: 'Two men were harassing him (Bill Bayeh) and I sort of came to his rescue. I hit one man so he couldn't do any more damage, then broke up the other two who were still fighting. The guy that I was helping ran off. I had this other guy pinned up against the wall. I didn't want to hit him because it would have been too easy, and I think he just acted out of reflex. He had a kitchen knife wrapped up in newspaper behind his back, and suddenly he just stuck me with the knife.'

Though it left him with a punctured lung and hundreds of stitches, the stabbing was the making of John Ibrahim. He spent six months in hospital, but when he came out he was suddenly a player.

'Getting stabbed certainly changed things … the person I'd helped (Bayeh) gave me opportunities. People liked having me around, they knew I'd always be there for them. They figured I had brains.'

Describing himself as a 'kept man', he said he and his friends were soon reaping the benefits of being 'in' with the Kings Cross criminal underworld.

'Wherever we went – in the coffee shops, the clubs, the discos – we'd get everything we wanted because of our association with certain people. At sixteen that was a big thrill.'

But over the next three years John began to see that being a gofer for the Cross crooks wasn't what he wanted for himself.

'If someone said, "Look, we'll be there for you – you can count us," that was good enough for me. But I came to know that it was all make-believe; that if the time and politics didn't suit them, they wouldn't be there, no matter what favours you'd done for them. I was getting burnt by all the conniving and lies and it started chipping away at me, a little bit at a time. I began to think, "This is ridiculous. These people aren't so magic. They're thugs and they're using me as their bat, that's all".'

True to John's reputation for foresight, he began to realise that life as Bill Bayeh's bodyguard wasn't going to bring him the success he yearned for. Bayeh was an illiterate, violent man who, despite being the head of a large drug syndicate, was eventually caught 'bagging' his own drug deals. John knew he wouldn't be around forever, and started eyeing off his own piece of the pie.

He got his security licence, created a company and made nice with a Surfer's Paradise nightclub owner. 'I liked him because he was his own man, a person I could learn from. On a holiday up at Surfers we looked him up and, after sorting out a blue outside his club, we got to talking. I suggested opening a nightclub in the Cross. He'd always wanted to but he was cautious because he didn't know the right people. I did, so we decided to go into partnership.'

At the age of nineteen, John borrowed $70,000 from a friend and bought a stake in a nightclub on Earl Place, in one of the seedy side alleys off the 'Darlo' strip. It was called Tunnel Cabaret. John signed onto the books in mid-1990, a month before his twentieth birthday, and is unofficially recognised as the joint's owner even today, despite removing himself from the club's books in 2001.

That club, which has since changed name three times – to Silva, EP1 and finally Dragonfly – remains the headquarters of the John Ibrahim clique, and on any given Saturday you can find John on the door or inside, mixing with his current crop of bad boys.

Some of the 'boys' have been by his side since the early days. Semi Pouvalu Ngata – better known as Tongan Sam, Uncle Sam or Sam the Taxman – has been the Ibrahim family's minder-in-chief for the better part of two decades. One of the most feared men in the Cross, Tongan Sam is known for his gangster look. He's not hard to pick – although only a fool would pick him. Men like Tongan Sam pre-date metric measure: he's a 'six-foot four' islander with a long black mullet and wears a black trench coat that makes people nervous. The close relationship between Tongan Sam and the Ibrahims is such that his son, Nimilote 'Nim' Ngata, has even begun to work for the family, as an apprentice standover man and bodyguard. Job security in a security job – all in the family.

Other well-known Ibrahim family hangers-on include Mehmet 'Turkish Mick' Gulasi; 'Big Fadi' Khalifeh; the current licensee and part-owner of Dragonfly, David Auld; David 'Samoan Dave' Lima; Alen Sarkis. And, of course, the photogenic sons of the deceased colourful Sydney identity George Freeman, David and Adam.

All can be seen at Dragonfly. Anyone wanting to speak to Ibrahim has to walk past at least one of these men. The club has been shut down on occasion since he became boss, and some new plaster and paint has disguised the night in 1999 when the club was sprayed with bullets.

In 2001, following a series of well-publicised raids, police applied to have the club shut down, alleging it was part of a well-organised drug trade in the Cross.

The people on the club's books at the time challenged the action and the closure application was thrown out of court, the drug dealing allegations never proven.

TWO men who haunt the back corners of Dragonfly, 'Samoan Dave' Lima and Alen Sarkis, have been key players in a new group linked to the Ibrahim brothers. This is the crime gang Notorious, which became a notorious crime gang after being just a little infamous.

Formed by the youngest Ibrahim brother Mick in 2007, the gang was originally a street gang known as the Notorious Scorpions. When Michael was jailed over the manslaughter of the brother of an Australian comedian and actor, George (Fat Pizza) Nassour, the group morphed into a well-organised band of crooks resembling a bikie gang with an image consultant.

With Sarkis, a former drag racer and chicken shop owner, as the putative 'President' and Lima as the sergeant-at-arms, the group began to push and shove to justify its name. It finally hit the police radar in mid-2008 during raids on city nightclubs linked with the Ibrahims.

Then, in mid-2008, residents of a quiet, affluent estate on Sydney's North Shore were woken by a bomb going off.

The bomb exploded under a late model black Jeep Cherokee owned by Sarkis, who had been living at the Lane Cove North Estate.

While the bomb didn't do much damage, it threw the spotlight on the gang, and marked the beginning of a six-month period of drive-by shootings and violence. Houses were shot at, young men were gunned down in dark places. It had taken time and effort but Notorious was now truly notorious, a name muttered among crooks and cops alike. Of course, the gang members immediately said they didn't like it.

In March 2009 Sarkis spoke to the Sydney newspapers to correct what he said were a series of misapprehensions.

'We don't want to be portrayed to the public as we've been. We want to be acknowledged and respected as a motorcycle club, not as gangsters. We're a group of like-minded friends that formed as a motorcycle club not to be dictated to by the other clubs – that's all we are,' he said.

He said the frustrations of police and other motorcycle clubs about Notorious were simply because the club represented the 'new age' of bikies.

'Australia has been used to the clubs that have been around for a while and the appearance of a new club has maybe been taken as a threat to them.' The only threat Notorious posed, Sarkis said, was to the fashion sense of the traditional bikie clubs.

'We ride bikes but we dress well, we shave and we train. If that's a problem, I apologise. If you want us all to be overweight and bearded – sorry, it's not going to happen.'

Since that meeting, and perhaps as a result of the New South Wales police's crackdown on the outlaw clubs,

Notorious has evaporated, with not a single sighting of their 'colours', even on a Vespa in Paddington. Samoan Dave is still an important part of the Ibrahim family inner circle of guards but Sarkis has all but vanished.

Well before Notorious, the Ibrahim clan had a much bigger and meaner gang on their side – the Nomads Motorcycle Club. The second biggest outlaw club in New South Wales, with more than 200 members across nine chapters, the Nomads were for a long time a powerful force in the Cross, and it was only a matter of time before they either clashed with the Ibrahims or brought them into the fold. History shows it was the latter.

In mid-1997 a secret police operation pounced on Sam Ibrahim and three members of the Nomads – the national president Greg Craig, his brother, and Scott Orrock, national sergeant-at-arms.

Only days before, on Wednesday 9 July, Greg Craig handed control of the Nomads' Parramatta chapter to Ibrahim.

It was a key moment in the evolution of both the Ibrahim crew and the outlaw clubs. For the Ibrahims, it meant they could tap into a powerful national biker organisation; for the clubs, it was the beginning of an ethnic influx of Lebanese, Turkish, Egyptian, Iraqi and Islander men. An experiment in multiculturalism that many of the 'establishment' bikies would later say they regretted. It is the same with many Gentlemen's Clubs.

Sam took over the chapter and the Granville clubhouse soon became not only an ethnic melting pot, but a rogue's gallery of men who have since become some of the most dangerous in Sydney.

A *Sydney Morning Herald* article by literary figure Malcolm Knox and Dylan Welch quoted a person who was part of the Auburn scene in the late 1990s and had been involved with the Parramatta Nomads:

'The way Sam ran it was: "Here are your colours, I'm your power base now, you've got the whole club behind you. Do what you want – you've got no one to answer to." Everyone joined. To our boys, the bikies were so up high in the crime world that if you were one of them, it's like you were so powerful that you were untouchable.'

The chapter quickly grew to become one of the most feared outfits in Sydney, and 'Sam' Ibrahim was the unquestioned chief of what police repeatedly alleged in court was an organised crime outfit.

Here, in the real world outside the social pages, 'Sam' was not playing the media-friendly game. He was, in fact, proving a headache for smooth-talking John because of his long involvement with the outlaw motorcycle club and his reputation as a violent standover man with a hair-trigger temper. If not a hair-trigger, full stop. Bikers were always big on guns.

The Nomads went to war with the Rebels – Sam even went so far as to challenge Rebels national president Alessio 'Alex' Vella to a 'fight to the death' – and feuded constantly with Mahmoud 'Mick' Hawi's Comanchero City Crew.

But in the end it was an internal feud, between members of the Newcastle and Parramatta chapters, which crippled the club.

In September 2004 a group of Sydney Nomads

travelled to Newcastle and attacked a group of senior Newcastle members, believing their colleagues were 'not properly catering for the financial needs' of a jailed member and his family.

Two men, Newcastle sergeant-at-arms Dale Campton and member Mark Chrystie, were bashed and shot in both kneecaps. This seemed unnecessarily robust, even by western suburbs standards. Sam Ibrahim, Orrock and Sydney West chapter boss Paul Griffin were charged over the double shooting two years later, when Campton agreed to give evidence. All three were eventually found not guilty by a jury in late 2008, but it meant that Sam, placed on remand in December 2006, was off the streets for almost two years.

In April 2007, only a few months after Sam's departure to jail, a van was driven through a roller door of the Parramatta chapter's clubhouse and torched. The fire destroyed several motorcycles and caused extensive damage to the building. The Nomads hierarchy, perhaps tired of the continual warring, disbanded the chapter and its members dispersed, filling the ranks of the Bandidos, the Rebels, other Nomad chapters ... and, for a small group of hardcore Ibrahim supporters, the newly formed gang, soon to be Notorious.

SOME dirt sticks even to Teflon. One of the reasons John Ibrahim has not been able to whitewash his past the way he would have liked is the voluminous contents of the Wood Royal Commission in the mid-1990s.

More specifically, a single sentence has haunted Ibrahim since his two days in the witness box at the age of 25.

Both Sam and John were called to give evidence before the Commission and John, with his trademark insouciance, seemed almost to enjoy being grilled by counsel assisting the commission, John Agius, QC, even when the prominent prosecutor dropped this bombshell: 'Well, you're the new lifeblood of the drug industry at Kings Cross, aren't you?'

With a smirk, Ibrahim replied: 'So it would seem, but no, I'm not.' But what he perhaps did not realise then was that Agius had placed on the record the central allegation that has dogged John and his brothers ever since: that they were – and remain – involved in the illicit drug trade.

A quick scan of newspaper articles reveals Agius's sentence has been referred to or quoted more than 40 times since, and has become the reflex allegation against the nightclub baron.

But that sentence wasn't the only revelation about Ibrahim contained in the pages of the Commission's transcripts, and his evidence gave an insight into his business life and his falling out with the Bayeh brothers.

Early in his examination of Ibrahim, Agius asked him whether the Tunnel nightclub had a bank account.

'We had one until four months ago,' John replied.

Q. *What happened?*

A. *We were in the process of renewing the lease and we didn't know we were going to be there. The chances of renewing the lease weren't very good at the time, so we'd stopped ...*

Q. *With which bank was the account?*

A. *Kings Cross State Bank.*

Q. *What was the name of the account?*

A. *Tunnel Cabaret.*

Q. *So you closed that account, did you, four or five months ago?*

A. *Could be longer.*

Q. *Since then you've not operated any bank account for the Tunnel Cabaret?*

A. *No, sir.*

Q. *Or for any business that's conducted there?*

A. *No.*

Q. *It's run as an entirely cash business for those last four, five or more months?*

A. *Yes.*

Q. *Is there any drug dealing going on there?*

A. *No, sir.*

Q. *Definitely not?*

A. *Never.*

Q. *Do you have trouble keeping the drug dealers out of the Tunnel?*

A. *Six years ago we had a bit of trouble, but there's been no drug dealers, there's been no mention of drugs in the place.*

Q. *How are you able to keep them out?*

A. *Well, by monitoring who they are and just not allowing them into the club.*

The examination then turned to a tape recording of a telephone conversation between 'supergrass' cop Trevor Haken and Bill Bayeh, in which Bayeh was recorded saying he wanted Sam Ibrahim, associate Russell Townsend and a man called John' out of the Cross.

Q. *What comment do you have to make about what Mr Bayeh was saying in those two pieces of tape? Did you suspect that he was referring to you when he spoke of Sam Abraham and John?*

A. *He's definitely referring to my brother, but I have no idea what Bill was talking about. I'm not sure that Bill has an idea what he's talking about half the time.*

Q. *Well, he seemed to be quite sure that Russell – which we interpret as Russell Townsend – and Sam Abraham and someone called John had lots of people working on the streets in Kings Cross in the context of selling drugs. Have you had any such involvement?*

A. *No, sir, I haven't.*

Q. *Definitely not?*

A. *Never have.*

Ibrahim treated the entire process derisively, and when asked by Agius what his relationship was like with Bill Bayeh, he was blunt. 'After hearing that tape conversation, not very good,' he said. He did not shrink from the persistent questioning, and when asked if he found the recent performance of a police officer forced to discuss corrupt activity 'amusing', John said: 'I find the whole thing very amusing, to be honest with you, sir.'

Q. *What do you find amusing?*

A. *That this is all – the way it is unfolding, it is just very amusing to me.*

Q. *What aspect of it is amusing to you?*

A. *Well, the police are finally sort of seeing how it is for your friends to dob on you, which they've been doing for years, managing to get friends to dob on each other and set each other up. Exactly the same thing is happening to them.*

In *People of the Cross*, John described the effects of the Commission in another way. 'Four years ago about six or seven people used to organise everything that happened in the Cross. They were always against each other but they were making so much money then that they controlled what opened, what closed, who worked, who sold the drugs. If you didn't go along with it, these people had the muscle, and the know-how, to make your business life hell. Unless you were one of them, there'd be nothing you could do about it.

'In the last three years, things have changed. The organisation element has gone. You can now actually ring up a policeman, tell him what the problem is and count on him to help you. Before, that policeman would probably know the person you've got the problem with and it would cause you even more trouble.'

JOHN Ibrahim is now one of the most instantly recognisable faces at the Cross.

On any given Saturday night he can be found standing outside Porky's with Frank 'Ashtray' Amante and the usual muscled strip-club touts. If not there, then on the door at his latest and greatest nightclub, the Piano Room, schmoozing with the A-listers. Or, sometimes, he'll be deep in conversation in a corner of Dragonfly, where it all began.

With Tongan Sam, Turkish Mick or Big Fadi in tow, John will walk the Golden Mile like a latter day mafia don, shaking hands, greeting people and checking on his businesses. Most Cross identities are loathe to talk about the sawn-off 'King of the Cross' but if pressed will simply say he's a 'well-respected businessman'.

At the time of writing, he was poised to be even better known, following his portrayal in the third of the drama series *Underbelly*.

When it was first announced that the show would portray crime and corruption in King's Cross, John was offered a consultant role but, at least officially, he declined. The ubiquitous lawyer Stephen Alexander was later quoted as saying the third series might present certain difficulties regarding his client's interests and activities.

'It's a lot easier to make movies or documentaries with people that have passed on,' observed Alexander, showing a remarkable grasp of the obvious. 'It's a free country and people are entitled to do what they do, but I hope they have their facts right.'

You may, Stephen. But does John?

3

WORKING BLUE

'You fuck one cop and the rest
hate you for life.'

WITH its flawless 180-degree view across the Pacific, John Ibrahim's eastern suburbs mansion testifies to his love of the finer things in life – but especially the water. To a boy raised in the hardscrabble streets of the western suburbs the big house with the 'blue view' is a constant reminder of how far and how fast he has come.

In an interview with much-impressed reporter Kate De Brito in 1996, Ibrahim talked about how much he liked to go night fishing from the rocks beneath the house. He also described his liking for scuba diving. Not surprisingly, he had two jet skis in his garage alongside the compulsory prestige cars.

It was this love of water and scuba diving that played a pivotal part in a more controversial episode in his history, a diving trip with a young Kings Cross policewoman called Wendy Hatfield.

Wendy Hatfield had joined the then New South Wales Police Service in April 1992, and two months later was posted to Kings Cross as a constable, where she would serve until May 1995. She had made an impression at the police training college because of her good looks and curvaceous figure – and the fact she sometimes seemed to speak with a Swedish accent. Although, as far as anyone knew, she came from well south of Scandinavia – from Melbourne, according to her fellow rookies.

One contemporary, still in the force, recalls that the energetic and obliging Hatfield cut a swathe through her male colleagues. She was no star recruit in the lecture theatre, shooting range or driving course, but made up for it with her enthusiasm to meet and make new friends. Often tired from partying late at night, 'She slept her way through the training', the former friend recalls.

'In fact, I think she failed the police driving test twice before she worked out how to get through,' says the policeman, an English migrant who was briefly one of Hatfield's boyfriends. 'It was the good old days, before everyone maintained a proper distance.'

Once she graduated and got to Kings Cross, says the former friend, it was clear to her rank-and-file colleagues that 'there was no major thought process going on.' But to the force hierarchy, the twenty-something constable with the beach girl looks seemed ideal for propaganda purposes. They dubbed her the 'new breed' of police officers when she presented herself with other young Kings Cross police who 'detested corruption' at the Wood Royal Commission in 1995.

Unfortunately for Hatfield, her involvement in the Royal Commission was not to end there. Just four months later she was outed as a regular at John Ibrahim's nightclub, The Tunnel, where she had formed a relationship with the man the Commission would tag as a new power in the drug scene.

The uncomfortable truth came out during a hearing of the Commission when the legendary criminal lawyer, Chris Murphy, representing a number of Kings Cross identities, was cross-examining Ibrahim.

The shrewd Murphy uncovered the story of how Hatfield had once told a highway patrolman that she was a Kings Cross police officer when she was in a car driven by Ibrahim pulled over for speeding.

Ibrahim, who at the time did not have a driver's licence, gave the officer his younger brother's name. 'She knew I was lying,' Ibrahim ungallantly told Murphy under examination.

Then came the story of the diving trip. During another appearance at the Commission Ibrahim was pushed to answer more searching questions about his relationship with Hatfield. At one point the questioning turned to a scuba diving trip he had taken with Hatfield to Forster, on the state's mid north coast, in April 1994.

Statutory declarations were produced from two people on the trip, the dive school operator and his divemaster. Both knew Hatfield but had never had the occasion to run into a genuine Kings Cross gangster type before, and took a keen interest in Ibrahim's battle wounds when he stripped down for a dive.

The dive school operator said of John: 'I took a closer look at this fellow and he had his shirt off which exposed what appeared to be stab wounds and bullet holes about his abdomen. This caused me to ask him how he received the wounds. He replied words to the effect, "occupational hazard", to which I replied, "Jeez, once is an accident, twice looks as though someone doesn't like you".'

The divemaster said: 'He stands out in my memory because when he was on the back of the boat at the wharf he stripped off his shirt to reveal what appeared to be stab scars on his body. I am an ex-Special Air Services member and the scars on this bloke's body appeared to be either from stab wounds or bullet fire.

'I then asked John if he had worked as an undercover cop. He laughed and said words to the effect, "No, I am on the other side, I'm a crook." I thought he was joking when he said that. He then told me that two of the scars were from 9mm bullets and the others were stab wounds.

John then went on to tell me that he worked for his uncle who owned nightclubs in Kings Cross. I may have mentioned to him that I would have to go to Kings Cross to have a look and he replied he would show me around. Personally, I thought he was a big noter.'

The divemaster, whose name was suppressed during the hearings, also noted that on a later dive – without Ibrahim – Hatfield told him that she had been first to a murder scene in Kings Cross and Ibrahim had been somehow involved.

'She said that she felt very embarrassed about it because she had been up here with him,' the divemaster stated.

That homicide, along with a number of other alleged improprieties publicly linked to her brief relationship with Ibrahim, would see Hatfield subjected to a withering media storm, hauled before the Wood Royal Commission, and in 1997 resign from the police force.

Unfortunately for Hatfield, the media scrutiny became too much for her, and a *Sydney Morning Herald* photographer, Nick Moir, was unlucky enough to be in the right place at the wrong time – that is, waiting outside as she came out of the Downing Centre court complex on 9 December 1998.

As Moir snapped her picture, Hatfield also snapped – but not with a camera. Instead, she threw a well-aimed right at Moir's head, hitting him across the left ear. He escaped with little damage but the image of the attack was captured brilliantly by another photographer. To this day the shot of a reeling Moir being pummelled by a 55-kilogram woman reportedly graces a number of Sydney newsroom desks, and is the subject of much amusement.

But it was the death she mentioned to the divemaster, of small-time Kings Cross drug dealer Talal Assaad on 21 April 1994, that did Hatfield's reputation far more damage than merely punching a photographer, a misdemeanour for which no jury would convict.

The killing of Talal Assaad also became an instructive glimpse into Ibrahim's role before the Wood Royal Commission. It happened like this.

In 1994 Russell Peter Townsend packed an astonishing 115 kilograms into a compact 177 centimetre frame, and often told friends he had once bench pressed a record 272 kilograms.

A former professional boxer who fought under the ring name 'The White Rhino', Townsend was also alleged to be one of the heavy players in the Kings Cross street scene.

Assaad had been dealing drugs for the Bayehs but had recently switched over to a rival syndicate, leaving a bad taste in the mouths of several Bayeh associates.

About 2pm, in the Springfield Mall at the north end of the Darlinghurst Road strip, Assaad was unlucky enough to run into the hulking frame of the White Rhino, who was with John and another man, Ali Sakr. There was little doubt who was going to be walking away from the encounter – and who wasn't.

One punch to the temple from Townsend was all it took. Assaad hit the ground and went into cardiac arrest. John called triple-0 and the first officer to respond to the call was, perhaps unfortunately for her, Wendy Hatfield, at the time Ibrahim's tame cop girlfriend.

A court was later told that Assaad had said to Townsend 'Do you want to score?' and that Townsend, described as a 'fitness enthusiast' by defence counsel Chris Murphy, took umbrage and punched Assaad.

A Supreme Court jury eventually found Townsend not guilty of manslaughter, but guilty of an alternative charge of assault occasioning actual bodily harm. In sentencing him to a four year good behaviour bond, Justice Alan Abadee told Townsend: 'You're a big man: keep your hands to yourself and exercise self-control and restraint at all times.'

Justice Abadee said he accepted the premise that Townsend had punched Assaad because he was offended by the offer of drugs.

'I accept it because, having regard to the prisoner's enthusiasm for fitness, as further supported by character references tendered before me this morning, that he might well take umbrage at being approached for the purposes of seeing whether he would be interested in buying drugs ... there is nothing in the prisoner's antecedents that I have had regard to which would suggest that he is the sort of person who has in any way, shape or form in the past been involved in drug activities, or even activities, more particularly relevant, involving personal use or abuse of drugs.'

After his close call, the musclebound fitness enthusiast returned to a safer arena – heavyweight boxing – and knocked down six men in ten months, most of them in the first round.

Hatfield was quizzed about the Assad death, the dive trip, and her alleged attempts to get Ibrahim off the unlicensed driving charge during the Wood Royal Commission. She took stress leave, eventually left the police and was later charged with perjury over another incident in 1993 when, working as an undercover officer, she was alleged to have tongue-kissed a Kings Cross nightclub patron and asked a bouncer for drugs.

Neither Townsend nor Hatfield frequent the Cross any more and prove elusive to find. Ibrahim, on the other hand, practically runs the joint.

Once, asked about the effect of the Wendy Hatfield episode, he quipped: 'You fuck one cop and the rest hate you
for life.'

After her fifteen seconds of infamy, Hatfield took about
that long to slip back into obscurity. Some think she married a horse trainer and moved north; others that she went
back to Victoria. If she learned anything from her time
caught in the harsh glare of the Royal Commission, she
should keep her head well down, her gear on and not throw
any punches. But some people never learn.

4

THE KILLING OF DANNY K

```
The dead man's colleagues did
not even pretend to cry - in
fact, they threw a party at a
Darlinghurst night club ...
```

IT was the underworld's version of the Last Supper. But instead of one Judas there were four – three of them armed.

The treachery of those he trusted was about the only Biblical overtone in the short life and brutal death of standover man and would-be drug overlord, Danny Karam.

Karam, 36, died in a hail of sixteen bullets from three guns fired by his most trusted lieutenants in a street in inner-city Surry Hills on 13 December 1998. It was a calculating and cold-blooded hit, even by gangster standards.

Minutes before Karam got the bad news, one of the accused men made him a cup of coffee and chatted with him, knowing his colleagues were set to murder him as soon as he went outside. Lucky it wasn't instant coffee, or they might have missed their chance to give Danny a wake-up shot that would take his head off.

But they didn't miss. Four men were linked to the murder but one fled to Lebanon and did not stand trial with the other three. One of those charged had to be brought to court each day from jail where he was already serving life for a double murder.

Danny Karam's twisted dreams – and a few vital organs – were blown away by gunmen in his own image, whose callousness he encouraged and exploited. Society might well be a better place with Karam dead – and his killers being locked up for most of their adult lives.

All of Karam's 'working' life in Sydney's drug scene had been aimed at creating a reputation for toughness and setting him up to move on to bigger and better criminal rackets. Now, at a pivotal moment in his career, he was handed a redundancy package by those who apparently nursed similar ambitions. Another example of the great cycle of criminal life.

It was not a time for genuine grieving. The deaths of criminals rarely are, apart from the tears of a few close family members. The public is glad that one less dangerous sociopath is off the streets. The dead man's colleagues did not even pretend to cry – in fact, they threw a party at a Darlinghurst night club called Rogues because Karam's exit put a new patch of drug-selling turf up for grabs.

'There was a saying at the time,' recalls self-confessed corrupt cop Trevor Haken, 'that if people really knew what happened on the streets of Kings Cross, they'd surround the place with barbed wire and flatten it with a nuclear device.'

Karam was a violent, unpredictable package of potential mayhem and heroin addiction who aligned himself to Kings Cross drug king Billy Bayeh in the expectation of taking over the throne if the opportunity arose. Bayeh used Karam as a human attack dog to savage all the opposition drug sellers on the streets.

Karam told the Royal Commission that he worked for Bayeh and Sam Ibrahim, brother of John, providing protection, violent if necessary, to enable their drug dealing to continue without disruption. It was lucrative. Karam said he made as much as $10,000 a week in 1995, with a regular $5000 a week from Billie Bayeh to run rival drug dealers out of the area.

Predictably enough, Karam's childhood and adolescence had been brutal and dislocated in war-torn Lebanon, where he left school aged eleven. He claimed to have been a commando during Lebanon's civil war. Most of his adult life had been on a battlefield or in jail.

In Australia, he began his criminal career in the mid-1980s by bashing heroin pushers and stealing their narcotics to feed his own $1000 a day habit. He told the Commission his raging temper was fuelled by addiction to muscle-building steroids.

Fiercely ambitious, Karam eventually fell out with both Bayeh and Ibrahim and joined a criminal group of other single-minded, ambitious young men who thought the answer to every problem was violence piled on violence. They were involved in at least four murders and sixteen shootings. Understandably, Karam was feared and hated for the measures he took to quash opposition and there were attempts at retaliation.

Haken says in his biography *Sympathy for the Devil* that Karam was typical of the hoodlums who sought success at the Cross. 'It was important to be tough in the Cross,' he says. 'Those with bravado seemed to get away with a lot, but it was a dangerous game. Danny Karam was a typical creature. His first convictions were in 1985 and included heroin use, theft and possessing an unlicensed pistol.

'In jail he built up a strong physique through weight-training and developed the jailhouse attitude that he used to his advantage when he returned to the streets. His record reflects this lifestyle with convictions for serious assault, robbery and the possession of drugs.'

It was almost inevitable that Karam would die violently and young. In fact, he was lucky not to be killed sooner. In 1993 a gunman arrived at the drug dealer's suburban house at Lugarno on an assassination mission funded by a cocaine and heroin supplier, a former Karam employer. It all went tragically wrong. The shooter was looking for Karam but murdered an innocent neighbour, Leslie Betcher, by mistake.

Karam's endeavours to become a gang leader were not matched by his people skills and his easily-triggered temper.

His own 'crew', known as Danny's Boys or DK's Boys, said he was self-centred, mean, abusive, greedy and violent. This was why they killed him, they said.

The three men charged were Michael Kanaan, 26, Rabeeh Mawas, 25, and Wassim El-Assaad, 25. They all pleaded not guilty to the murder of Karam 13 December 1998. Police said the fourth man in the plot, Charlie Gea Gea, bolted to Lebanon to escape prosecution.

Karam was shot in his car after leaving the Surry Hills apartment the gang used as a safe house. The impact of sixteen bullets fired from high-powered guns left his body mangled and spread over the front seat.

The details of what happened came from another of DK's Boys, Alan Rossini, who was given immunity from prosecution for revealing the events leading up to the hit.

He said that from 1997 until his murder, Karam's regular routine was to collect 'rent' payments on Sundays from drug distributors for the right to sell cocaine on the streets of Kings Cross. Payments ranged from $4000 to $28,000 a week. The money was collected by Rossini and Kanaan but they saw very little of the cash they were gathering. It all went to Karam, they claimed.

Frustrated by Karam's greed and refusal to share the huge profits he was making and angry at what they claimed was the occasional $100 he threw them as wages, his 'boys' became murderous.

'Danny said he was putting the money away for us and he'd give it back,' Rossini alleged, giving an insight into the sophisticated distribution network that put cocaine on the streets.

'Rent' payments depended on the number of sellers involved. 'If you wanted to have four (drug) runners on the street it was $4000 a week rent,' Rossini told the Supreme Court.

Rossini said he and Kanaan helped put cocaine into capsules and took it to distributors at the Cross who passed it to drug runners. 'They put it in their mouths and walked around the streets of Kings Cross selling it,' he explained.

The cash would be passed back to Rossini and Kanaan to give to Karam.

'We did not get any of that money. Sometimes Danny gave us $100 a week,' he said.

There were times when Karam would become violent because the rent was too low. He would threaten to kill anyone who displeased him. And he used the three men as largely unpaid personal servants who grew marijuana and packaged cocaine to be sold to distributors as well as collecting money from drug runners.

When Karam decided to stay home, his men would also go out to buy his food, get videos, do his laundry and go training with him. At least, this was the picture they painted at trial. As everyone knows, the survivors get to tell the story.

Rossini told the Supreme Court that Karam had also borrowed $10,000 from Kanaan to set up a computer shop to launder money and had never repaid the loan. Kanaan said he had borrowed the money from his parents and that Karam's disrespect and failure to pay caused great friction in the group.

'Kanaan was upset about being used. And told me "after all the work we've done for Danny to build up his business we have got nothing for it",' Rossini said.

The idea of killing Karam had been discussed by the three accused men and Charlie Gea Gea for around nine months before the actual shooting. 'It was almost every day,' Rossini said.

A failed attempt to give poisoned heroin to Karam, so he might kill himself with a lethal injection while feeding his habit, convinced the trio that shooting him was the only sure way to nail their tyrant.

'I remember them (the shooters) talking about where they would stand when they shot (at him),' Rossini said.

One man, he thought it was Kanaan, emphasised that the men should stand at an angle so they would not get caught in cross fire.

The scenario suggested Kanaan, Mawas and Gea Gea murdered Karam in his four-wheel drive after being tipped off by El Assaad that the standover man had left the apartment.

Rossini conceded in the Supreme Court that he could have alerted Karam to the murder plot against him and stopped him leaving the unit.

Barrister (for Kanaan): *You never warned him: 'I think there's a plot to kill you Danny?'*

Rossini: *There's no way I could have done that. No.*

Barrister: *Why didn't you warn him that he was about to get ambushed?*

Rossini: *I was concerned for my own safety. I wasn't game enough to tell him what was happening.*

Rossini said that although he was not involved with the murder plan he did not disagree with it.

Judge James Wood, co-incidentally the same man who heard Karam's original revelations when he chaired the Wood Royal Commission six years earlier, called Karam's murder cold-blooded and motivated by greed.

'The principal motive (of) Michael Kanaan, I am satisfied, was to acquire an entrenched position for his subgroup in the trade of narcotics and to increase their standing within that section of the criminal milieu,' he said.

Judge Wood sentenced Kanaan to life and the other shooter, Mawas, to 25 years with a non-parole period of nineteen years.

El Assad, who made the crucial telephone call to alert the killers, was given 24 years, with eighteen years non-parole.

Kanaan was already serving two life sentences for murdering former National Rugby League players, 23-year-old Adam Wright and 24-year-old Michael Hurle, in a drive-by shooting as the two men stood outside a hotel in the inner-city suburb of Five Dock on 17 July 1998.

When her son's third life sentence was read out by Judge Wood, Kanaan's mother made a lengthy outburst from the public gallery, shouting her son's innocence. 'I want to be beside you,' she called as she was led from the court room. 'God be with you. He will prove you innocent one day.'

Kanaan called back: 'It's all right. Don't worry about it.' He was more expansive in addressing Judge Wood saying: 'Your Honour, I didn't kill those footballers and I didn't kill Danny Karam.'

Putting murderers in jail was a triumph but a bonus was the overflow of evidence collected in the Karam killing. The killers and their victim were linked to a renegade crime gang inflicting death and destruction at random to try and muscle in on Sydney's lucrative drug dealing.

The gang was suspected of sixteen shootings and four murders, including that of an innocent schoolboy. Ballistic experts linked the sixteen bullets taken from Karam's body to a gun found at the scene where a policeman, Chris Patrech, had been wounded.

They were also linked to a notorious drive-by shooting of Lakemba Police Station in November 1988.

Police are also convinced some of the dozen members of the outlaw gang were responsible for the stabbing murder of young schoolboy Edward Lee on a Punchbowl Street a few weeks before the Lakemba incident.

Karam had a 12-gauge shotgun in the back of his four-wheel drive but didn't get the chance to reach for it because his assassination was so swift. Police linked the gun to shots that were fired outside the EPI nightclub at Kings Cross in September 1998 and another shooting at a panel-beating shop.

Karam's shotgun was also forensically linked to a wild drive-by shooting in the inner-city suburb of Redfern, known for its indigenous population. As many as fifteen houses were sprayed with lead fired by shooters driving a stolen Mitsubishi Pajero later found torched in nearby Alexandria.

The attack was retaliation for a bashing in Lithgow Prison days earlier when Aboriginal inmates bashed Middle Eastern prisoners so badly that three had to be admitted to hospital.

The gunmen, who fired shotguns and rifles in the dawn raid, left an Aboriginal flag with a luridly painted message: 'Fuck with our brothers inside and we fuck with your families outside. Blood 4 blood. P.S. Lithgow Jail 2 die 4.'

'It was a most wanton act of indiscriminate shooting and at least fifteen homes were peppered with high-calibre projectiles. It is amazing no one was injured,' police said.

Indicating the gang's callous and casual attitude towards murderous violence, Assistant Police Commissioner Clive Small said not all of the incidents were against targeted people. Others seemed random and could have been just spontaneous thrill killings.

'Some of the crimes were committed by a small number of people who we believe targeted the victims following their association with the group,' he said. 'Tragically, it would seem the shootings of Edward Lee, Michael Hurle and Adam Wright were not premeditated.'

He described the gang as a small group of very dangerous people without morals or compassion. 'They are motivated by greed and have little loyalty to anyone around them.'

He said anyone associated with the group ran the risk of becoming the next victim. Just like Danny Karam.

– WITH RAY CHESTERTON

5

THE POLICEMAN'S DAUGHTER

'He held a gun between my legs
with the hammer cocked ...'

BY the time the stripper starts, the men leering at her are half-pissed. Her moves to the taped music are not so much erotic as a parody of eroticism – but who cares? It does the trick for the mob of punters around her: they hoot, holler and whistle as the gear comes off. It's a bucks' night, a sleazy convention in their circles – a bogan brotherhood whose borderline criminal bravado is fuelled by booze.

The girl is in her twenties, more girl-next-door than vampy bombshell, not necessarily a disadvantage in a business with enough tricked-up transsexuals to make punters wonder what's real and what isn't.

But there are signs that not all her assets are natural and that at least one of the many contacts she has made since arriving in the Big Smoke is a plastic surgeon. Up close, the pert nose is a little too neat, the pert breasts a little too big, the teeth even and white. It's not overdone – not a Michael Jackson nose above Pamela Anderson breasts but it's obvious she has been 'pimped' in more ways than one. It's the thing old school friends notice when they see pictures of her, especially other women. She's instantly recognisable – but recognisably different.

She has the same, dark curly hair and white skin she had at high school but is more physical than the quiet, bookish schoolgirl she was back then. Not sporty as a teenager, now she flaunts the body of someone who works on fitness for a living, with the defined muscles that come from exercise and diet – strict vegetarian in her case – and with no signs of the drug use so common in her game. She looks like a professional and she is. And her profession, at least proverbially, is the oldest of all. That's part of the attraction for the men crowding around, waiting for what they know will happen next.

She begins the strip wearing a version of police uniform: blue culottes, crisp white shirt and swinging baton. Off comes the uniform, piece by piece tossed among the tossers in the crowd, until she is naked, bar a tiny G-string. Then she gets down to some dirty work with the baton. The watchers are getting rowdy, making remarks ranging from suggestive to obscene but, some time in the years since leaving home and school, she's been inoculated against that. Words are weapons but in a game where robbery, gang rape or bashing are occupational hazards, they can lose their sting.

She finishes the strip but the show's not over: stripping was only the entrée, a tease for 'fans' now lining up in an unspoken pecking order behind the unblushing bride-groom-to-be. He will have sex with her first. Then his mates will. Any or all of them: first served, first come.

'There were hands coming from everywhere,' she would later tell a reporter. 'They were all drunk, throwing beer cans at me and out of control. They were fond of me dressing up in police uniform and I had the complete outfit. I had such an effect on them that they were literally lining up afterwards for sex.'

At one strip show 'about 60 of them were lined up and there were even punch-ups out the back over who would be first,' she remembered. There were two other girls in the show but some of the policemen would be furious if they were not 'the first to get the girl of their choice.'

If she were getting cash from each man the sordid deal would have at least some crude equity to it. But there is something different about this scene. It is not only – or maybe never was – strictly commercial. The stripper-turned-hooker is not dulled by narcotics – or strung out and getting cashed up for her next hit. Her bright and brittle bravado obscures the fact that tonight she's debasing herself for next to nothing: working at a 'discount'.

Why would she do that? Because the men queuing up for her are police – and she wants to be like them. Wanted to, she sometimes said later, ever since reading her father's detective manual when she was a child. 'I used to mess around in my Dad's shirt playing police with my sister,' she once revealed. A lot of children play dress ups but this one was different: Daddy's little girl turned into a cop groupie who'd do anything for police because she wanted to be one, like her father used to be.

It was only when the 'big blue gang' rejected her that the trouble started. That's when everyone got to hear about Kim Hollingsworth, the stripper who took on the New South Wales Police Force – and proved the truth of the saying about the fury of a woman scorned.

SO how did a nice girl like Kim end up in places like that, spending the best years of her twenties stripping for mobs of men, sometimes providing sex for as many of them as wanted to line up?

And what sort of police force would tolerate the fact the men in the queue were often serving officers, given that she performed for at least 30 police functions for crowds of up to 300 cops and their mates?

No wonder, perhaps, that Hollingsworth thought she could leave the sex game behind to become a New South Wales police officer: after all, she knew from personal experience that members of the force weren't fussy about matters of morality. In the end, of course, it wasn't morality that got her. It was hypocrisy.

Given her profession, Hollingsworth's view of police and the sex industry seemed oddly naïve. It began to sour when she felt the undertow of corruption as police put pressure on some of the brothels where she worked.

'We thought we were earning a lot of money as prostitutes but the police were earning much more,' she would claim later. She saw how brothel madams who paid protection money to police were given special treatment – and saw that police demanded special treatment in return, with some demanding free sex as well as the cash.

'They expected it and got it for free. You wouldn't dare refuse, after all. You do as a police officer tells you.'

One officer threatened to kill her when he didn't get his own way, she would say. 'He held a gun between my legs with the hammer cocked and there were six bullets in it at the time. When it's in that position a gun only needs a touch of pressure on the trigger to go off, so had his finger slipped I would have been dead.'

But Daddy's girl was dogged. She still wanted to wear the uniform for real, not as a prop in a sleazy strip act. So she applied as a recruit in the New South Wales police service and began training in May 1995, when she was 28.

The public did not hear of Kim Hollingsworth until two years later but the events that led to her hitting the headlines happened in mid-1995. In July that year, Hollingsworth's short career as a trainee police officer ended abruptly after a gruelling interview with her superiors in a suburban Sydney police station, Daceyville. When she went into the room she noticed a document headed 'Termination of SPO Hollingsworth'. It was obvious the dice was already loaded against her: they were just going through the motions. Next day, little more than two months after joining the force, she was sacked.

Her offence, officially, was that she had failed to disclose her previous career as a prostitute and stripper on the application form to join the force earlier that year. In legal terms, this threw doubt on 'her veracity'. In fact, the application form was the perfect Catch 22 booby trap, able to be used against her at the whim of anyone in authority.

It was reasonable to assume that if she had volunteered every detail of her employment history on the form – as most shrewd people would not – it would have jeopardised her chances of entry into the force despite her physical fitness, engaging personality and higher than average intelligence.

Like a lot of police recruits her age, Hollingsworth had plenty of jobs on her resume – she had worked in shops, as a model, a flower seller, waitress and pharmacy assistant and on horse properties and in stables. In fact, she would later tell the authors of this book, her main motive in signing on was to join the mounted police. This was slightly at odds with her claim to journalist Ben Hills in 1997 that she wanted to work with dogs, but that doesn't matter. Either way, it reflected her professed love of animals.

One of her friends was a mounted policeman. The friendship didn't bring him luck. He would later commit suicide after being questioned about writing her a reference on police letterhead. But Kim Hollingsworth was made of sterner stuff. When she was faced with the prospect of being humiliated and rejected, she didn't kill herself – she did something braver. She killed any chance of safe anonymity – of quietly reinventing herself away from the sex industry – by airing her grievance on the most public of stages.

The irony was this: the real reason for her sacking was not for her supposed dishonesty in airbrushing her past on the application form – but her honesty in blowing the whistle on a fellow police recruit with bad intentions and shady connections.

It happened like this. When she applied to join the police force in early 1995, she was routinely vetted by a sergeant assigned to that mostly tedious task. The sergeant would later claim to have checked police records, spoken to her neighbours and her landlord, as well as interviewing the would-be recruit herself.

The sergeant could find 'nothing of an adverse nature' and reported the applicant was 'of good character' and 'a suitable person for police employment'. For her part, Hollingsworth left out colourful details of periods of 'self employment' over several years. She would later say there was no space to do so on the form, the sort of answer any serving police officer would be pleased to make under cross examination by a pesky lawyer. If she was not specifically asked details of her self-employment, why volunteer them? No copper in their right mind would. As the daughter of a detective, and street smart from time spent working variously as a stripper, as an escort and as a $400-an-hour pro in expensive brothels such as Sydney's famous Touch of Class, she knew when to shut up. Although not enough, as it turned out, to bury her past.

She had been inducted into the police academy at Goulburn in May, 1995. For a few weeks, all was well. Fit, friendly and good-looking, with a breezy line of chat, Recruit Hollingsworth seemed to fit in. Had she gone to Perth or Darwin to join up, she might have been a police officer to this day, perhaps a good one. But to imagine she would go unrecognised – or that it wouldn't matter if she were – was optimistic, if not naïve or even a touch arrogant. Sydney was too close for comfort. It was inevitable that the past would point a grubby finger at her.

It happened when a young detective who had seen her working at police strip nights recognised her. It wasn't as if he were shocked – or motivated by altruism to identify Hollingsworth's past to his superiors. He was (name deleted) later identified by the Commission as MK2, and a man with an eye for an opportunity. Hollingsworth said he asked her to act as a madam in a brothel he said he was planning to open in Sydney's western suburbs, a fact that would imply he was probably associated with the Lebanese gangsters who were expanding from their western suburbs strongholds into the more profitable fleshpots of Kings Cross.

At first she thought it was a joke, she would claim. Then she realised she was being forced to make a choice. Faced with the unspoken but explicit threat of her past being revealed, she decided to fight. She had wanted a clean break from the sex industry but now, dragged back to face her past, she decided to tell the truth. She blew the whistle on the dodgy detective. This, she would tell the Wood Royal Commission (and the New South Wales Industrial Commission), was the real reason for her sacking. Her sin was that she wouldn't play the game by joining 'the joke' to become a bent cop moonlighting as a brothel madam, an outrageous dual role to which the force might well have turned a blind eye at the time.

'One day I was told I was a human being by senior staff at the police academy but after blowing the whistle it was a very different story,' she would say later. 'It was the end of my career. The police knew that I had a wealth of knowledge about corrupt police officers, having been involved in the sex industry.'

The Commission had no choice. It had to be seen to act. Its investigators came up with a faintly farcical scheme to set up Hollingsworth's flat with a hidden video camera to mount a sting on the bent detective. It took a month, and the cast included a tow-truck driver pretending to be a crooked police inspector and Strip-O-Gram operator, a mechanic with ambitions to open a brothel above his garage, and a maintenance man from a Sydney escort agency. Eventually they filmed the detective accepting $100. He was dismissed from the force but denied being charged with taking a bribe or anything else. Nor were any of the other twenty police that Hollingsworth had named as having links with the sex industry.

Supposedly, her background as a stripper was not officially 'discovered' by the police hierarchy until half way through the sting operation. She was kept on until the sting was done, then sacked at short notice after the interview at Daceyville.

It was a cruel lesson about being a Crown witness – especially against police. The investigators had promised protection, support and a new identity, but now that they'd used her and the fun was over, it seemed they didn't love her in the morning. In fact, they treated her as if she were just a hooker with a big mouth; she had done her trick for the boys and was now an embarrassment to be bundled down the back stairs and out of sight. Literally out of sight, in this case: they gave her a one-way ticket to Adelaide and (she would later testify) encouraged her to go back to work in a brothel to repay money she had borrowed from the Commission.

Realising her life could be in danger, she spent a couple of months 'crying myself to sleep' before sneaking back to the bright lights of Sin City, angry and determined. That's when she decided it was payback time.

She engaged a lawyer and, ignoring threats, demanded that the authorities make her case public. Having run foul of bent police, it might have seemed that the safest place to stand was right in the spotlight – or maybe it was just that part of her craves publicity. Either way, she got it: an army of journalists turned up at the hearings of the New South Wales Industrial Relations Commission to catch the jilted stripper's tale. She didn't disappoint.

Among the onlookers was veteran investigative reporter and author Ben Hills, who was bemused but not quite convinced by the stripper's spirited performance. To him, the young woman suing the Police Department seemed more happy hooker than bitter whistleblower. There was a pattern to the coverage. Another hardbitten reporter, Ray Chesterton, wrote at the time that she worked the crowd, flashing 'a smile that would empty your wallet at twenty paces.'

Hollingsworth could be alarmingly frank. Once, sitting outside the court room, she told Hills that her breast implants enabled her to move her breasts independently – and offered 'to demonstrate this phenomenon to me', he noted later. (He politely ducked the demonstration, but accepted a short-lived invitation to write a book. The negotiations didn't end well.)

Anatomical entertainment was in the court room as well as outside it. Hollingsworth's artificially enhanced breasts weren't the only ones before the bench. In what one reporter called 'theatre of the absurd', the police service engaged a transsexual attorney to represent it.

The barrister, formerly known as Terry Anderson, had swapped regulation dark suit and tie for a dress, handbag and frizzy ginger hair and asked to be called 'Teresa Anderson'. If briefing Anderson were an attempt by the police brains trust to prove its broad-minded equal employment credentials, it didn't work that well. When not alarming natural-born women by using the female toilets at the court, the new Ms Anderson scored a few points along the way. She said Hollingsworth had admitted 'lying' on her application form and scoffed at her portrayal as a whistle-blower motivated by conscience. Instead, she painted Hollingsworth as a cunning and manipulative liar who would 'say anything at any time to achieve what she wants.'

But after a nine-day hearing, Industrial Relations Commissioner Peter Connor decided that most of the lies and manipulation had not come from Hollingsworth's side. He found that she had been denied natural justice and ordered that she either be reinstated as a trainee police officer – or paid compensation. The compensation figure was later set at $35,000 – but Hollingsworth wasn't going to be brushed off with that. She wanted to be back in uniform as a police recruit.

'I do hope I get the job back in future,' she told reporters. 'That's been my ambition since I was a six-year-old and corrupt police will not be spoiling that for me. I have no ill-feeling towards the police service. I don't think I ever will have. It's something that happened in the past and all I can do now is try and get reinstated.

'Of course there are going to be some police officers who won't be happy,' she conceded.

She was right about that. And the officers unhappy with the ruling included senior people running the force, according to anonymous sources who briefed reporters.

If the commission ordered she be reinstated, it would be unlikely she would successfully complete recruit training.

'She'd be better off taking a compensation package,' one source told a reporter.

Meanwhile, before the media caravan moved on, there was a chance to make a little extra cash. The Nine network's *Sixty Minutes* reportedly paid her $19,000 to appear, and it was well-known that a division of Penguin had offered a hefty advance for a tell-all book.

Ben Hills was approached to write the book but says he pulled out when a lawyer advising Hollingsworth demanded the lion's share of the advance for her. Hills, famously frank, told the lawyer where to go and no book was written. The approaches from film and television producers also came to nothing for many years. It was only when the makers of the *Underbelly* drama series revived contact with Hollingsworth years later because of her colourful Kings Cross connection that it looked as if a version of her story would reach the small screen.

By mid-1997, Hollingsworth was locked in a Mexican stand-off with the police force. She insisted she still wanted to join it – and the force insisted she wasn't wanted. One tactic was to refine the charge against her. According to a barrister acting for the police at a new hearing before the full bench of the New South Wales Industrial Relations Commission in October that year, Hollingsworth's time as a prostitute would have exposed her to 'the criminal milieu'. The barrister said the police service wanted to draw a 'very, very distinct, clear line' in the case. The trouble was that the line was not clear because prostitution is not a crime in New South Wales. The case polarised – and titillated – public opinion as old morality collided with new political correctness. If there was no law against being a prostitute, then how could the fact of being one in the past legally be used against a job applicant for the police service or anywhere else?

The mix of sex scandal, corruption and political correctness was irresistible to the media and the public. Among the reporters who swarmed to the case when it was resumed in late 1997 was Luke Slattery of *The Australian*. Like Hills, he was not quite convinced by Hollingsworth's portrayal of herself as a simple country girl-turned-fearless whistleblower confronting a corrupt and hypocritical system that denied her the chance to turn over a new leaf.

The astute Slattery wrote of 'the rather theatrical form' of Hollingsworth's dual personalities as the police woman/prostitute: what he called 'Good Kim. Bad Kim.'

'Kim Hollingsworth's eyes are a deep, lapis lazuli blue,' he wrote. 'Her skin is pale, sun shy. Her nose has been so finely shaped by a surgeon's scalpel that it resembles more closely a piece of ornamental filigree than a breathing apparatus.

'She is beautiful yet severe – all angles and planes. Too pointy, you'd think, to melt hearts. If she sashayed into a Sean Connery-era James Bond thriller as a wily seductress, you would wonder, as she and Connery slide between the sheets: KGB or CIA?'

But he made the point that the severity is softened by an open 'at time naïve, country manner, a mouth that curls readily into a schoolgirlish grin, and a repertoire of broad Aussie dipthongs: "yes" is a husky "yieah" ...'.

One of several contradictions about Hollingsworth was this: why she would want to return to the police service at all, given the treatment she swore she had endured during her two months there in 1995.

According to her affidavit, what began as a few sarcastic remarks at a nightclub about her past turned into sexual harassment and bullying by fellow police. One classmate said: 'Tell me, did you get your gear off?' and then two trainee detectives approached her and said words to the effect: 'We remember you from the strip shows. How would you like to make some money and do another show? We could organise one on a boat.'

Soon, she said, notes were pinned on her door, such as: 'Strip moll', 'Blow me, Kim', and 'Fill me up, Kim'. She got obscene telephone calls and male recruits banged on her door late at night demanding sex. She would later tell reporters that she was 'treated terribly', ostracised and ate her meals alone.

In an affidavit, she said: 'The harassment got so bad that, at night, I would sit in my room alone with only the desk light on and put towels around the bottom and paper up the top of the door so the light did not shine through, so that no one would know I was in there.'

It was hard to keep the subject of sex out of the Industrial Commission hearing. The court tittered with laughter when the transsexual barrister Terry/Theresa Anderson tried to nail Hollingsworth on the issue of 'trick sex' because Hollingsworth had claimed earlier that she simulated sex with clients rather than providing the real thing.

The transcript reads:

Q: *Ms Hollingsworth, the men who you performed trick sex on or simulated oral sex on …*

A: *Yes, yes …*

Q: *– were men who had in fact sought from you that you participate in true sexual intercourse?*

A: *That's correct.*

Q: *And that you participate in true oral intercourse?*

A: *Yes.*

Q: *And to the extent that they did that, they paid you upon that basis?*

A: *That's correct.*

Q: *And to that extent, you deceived them?*

After objections from Hollingsworth's lawyer on the grounds of relevance and some legal quibbling, a bemused Commissioner Peter Connor shot down the barrister's line of attack that Hollingsworth was nothing but a crooked hooker: a mattress actress who short-changed honest johns by simulating sex.

Connor said testily: 'Are we going to prosecute every prostitute for –' before interrupting himself to answer his own rhetorical question. 'No, we won't. You can't answer that question.'

Apart from such diversions, the case would drag on, turning into a saga. In the end, Hollingsworth landed a punch on the police service because Commissioner Connor found she had been unfairly dismissed and ordered her reinstatement with the next intake of recruits in November 1997. This result prompted one tabloid to run the inevitable headline 'Happy Hooker' but she wasn't happy for long, because the police appealed for a stay against her reinstatement.

Hollingsworth turned up in a dark blue suit over a light blue silk shirt, a businesslike outfit that did not hide her striking figure. A reporter watching her walk into court noted a passing businessman swivel around to stare at her.

Hollingsworth was represented before the full bench of the Industrial Commission by Ian Barker QC, famous for his notoriously successful prosecution of Lindy Chamberlain – who was, of course, subsequently cleared of murdering her baby daughter Azaria.

Barker, who had played the Chamberlain jury like a violin, this time took the softly, softly approach – arguing that his client be allowed to start again as a trainee police officer rather than be fully reinstated as a police officer. That way, he said soothingly, the police service would have time to assess if she were suitable for the job. If this were meant to appease the police, it didn't work – at least, not judging by the language used by the police barrister, Paul Menzies QC. He gave a caustic critique of Hollingsworth's character, talking of her 'absence of credibility, absence of credit', accusing her of avoiding tax and stating: 'The Police Commissioner does not wish to have such a person in his police service ... The Commissioner does not want her there.'

It worked. After a few minutes the commission president delivered judgment: the stay was granted. Meanwhile, however, Hollingsworth was to be paid the equivalent of a trainee salary: around $200 a week. In other words, about what she could make at the Touch of Class brothel in half an hour. But it wasn't about the money for Kim Hollingsworth. She had a point to prove, maybe to herself.

All the scurrilous stuff about her had already been aired and couldn't hurt her any more, so she was free to cause as much grief for the police service as she liked. Which is exactly what she did. She posed for photographs with her pet rat Caspar on her shoulder and became an evangelist for animal rights as well as for herself, a poster girl for positive thinking.

From Kings Cross to animal liberation. It was all a long way from her hometown.

TEACHERS don't need crystal balls to predict the futures of most of the kids that pass through their hands. There are plenty of signposts pointing out the likely course of adult lives.

Here's a placid girl, friendly and mature, the part of wife and mother already written for her. There's the cocky, overgrown boy strutting around near the top of a pecking order that will make him a small town hero on the sports field until he ends up a bar room bore, unless he is the one in a hundred who can make the big league.

There's always a few troublemakers – often from troubled homes – smoking in the toilets, drinking at the dance, doing drugs, fighting and fornicating. Some are only temporarily wild, hostages to hormones or easily led, but among them are the ones doomed to end up on the wrong side of the law.

Then there are the studious few, bent over their books and ignoring the temptations of the present because they dream of the future, an escape to the outside world.

At Wodonga West High in 1984, Kim Hollingsworth was one of the studious ones. She was never loud or vulgar, one of the so-called class 'tarts' with short skirts and long fingernails and cigarettes in her handbag. In fact, in all her time at Wodonga, no one would later recall her doing anything that made her stand out from the middle ground. She was quiet, like her brother Jason and sisters Melissa and Melanie. Quiet, in fact, like their mother Glenys, who lives in the same mission brown double-storey house and is so reserved she rarely speaks unless spoken to first if an acquaintance sees her in the street.

What little that Kim Hollingsworth's contemporaries and teachers recall of the quiet girl is what she didn't do, rather than what she did.

She didn't smoke in the toilets, 'pash' boys behind the bus stop or pinch stuff from the shops down the street. She didn't turn up late for school and didn't disturb others in class when she got there. She did her homework not only on time but well. About the only thing that stood out was that she and her closest schoolfriend, JoAnne Wiltshire, were Boy George fans. Even then, Kim wasn't the leader nor remotely outrageous. Teachers remember that it was JoAnne, who still lives in Wodonga, who wore the androgynous Boy George outfits and joked about going to England to see him sing.

Nothing about Kim's school days hinted at what was ahead: that she would not only become a stripper and a hooker but such a relentlessly extroverted cheerleader for her own cause – not addicted to drugs, like most sex workers, but to self-promotion, like many showbiz performers. When she left school – and the town – she left barely a ripple behind her. Ask people in Wodonga about her and they shake their heads and wonder what happened to change the girl they now realise they barely knew.

Even the few who did know her are puzzled about what happened to the studious schoolgirl. Even in hindsight, none of them claims to have picked anything in her behaviour to indicate that she would end up in the sex industry – or wanting to be a police officer, for that matter.

Kim's embracing of causes – not just her own crusade to join the police service but that of animal liberation – bemuses one of her few close friends from school. The friend, who doesn't want to be named, became close to Kim in Year 11.

'She was pretty straight but a bit of a loner,' she says. 'Neither of us made friends easily. She was definitely brighter than most of the others and always studying.' She was good at English and German.

She recalls the Hollingsworths having cats and a collie dog but little to indicate Kim's later passion for animal rights. 'That could have come when she went to Sydney and got in with a new group of people,' she ponders. Nor can she recall Kim the devoted vegetarian, more that she was interested in music.

Half a lifetime later, the details have faded but she recalls vaguely that something went wrong for the Hollingsworth family that she can't quite identify. Kim's father left the police force before the girls finished school, and soon after separated from his wife.

'It was a big house in the snobby bit of Wodonga. I think they (Kim's parents) were still together when we met but they separated and he moved downstairs. He was always very friendly to me. I think he made stuff out of glass (for sale) in the garage. Kim's mum didn't like visitors but she didn't mind me.'

Whatever it was that went wrong for the Hollingsworths might well have derailed Kim's final year at school. At least one teacher recalls that she didn't see out the school year in 1984. Her former classmate's memory is that she moved out of home and across the Murray to Albury, renting a flat and working in an ice cream shop, first of a series of casual jobs that would lead her to the sex industry.

It sounds like the start of the independent, sexually adventurous life but the friend says not. 'She didn't have a boyfriend. She was never into boys then – apart from Boy George. It wasn't until later that she became more of a show pony.'

The friend claims to share Kim's philosophy: 'I do what I like as long as it doesn't hurt anyone else.' But she concedes that Kim changed after she left the district and joined 'the scene'.

A lot can happen in three years. When Kim returned to Wodonga for her classmate's 21st birthday in 1988, she had changed – in more ways than one.

'She was a "dancer" then. And I think she'd had her boob job done by then, and I reckon a nose job.' But what she remembers most is Kim giving 'my Dad a real big kiss – almost a pash. No inhibitions at all.'

After that, they kept in touch intermittently but rarely saw each other. The friend had married young and they were taking different paths. Interestingly, she says, Kim's sister Melissa also joined 'the scene' in Sin City, whereas brother Jason stayed back in Wodonga with his mother, working steadily and not having much to do with his father or his well-known sister in Sydney.

KATRINA Francis was – and is – a friend of the Boy George fan JoAnne Wiltshire more than she ever was of Kim Hollingsworth. She recalls Kim wanting 'to be a vet' and loving animals.

'I don't think Kim had many friends,' she says. 'She was one of those students who would sit and study. Always had her head in a book. She wasn't out to make friends – was what you'd call a nerd.

'She wasn't a very attractive girl when she was younger. She looked anorexic to me – like a stick figure.'

Katrina was living in Sydney in the late 1990s and was surprised that Kim contacted her and arranged to meet her. 'We met at the train station and she gave me flowers,' she recalls. She had been a little bemused by the unexpected gesture – wondered if there were a motive – because they had not really been friends at school.

Like other Wodonga West teachers, Brian Rock recalls the high school fondly. 'We had some of the most magical teaching ever, there,' he recalls. 'The school was built in a paddock and grew form by form each year. It was more a country style school then – friendly and part of the community. Relationships between staff and students were strong.' The sort of place, he says, where 'if the circus came to town we'd close the school for the day and go to the circus.'

The school had its success stories: two of the best from battling families not as well off as the Hollingsworths. One former student, Mark McDonald, became a senior researcher at the British Museum. Another, Michael Clifford, is a surgeon who has distinguished himself overseas.

But Kim from Castle Heights, the 'dress circle' middle-class enclave where the principal lived, didn't kick on the way Brian Rock and his fellow teachers thought she would.

'She was the last kid you'd pick to end up as a stripper or in prostitution,' says Rock. 'My first reaction was that she must have been affected by drugs or mental illness – but that wasn't it. She was quiet, studious, shy, not outspoken.'

He thinks she didn't finish the year's study (in 1984) because of some domestic upset but can't recall the details. 'I've got a niggling suspicion that something went wrong at home.'

One thing is clear: by the time Kim reached VCE in 1984, her police sergeant father was on extended sick leave for reasons that time has partly obscured. Fellow police recall unproven suspicions that some members had been 'milking' petrol from police cars. And that, angered by rumours that bounced around the station, Alan Hollingsworth had taken a stand: he would take all his accumulated sick leave then resign. He was a proud man and wasn't going to suffer the humiliation of being questioned over nonsense like allegations of siphoning petrol as if he were some supposed petty thief, even if it were only a departmental matter. At around the same time, tensions at home came to a head and he split with his wife, Glenys, living for a while under the same roof. Then he left, heading for Sydney and a job as 'a chauffeur', according to one bemused former police officer who worked at Wodonga at the time.

Whether it's right or not, the impression he left behind is of a strict and secretive man who dominated the family until he left it. A police officer stationed at Wodonga at the time recalls that Alan Hollingsworth transferred there from Melbourne's outer eastern suburbs in the late 1970s, before Kim was ready to start high school. He was a sergeant in uniform but not one to curry favour with the public and fellow police. He kept to himself – and so did his family.

'The wife and kids never really spoke to you unless they had to,' the officer recalls. 'It was as if they had been instructed by the father not to talk to people. No "nice day today" or anything like that. If he brought them into the station to collect his mail or anything, the kids would never talk to you. I don't think many people would go to the house. He was a bit of a mystery man.'

THE only paying customers who get to see Kim Hollingsworth these days aren't buying sex. They are riders who pay by the hour to do trail rides at the Scenic Hills Riding Ranch near Campbelltown. It's easy to find, she says: the name is spelled out in big, white letters, Hollywood style, on a hill near the M5 freeway south-west of Sydney.

She's a casual riding instructor – saddling horses to ride out with the public who turn up at the 'ranch' on weekends and holidays. It is the latest in a line of jobs she has had with horses since quitting prostitution and being forced to abandon the police service after a determined effort to embarrass the authorities for snubbing her. She has worked at racing stables – riding work for various Sydney trainers. She is light but strong for her weight – testament to a vegetarian diet, exercise and the fact, she says, that she has never done drugs. At 42, she looks years younger in photographs, with few of the tell-tale signs of surviving the sex industry.

She refuses to deny or be demeaned by her past. Luke Slattery wrote of her in 1997: 'She carries herself with a confident air, all the while striving to lay claim to a fresh self.' She still does.

When the authors spoke to her in 2009, she was living at a small property at Appin, between Picton and Wollongong, and working part-time at the riding school, half an hour's drive away. She was as bright and engaging as any sales person – or well-schooled escort. She tells her stories with apparent frankness, but there is a sense that they are well-honed anecdotes of the sort that performers roll out on chat shows. Cute on cue.

She tells, for instance, how a little girl at the riding school asked her innocently one day, 'Were you a policeman?' and when asked why she'd asked, said it was because of the way Kim sits up straight, shoulders squared, hands neat and low. There is a discipline and precision in the way she does things that is at odds with the sex and drugs and dirty money of life in the Cross.

In the end, of course, the big question is: Why? What made her take up the sex industry?

The story she has told everyone for years hasn't changed.

'I was a late starter,' she confides, beginning her routine as if it's for the very first time. It isn't. 'I didn't do anything in Albury-Wodonga. But then I had a bad boyfriend.

I thought everyone was out of a Jane Austen book but I walked in on him with two prostitutes. I was all sad and crying and they looked after me and ended up offering me a job. When I asked, 'How much?' they said I could make at least a grand and more likely two grand a week. My wage at the time was $160 as a waitress.'

But the motive wasn't the money, she says. At first she was just trying to get back at the bad boyfriend. But once she tasted the money it was hard to go back to low pay.

She says when she started stripping, she and her sister and another woman ('two blondes and one brunette') took their skimpy stripper costumes and tape player into the grounds of a kindergarten next door to their apartment and practised on the hopscotch court. Once they got their moves down pat, they were in business.

She doesn't avoid talking about her years in the sex industry but is happier talking about her love of animals. She claims to have declared herself against eating meat when she was a tiny child, to her parents' astonishment, and to have stood by those principles all her life. It hasn't been easy, she says.

Her ill-fated mounted policeman friend was called Roy De Coque. Because she wanted to get into a Bachelor of Applied Science course in equine studies she needed a reference stating that she was an experienced horse handler. De Coque obligingly wrote one for her – on police letterhead. When he was summoned to the Wood Royal Commission to answer questions about this he panicked and shot himself. But the story does not quite end with that senseless tragedy.

The postscript Hollingsworth adds is that the fatal reference got her into the course but she couldn't stand it. Why? The college had a pig production unit that upset her. And her lecturers put down a pregnant mare so the students could study the foetus. She ditched the course. So De Coque's fatal favour didn't do anyone much good.

IN mid-June 2009, in the news room of the Albury newspaper, the *Border Mail*, the chief of staff fielded a telephone call. On the line was Kim Hollingsworth, calling from Campbelltown. She said she wanted to announce that she – meaning a character based on her – was going to be in the next *Underbelly* television series, to be screened in 2010.

The chief of staff, Anthony Bunn, was mildly surprised at the naked self-promotion but happy to play along. Hollingsworth, an old hand at the publicity game, was only too pleased to pose with her clothes on in front of the Campbelltown police station so that her local Camden newspaper could photograph her. The same picture (and story) could be used in both that paper and the Border Mail. She told Bunn the Campbelltown police weren't happy at her using their station as a backdrop – but not to worry, she'd do it anyway. And that's exactly what she did.

Kim Hollingsworth pleases herself. There was a time when that meant she provided happy endings for the police, but not any more. She's a big girl now.

COOKING CHOOK

> Lagging bent colleagues wasn't
> good for your nerves, your
> health or your police career.

DETECTIVE Inspector Graham 'Chook' Fowler was filling his car with petrol at a service station when the Royal Commission investigators swooped. But Chook was used to having anti-corruption officers breathing down his neck and kept his hand calmly on the nozzle.

For once, his confidence was misplaced although it would take a while for the bad news to sink in. Until then, somehow he had always survived. None of the seventeen disciplinary charges brought against him by police Internal Affairs while he was head of detectives at Kings Cross had been able to land a punch on the 51-year-old police veteran.

And each escape, narrow or not, added to his belief in his own invincibility and the solidarity of the 'big blue gang'. Honest police might detest corrupt ones but would rarely expose them, even if they wanted to. Lagging bent colleagues wasn't good for your nerves, your health or your career.

That's why he was so sure of himself. That's why he knocked back the deal the officers offered him to 'roll over' and work undercover for the Royal Commission to expose other corrupt police. 'Thanks but no thanks,' he said.

From where Chook Fowler stood, it was a pragmatic decision. Why risk changing direction after decades of getting away with standover tactics, intimidation, bribe taking, fraud and offering protection for drug dealing, prostitution and pornography?

But Fowler didn't know there was a marked card in the hand he was being dealt. The deal he rejected had already been accepted by his friend Detective Sergeant Trevor Haken, who would become the Commission's star witness – and ultimately send Fowler to jail.

Under Haken's direction, Fowler would be among the most celebrated, exposed and humiliated individuals in the chequered history of Australian law enforcement. He would emerge as a blustering, antiquated, comical embarrassment: an old-time corrupt copper unable to cope with radical new technology that caught the sins of bent cops and their criminal collaborators on film and tape.

All he could do was watch in bewilderment as irrefutable evidence of his corruption flowed from his own mouth, leaving him no avenue of escape and giving him worldwide exposure as an incompetent, bumbling crook.

'Car-cam', as it came to be called, comprised tiny cameras hidden under the dashboard of a specially modified Toyota driven by Haken. The cameras captured perfect video images of anyone sitting in the front seats – and recorded anything they said.

It was impossible to argue with the evidence supplied by the hidden camera because usually the suspect was recorded blithely implicating himself in crime. It was as effective as a full confession. The revolutionary electric surveillance included bugs on phones, cameras in cars, and long-distance recording devices – most of it involving poacher-turned-gamekeeper Trevor Haken. He made 80 secret car-cam videos of corrupt dealings.

Corrupt police watched, at first befuddled, then in mounting horror, as the recorded electronic evidence was played to the Commission. Like cavemen watching a rocket ship, they were dumbstruck as they heard their own voices detailing crimes and corruption that would destroy careers and lives. 'Rolling over' immediately became a brutally effective psychological tool. There was nowhere to hide any more, so police jostled to rat on each other in return for leniency and destroyed forever the 'blue wall' of solidarity.

They were exposed as just as cowardly and just as disloyal as the criminals they had intimidated into 'admitting' to crimes they had not committed. In Fowler's case, he repeatedly denied questions from counsel assisting the Commission, Gary Crooke, asking if he had ever accepted bribes from Kings Cross night club owners and drug dealers. But the video told a different story.

Haken's Toyota might have been in perfect running order but it was still a death trap for a police career – as Fowler found out on half a dozen occasions as tape after tape was screened to an enthralled hearing. It was like watching a car crash replayed in slow motion.

Ironically, one videotape included Fowler rejoicing in his security as he accepted a $500 share of a bribe from Haken while laughing at police investigative procedures: 'They don't bug cars. They just follow them,' he scoffed.

Overweight, bombastic, his evidence riddled with four-letter obscenities, and long suspected of being corrupt, Fowler would nonetheless become the Royal Commission's pin-up boy.

He was the first one to appear on car-cam and generated massive public interest when video of him talking about his corruption was played. It dominated headlines around Australia next day and was replayed endlessly on TV news shows and overseas services.

It stunned the public. More importantly, it frightened the dozen or so other high-ranking police who suddenly realised their futures were in jeopardy because of their suicidally frank talks about corrupt activities during the previous nine months with roll-over cop Haken – either in his car or when he was 'wired for sound'.

But no victim was as staggeringly obtuse as Fowler. He even admitted he had heard rumours Haken had rolled over but chose not to believe them – or take precautions. He took bribes and was linked to a $10,000 offer to an alleged murderer to 'fix his case.'

Another car-cam tape showed Haken receiving a $2000 bribe from Kings Cross sleaze merchant Steve Hardas, also being monitored by Commission investigators. As soon as Hardas left the car, investigators counted the money and confirmed with Haken that $1000 of the bribe was to be passed on to Fowler.

With so much evidence at its fingertips, the Commission calmly ignored Fowler's witness-box bluster, revealing for the first time its pattern of attack.

Crooke, the counsel assisting, ran Fowler through the usual inquiries about whether he was corrupt and got the expected denials. In fact, 25 times Fowler denied being corrupt. In the past, such verbal denials had been enough to get corrupt police off the hook. But not with car-cam.

A stiff exchange between Crooke and Fowler in the witness box disguised the dynamite about to detonate.

Crooke: *Mr Fowler, it has been your position, hasn't it, that you've never been in receipt of corrupt monies?*

Fowler: *That's correct.*

Crooke: *And so it is today?*

Fowler: *That's correct.*

Crooke: *And by that you mean to say that you haven't been involved directly or indirectly in the receipt of corrupt funds?*

Fowler: *That's correct.*

Crooke: *It's just a blanket answer as far as you are concerned. Corruption and you are strangers, in other words.*

Fowler: *That's correct.*

Then came the big bang.

Crooke: *Would you look at the tape, please?*

And there, in black and white on half a dozen video screens around the room, Fowler was seen stuffing the bribe Haken had given him into his pocket while bitching about the size of the payment. The audio made misunderstanding impossible.

Haken: 'Hardas gave us a grand, right. That was just a fucking drink to keep going as far as I understand it anyway. Are you happy with that?'

Fowler: 'Yeah. Fucking yeah... the fucking duds.'

Haken: 'That ought to pay for this morning's shopping so what are you fucking blueing about.'

The tape ran for 22 minutes. To Fowler it must have seemed an eternity. He watched the early frames with a puzzled look then, as reality hit him, he went white and started fidgeting as if a wasps' nest had fallen down his pants.

The end of tape one brought no relief. The Commission had more films than Hollywood. Another one showed Fowler talking about a future accident he planned to have: it involved slipping on a spilt milkshake in the foyer of the City of Sydney police station to get a hurt-on-duty discharge and a hefty accompanying payout.

The conversation included what were known to be Fowler's short term plans to handle what seemed to be increasingly dire straits and financial pressures.

As a result of the milkshake 'accident' Fowler was on indefinite sick leave and used it as a reason to delay his appearance before the Royal Commission for more than six months. It finally took a threat from Commissioner Wood to jail him if he did not appear, to force him to front in December 1994 and answer some more tough questions.

Although he had beaten charges from Internal Affairs while working at Kings Cross, he was becoming increasingly tainted. In fact, he was a carcass swinging in the breeze, stinking to high heaven.

During his time at the Cross, one of Fowler's colleagues, former sergeant Larry Churchill, had been jailed on a variety of charges including protecting drug dealers and involvement with a $4 million importation of amphetamines. Another officer was sacked.

This time Fowler had run out of protectors. His loud denials started to unravel as the evidence mounted. He claimed that a lump sum of $30,000 he used to help pay for a house on the Central Coast – plus the monthly mortgage payment of $1300 – came from punting on horses.

'I win at least $200 a week on the horses,' he said. 'I'm more successful at picking winners (than losers).'

Fowler would admit he had anything up to $30,000 (in lots of $5000) hidden around his house at any one time, including in the pockets of suits. And his recorded conversations with Haken made it clear he had an intimate knowledge of who paid bribes at Kings Cross and how entrenched various police were in the corruption.

In the weeks leading up to the Royal Commission, Fowler's exasperated bosses had moved to limit his activities. They decided to at least move him as far away as they could from opportunities for corrupt payments. He could go to Chatswood station on uniform duty. Or he could go to a country station.

Chatswood or the bush was no choice at all for Fowler. It would mean an end to his established lines of graft and corruption and slash his revenue by hundreds of dollars a week. That's why he devised the third option: he would stage an accident and be discharged with a payout.

He spoke to Haken about suffering a 'career-ending' accident in a staged car smash but then switched to the idea of slipping on a milk-shake at the City of Sydney station when he walked out of a lift, injuring his back on the marble floor.

'I've got to have an accident tomorrow at work,' he told Haken in a taped conversation which was played to the Royal Commission only minutes after Fowler had denied any such conversation had ever taken place.

'I'll have to set it up.' It would have to be a `fucking nasty accident – nothing else would suffice,' he said. 'I need a payout. Stress isn't enough.'

The payout would go towards the down payment on a caravan he was planning to buy to travel around Australia. Right on cue next day, as Fowler had foretold, he slipped on a pre-arranged spilt milkshake near a lift well and was carried out of the building on a stretcher.

In his book *Sympathy for the Devil*, Haken says Fowler survived only a few days in hospital before being sent home, 'following a number of incidents involving alcohol.'

Fowler's ability to predict his accident and his inescapable collusion caused Commissioner Wood to be almost light-hearted at one stage in his questioning.

Wood: *You say you genuinely fell on a milkshake?*

Fowler: *Yes.*

Wood: *Is it a co-incidence that you happened to talk about slipping before it happened?*

More damning was Fowler's taped conversation with Haken in planning the accident.

Fowler: *Stress is not enough. I have to go for a payout.*

Haken: *HOD (hurt on duty) are you?*

Fowler: *Yeah HOD and fucking injury, long term.*

Haken: *At work.*

Fowler: *Yeah, don't fucking mention that to any cunt. Doctor said all I have to do is make it happen. I'll do everything, everything is organised.*

Stunned by the secret tapings, Fowler tried to fall back on his dismal record as a policeman – and even tried to call the Commission corrupt. It was the raving of a desperate and ruined man.

'This Commission is as corrupt as anyone it is investigating,' he almost shouted from the witness box. He emphasised he had been exonerated on all seventeen charges he'd faced at Kings Cross but said he remained tainted by what he called 'rumour and innuendo.'

'After 32 years in the police trying to uphold the laws of this state I have always believed a person is innocent until proven guilty,' he stormed. 'We've come back to the French Revolution. Where's justice?'

Watching Fowler stumble into the Commission's well-laid traps made compelling watching. He typified the stupidity of corrupt police who believed in their own invincibility long after it had crumbled.

Despite overwhelming evidence, Fowler blocked out reality. He became a pathetic figure as he continued to maintain his innocence, saying at one stage that the money Haken was handing over was to repay a loan. He also came up with a novel alternative defence: that the man on the video taking bribes was not him. It was, he said, an actor hired by the Commission to impersonate him.

'Do you think we'd hire someone to play Graham Fowler?' asked an amused Crooke.

'Funny things happen here,' said Fowler, clearly rattled.

The revelation that Haken had sold him out shattered Fowler's self-proclaimed integrity and blind loyalty to police unity. The blue line was no more. It was now a race to the lifeboats, every man for himself.

It was well-known that certain senior police were out for all they could get from bribes or dodging work. Haken said that after a certain hour each night Fowler could be more easily found in the Sir John Young Hotel than on duty. He was one of several officers-in-charge whose nocturnal activities were not textbook policing.

One would come to work with his fishing gear. Wearing a jumper to cover his police uniform, he would spend the night sitting on the sandstone wall around the Opera House, fishing. Another would bring a kayak to work and row in Centennial Park lakes to keep fit. Fowler's antics were more mercenary than sporting. His only known exercise was counting the cash he got in 'slings'.

Although his decision not to roll over to the Royal Commission would ultimately send him to jail, Fowler's decision to take his chances was backed by the sound logic of the past. Previous inquiries in New South Wales had inflicted few casualties on police united in lies and denials and he must have thought the line would hold. One reason for his confidence was that two senior police had told him (so he told Haken in a bugged conversation) that his 'loyalty' to the bent brotherhood would be rewarded.

The senior men made it clear that protecting the force was top priority. Those who stayed silent would be given a choice of jobs when the Commission was finished. Or they would be given a pension.

This was backed up by Haken. When warned by a lawyer that if he had not rolled over, his assets would have been seized and he would have been imprisoned, he had retorted: '... if I hadn't (helped the Commission) I might also have become a superintendent in the CIB.' It was a fair point.

Eventually, even Fowler's loud and repeated denials of corruption started to unravel as evidence mounted. The Royal Commission asked him to explain how he could be such a successful punter when his TAB account, which they subpoenaed, indicated that in three and a half years he had lost a large part of the $9000 he had wagered.

Despite his profitable working relationship with Fowler and the friendship between them, Haken had no compunction about trapping him. It was, he said, just a continuation of his role as an undercover agent for the Commission. Survival of the fittest – and the quickest thinkers.

'Detective Inspector Graham Fowler had been a colleague of mine for a number of years,' he said on *60 Minutes*, appearing in heavy disguise. 'The video that I recorded in my car was typical of many previous transactions where money had been picked up from a criminal and was being divided among the police involved.'

He told the ABC's *Australian Story*: 'I was a close associate if you like, if not a friend. They were hard times but that was the job I undertook. That was the way it went.'

Asked what was going through his mind as he betrayed Fowler, he answered: 'That I was doing a job... Purely and simply a job.'

He said he blocked out the fact that somebody he had known and presumably liked was being set up. But after a couple of rambling sentences that said nothing, he came out with the truth: 'There is no nice way of putting it – yes, I was destroying him.'

But in his book he made a cooler and less-emotive assessment of Fowler. 'He was nice enough when you were on a par with him but he was a standover man both to his staff and to people in the street,' he wrote. 'He was called GOC (Grumpy Old Cunt) or GOP (Grumpy Old Prick).

'I didn't mind the guy but he was an horrendous "dudder" – that is, he would rip you off. If there was a quid around he would take 75 cents in the dollar. I didn't worry because there was plenty around in the Cross ... Perhaps that is why I survived so well, I played the odds.'

As for Fowler, as people all around him rolled over he blindly clung to his belief that somehow his faith in the brotherhood would rescue him at the eleventh hour. It didn't. Allegations mounted, including one that he and Haken had taken thousands of dollars from Hardas to help him beat charges of having bribed a police sergeant in Sydney's west.

He claimed that his bugged conversations with Haken had been tampered with to provide the wrong interpretation.

Counsel assisting, Gary Crooke: 'Are you suggesting that the Commission might have got actors or cobbled these videos together? Is that going through your mind?'

Fowler: *That's a possibility. You could have dubbed the tape, yes.*

Crooke: *Has somebody taken the part of Graham Fowler and taken the money?*

Fowler: *Funny things happen, don't they.*

Wood: *Are you suggesting we've doctored all those tapes. Last time you suggested we provided an actor to play your part. Do you still suggest that is the case?*

Fowler: *I don't know what to believe, sir. I wouldn't believe you're part of it, sir, but I wouldn't put it past some of the people.*

Crooke: *Where's it going to get you, Mr Fowler? Why don't you be a man and confess?*

Fowler, who was suspended without pay straight after the car-cam screenings, was eventually tried and convicted on charges of defrauding an insurance company over his milk-shake 'accident' but served only a couple of years in jail.

He was never charged with any corruption offences arising from his taped conversations and video evidence.

IF Trevor Haken and Fowler were the established face of perennial police corruption, Detective Senior Constable Duncan Demol represented the next generation of officers being swept up in 'the joke', often against their will.

To succumb to temptation was to spurn the vows of public service and integrity they made as police officers. But to knock back a share of the spoils was to risk being ostracised – and could even cripple careers.

Demol was tortured by the dilemma from his first days on the job, when his minder and work partner Senior Constable Stephen Worsley had taken him to a brothel called the Barrel, where they sat drinking with naked women. Free women, food and drink: you don't see those job opportunities on police recruitment posters.

Demol picked up the idea of warped police work pretty quickly. During his first week he signed a false affidavit about a crash involving a police car. Demol's first bribe was $50 from Haken, who took it from two shoplifters. The next time he had a search warrant he stole $5000 from a cupboard in a raid on a drug dealer's house and split it with Haken.

Demol rolled over to the Commission after being confronted by video evidence, taken in Haken's car, of him lying. Although they by then worked in different areas, Demol idolised Haken, staying close even though rumours were pinpointing the older man as a turncoat collecting evidence for the Commission.

So when Demol read a confidential memo from a New South Wales Crime Commission mentioning Haken he rushed to tell him, not knowing he had rolled over. In return, Haken deliberately lured him into the car-cam vehicle so his confessions could be recorded and handed over.

A disillusioned Demol, overweight and bald, then rolled over himself. He told of police fitting 'someone up with the trifecta' – cop slang for charging someone with offensive language, assaulting police and resisting police, whether they had committed offences or not.

Kings Cross police were served free beer in teapots in restaurants so no one could see them drinking. It was protocol that money stolen during drug raids would be shared among other police. So warped were the values that the only notion of 'dishonesty' was failing to split a drug dealer's dirty money with others cops on the shift.

Demol volunteered two police maxims drummed into him as a probationary officer: 'You're not a copper until you can work pissed,' and, 'Everything you did was to cover your arse.'

Police drank on duty and held parties at the back of the station while someone watched the front desk. Any member of the public who came in with a problem was processed as quickly as possible.

He told of police getting together in 'scrum downs' to fabricate evidence. Perjury was rife because police considered the odds were against them making a case on the facts alone. He admitted he would fake evidence against someone who was guilty if the case needed strengthening. And theft and corruption payments for protection were widespread.

'It is a common belief that you have got to do what you can to get a conviction because nobody believes you,' Demol said. 'Juries won't believe you, judges won't believe you.'

Demol, who was with the Drug Enforcement Agency, said street police hated all investigative organisations like the Royal Commission and the Independent Commission Against Corruption (ICAC).

Demol was among eight police, including Haken, dismissed from the force after either giving self-incriminating evidence or being confronted by indisputable evidence on video.

The others included Fowler, Detective Senior Sergeant Denis Kimble Thompson, Detective Sergeant Neville John Scullion, Detective Sergeant Wayne James Eade, and Detective Sergeant John Gordon Swan.

Eade, head of the Police Drug Unit on the New South Wales Central Coast, was caught on video taking drugs, having sex with a prostitute and asking her if she had access to child pornographic films.

The eighth 'scalp' was one of the highest-ranked officers to be caught up in the corruption investigation, Detective Chief Superintendent Bob Lysaught, who allegedly arranged bribes from drug dealers. Betrayed by a close associate and long-time friend of the family, he crashed and burned and the flames singed everyone who had ever been close to him.

The bigger they are, the harder they fall.

– WITH RAY CHESTERTON

7

NO SYMPATHY
FOR THE DEVIL

The prisoners were ordered out
of the van one at a time and
bashed as they ran the gauntlet
between two lines of police.

THE boys were out for a bucks' night when they learned
the hard way not to cross the crooked cops who were the
uncrowned kings of the Cross.

The young bucks were aggressive and confident they
were tough enough to match any challenge to come their
way. They were wrong. In the street brawl that erupted on
that winter night in 1992, bouncers from nearby nightclubs
joined forces with the off-duty detectives to throw punches
and crack heads. It was only going to go one way.

But winning the battle wasn't enough for the Kings
Cross coppers. Like any other street gang members, they
wanted to make a point. The more violently the better.

Back-up police arrived swiftly to look after their mates – and 'fix up' the would-be troublemakers. They threw them into a paddy wagon, took them to Kings Cross station and systematically beat them with batons.

It still wasn't enough. To rub salt into their wounds, the bruised and bloodied crew were charged with various offences. Naturally, the police would later collaborate with each other to give false evidence that would ensure convictions – and protect them, they thought, from any possibility of a comeback.

At the time, it was just another violent night in the Cross. But it would prove one of many incidents to come back and haunt the police that took part because one of them was going to tell the truth about it.

Not that he was guilt-stricken or had got religion. It was more cold-blooded and selfish than that. As any cop knows, most crooks will cut a deal to avoid punishment. And that's exactly what happened when investigators from the Wood Royal Commission came knocking at Trevor Haken's door.

TREVOR Haken was as bent as a three-dollar note, as crooked as most of the scum he'd ever locked up. He just looked better from the outside.

In nearly three decades of graft and law-breaking he had risen through the ranks to be a detective sergeant at Kings Cross.

He had earned his spurs as a black knight at the Drug Squad at Darlinghurst, called 'Goldenhurst' by police in the know because of the easy money they could make from rackets there. He'd been a member of the CIB and of a

NO SYMPATHY FOR THE DEVIL

Joint Task Force of State and Commonwealth officers set up to combat drug trafficking in Chinatown. Finally, he had risen to be in charge of Kings Cross detectives, his dishonesty apparently overlooked (or quietly appreciated) by the many senior police who were already on the take.

In his final year as a corrupt officer, Haken pocketed around $90,000 himself – and acted as the bagman to distribute 'slings' to other bent officers. When investigators turned up on his doorstep at Hornsby in north-west Sydney, the ghosts of Trevor Haken's past came back to haunt him. The investigators had been probing him for weeks and following him everywhere he went. And they had enough evidence to prove what they already knew – he was corrupt.

They gave him a simple choice. He could take responsibility for his crimes and face charges – or he could 'roll over' and co-operate with the Wood Royal Commission.

'Roll over' was a term that would be heard more and more often as the inquiries and evidence became public and it became increasingly obvious there was nowhere for bent cops to hide.

Haken rolled, choosing to be an informer and turning on crooked police mates to mitigate his own involvement. In return, he and his family would be given new identities and go into witness protection once he'd told the Commission everything he thought he could.

To his former mates, he was a 'dog' and a 'maggot' for 'lagging'. But to the Royal Commission, and the majority of the public, he was a one-man force for redemption, the mother lode of information for a sophisticated investigation into police corruption.

Not that it was easy for him – it wasn't a decision driven by morality or conscience. He would later say he sometimes regretted the decision to roll over because a couple of years in jail might have been better than a life in hiding, constantly fearing recognition by criminals and rogue police he had named in the Commission. By rolling over he had broken a code he'd followed all his working life.

His decision to become a whistleblower underpinned the Wood Royal Commission's success. Without Haken's astonishing recall of his own corruption, and the involvement of so many others, the inquiry might have floundered, as others had in the past, when faced with police willing to unite in their lies.

Haken changed that. Using cutting-edge electronic equipment, the Commission's officers tapped phones and eavesdropped on police doing deals with criminals and talking to other corrupt officers.

A highlight of this remarkable covert investigation was that Haken used his street smarts to fight for good just as skilfully as he had evilly used it to pocket hundreds of thousands of dollars over the years. He wore electronic gear to meetings with corrupt police and criminals so they would incriminate themselves.

Another sting was referred to as 'car-cam', where a secret camera was hidden in Haken's car to record irrefutable proof of police taking bribes.

Haken's allegations dredged up treacheries and acts of dishonesty that those involved might have imagined were long forgotten. The bashing of the Kings Cross bucks' night revellers described above was just one 'routine' offence, and by no means the most serious. Protecting drug dealers was worse – but the bashing was graphic proof that Kings Cross police were out of control and believed they were untouchable.

The combination of a well-placed whistleblower and advanced electronic equipment would supersede all the stillborn attempts at anti-corruption investigation that had gone before it, exposing thuggish police behaviour that had gone unchecked for decades.

As Haken recounts in his own account of his Kings Cross escapades, *Sympathy for the Devil*, that violent night of 22 July 1990 was one to remember for all the wrong reasons.

The detectives and their wives and girlfriends had just finished dinner at the Gazebo restaurant. They decided to take a stroll around the area to have a look at places of interest.

The group ran into a bucks' night group of eight to twelve young men from the western suburbs who (as Haken would tell the Royal Commission) had been drinking and were behaving badly. One of the young men brushed shoulders with one of the detectives – a misjudgement that led to a detective throwing one of the revellers against the side of a tow truck in retaliation.

Haken writes: 'We were set upon by a group of thugs who were later referred to in court as a "group of young men".

'But thugs are always a "group of young men" in the eyes of mum and dad. They come along to court in their suits and short hair but on the night they had blood in their eyes and were out of control. They were intent on beating the living daylights out of anyone who got in their way.'

The confrontation quickly became an all-in, bloody brawl.

A constable, Duncan Demol, was kicked in the face and collapsed. He would later need stitches to a cut in his head. Another policeman was kicked and punched. Horrified on-lookers scrambled out of the way and as the brawl spilled over the footpath, bouncers from nearby nightclubs rushed to help their police buddies.

With the bouncers in play, who would win the fight was never in doubt. But it took the party boys a little while to work out what they'd let themselves into. Still unaware of the identities of the men they had been fighting, they continued to yell abuse and bang the inside of the police van after the uniformed police arrested them.

It was not until one of them looked out the back door of the van as it pulled into an underground car park beneath Kings Cross police station and saw the men they had been fighting lined up, carrying batons, that the truth dawned on them.

'Fuck. We're dead,' one lout said to his mates. He was almost right. No one died in the resulting bloodbath, but it was a wonder.

The vengeful police started by rocking the van and bashing on the sides and telling the men inside they were 'dead.' The prisoners were ordered out of the van one at a time and bashed as they ran the gauntlet between two lines of police to get to the holding cell.

'It was full on anger and there was plenty of "Get the fuck in there" and "We'll teach you to fucking belt us" and that sort of thing,' the Commission heard.

In *Sympathy for the Devil*, Haken tries to rationalise the attack, saying it squared the ledger for other incidents that had gone unpunished.

'This type of behaviour used to happen all the time in the Cross,' he writes. 'People would come on bucks' nights and flog someone and get back on their bus and disappear, leaving the damage behind for us to clean up. But this was where we worked, this was home for us and they picked us. They expected to get away with it but they didn't this time.'

The systematic bashing with batons was not enough. There was simply a change of personnel. While some police got started on paperwork for the arrests, others took over the beating.

Husband and wife police David and Christine Langton, who had been part of the police-and-partners night out, joined in. Langton had a reputation for losing control when dealing with arrested men and would eventually be sacked from the force for breaking the jaw of someone who objected to being searched.

Haken told the Royal Commission that the two ring leaders of the revellers were 'flogged unmercifully.'

'Langton was handy with his fists and was a good bloke to have on your side in the Cross but he ... was out of control.'

Evidence from one of the revellers supported this. He said Langton shouted, 'You little fuck!' at him, punched him hard in the face and then on the head and nose. Yelling at the terrified man to stop crying, Langton had to be stopped from inflicting further punishment.

Meanwhile, Langton's wife Christine did her bit, bashing the unresisting mens' heads on walls and desks. She would tell the commission she was motivated by injuries inflicted on two of her friends in the brawl and because 'a perfectly lovely night had been upset.'

Newspapers quoted her telling the Royal Commission that she had pushed a fingernail into the throat of an arrested man and said: 'You didn't know who you were messing with.'

One prisoner says he was thrown against a wall and repeatedly struck in the face by different officers. Even feigning unconsciousness did not help. Haken says the man was told to 'get up or get more.' Langton allegedly told one man to 'stop bleeding on the floor.'

The prisoners were then forced to run the gauntlet of another line-up of baton-wielding police back to the van to be taken to the Sydney Police Centre. When they got there, the two ringleaders were so obviously injured that police receiving them asked the Kings Cross crew for help to 'explain' what had happened in a way that would counter any allegations of police brutality.

Asked about the injuries, those that had inflicted them brazenly denied responsibility saying any wounds must have come from the street brawl before arrests were made.

The police apparently returned to their wives and girlfriends and retired to the Bourbon and Beefsteak nightclub to salvage what was left of the evening. The prisoners, nursing bruises and shredded egos, decided it was prudent not to mention the police thuggery and to plead guilty. All, that is, except one of them.

As Haken says in *Sympathy for the Devil*, the exception was a security guard who would lose his licence if convicted – so he was determined to tell the truth about the bashing.

But, at the time, this seemed no problem for the police. Haken and his men did what they had done many times before. They had a 'scrum down' among themselves, decided on the statements they would make and simply went into court denying the bashing.

'In those days there were no problems that couldn't be overcome somehow,' he writes.

But Haken's subsequent evidence to the Royal Commission, corroborated by some of the victims, scuppered the cover-up and the guilty police were prosecuted. This was rare: police authorities and the government had always been more interested in ensuring corrupt cops were sacked rather than charged. Not prosecuting crooked police after inquiries was the norm in New South Wales. There were sackings, reprimands and hand-wringing by the government and police authorities. But jail? Hardly ever.

The decision to pursue the bashing case through the courts was no doubt justified but overall it was far less significant, and less deserving of prosecution, than many other matters that Haken's electronic surveillance and personal involvement had revealed.

'There were a lot of matters exposed at the Commission to show what went on at the Cross, but they prosecuted the cops for that bashing. You think, how the fuck did I get into this?' Haken said.

TREVOR HAKEN'S evidence shook the previously iron-clad belief of corrupt police that everything would be all right if they stuck together. In nine months of tense under-cover work, he collected more than $30,000 from crimi-nals for distribution to crooked police and he caught cor-rupt police on tape and on camera revealing themselves as thieves who sold their ethics to the highest bidders in the Sydney underworld.

It was a dangerous choice. Potentially fatal, even.

As word swept through Kings Cross that someone had turned informer, criminal bosses with huge fortunes at stake made their intentions clear. One of them was drug czar Billy Bayeh. A curious mix of cunning and stupidity, Bayeh reflected the inability of the underworld to come to grips with modern surveillance technology. Or maybe it was just greed and ego that made him and others like him push their luck.

'I met with Bill Bayeh on a number of occasions and I received large sums of money from him,' Haken would tell the ABC programme *Australian Story*.

'He had problems at that stage. He was losing his au-thority on the streets of Kings Cross and wanted police pro-tection to get back into a better position. At one meeting with Bayeh, he told me that another police associate had told him he must have balls to be meeting with me because the rumours were all over town that I'd rolled.

'And he said, "If anyone goes against me I'll kill them. I'll kill their wife and I'll kill their children".'

Haken says the threat jolted him. 'I did not take it idly. Not then. Not ever,' he says. 'It was an extremely frighten-

NO SYMPATHY FOR THE DEVIL

ing time. I got through it by being a walking pill bottle. I was on all sorts of medicals.'

Haken's last meeting with Bayeh was heart attack material. Bayeh had got hold of an electronic alarm that sounded if anyone was wearing a hidden recording wire. The alarm went off when Bayeh approached Haken.

'I managed to get out of it all right and that was the last time I saw him,' Haken would say.

There were other tense moments. Such as when another criminal told Haken of the rumours he had rolled over and that a lot of crims and some police believed it. Haken, who was wearing a wire at the time, said it was 'fucking shit'.

The criminal accepted the denial and the incriminating conversation continued. His mistake was to think there is honour among thieves.

TREVOR Haken switched from alcoholic bent cop to non-drinking white knight as easily as if he were an actor swapping roles. He seemed unswayed by friendship or any past associations.

He agreed to be 'wired up' to trap his colleagues without hesitation. He used the car camera set up by the commission to record and film a detective, Graham 'Chook' Fowler, talking about bribes and pocketing money he had taken from Haken as a share of a supposed bribe.

The 'car-cam' footage devastated senior police who had insisted the force was corruption-free. And it shocked tainted police when they realised too late that the electronic surveillance was so sophisticated and the evidence so compelling that there was nowhere to hide.

By the time Haken finished giving evidence, the police force was in tatters. Dozens of senior police had been exposed as drunken, drug-dealing criminals prepared to do anything to get an illegal dollar.

They had stripped vital evidence from prosecution briefs to get guilty drug dealers and killers off; taken money from dealers to protect criminal rackets from police intrusion; and helped wipe out competing drug dealers who were not paying bribes.

There were plenty of dirty deeds – but rarely done dirt cheap. And, for years, Trevor Haken had enjoyed a front row seat.

His apprenticeship in 'the joke' had begun at North Sydney police station, soliciting $10 bribes from tow truck drivers for access to car crashes and telling undertakers about dead bodies at $20 a time.

'Over the years I became involved to the extent of being the bag man, picking up money from people who were conducting businesses like prostitution, night clubs, gambling clubs and drug dealers,' he would admit.

'I was involved in stealing money, verballing people (giving false evidence in court), gutting briefs – which is removing information from briefs to allow people to be exonerated.

'There was no form of improper behaviour that we were not involved in.'

Haken's biggest coup was coolly trapping Fowler – one of his mates – by luring him into the car fitted with recording and videotaping equipment. The sting came early in the Royal Commission and had an explosive effect on media coverage. In the past, inquiries had floundered because accused officers would brazenly deny any accusations, but now there was irrefutable proof. Corrupt police were damned by their own words and actions, all caught on tape and film that made headlines for the life of the inquiry – and became its signature 'grab' on the electronic media. In isolation, the Fowler 'sling' was a small amount but the image it created was immensely damaging.

A fascinated public watched in amazement as a police force repeatedly touted by its bosses and politicians as the best in Australia fell apart under the weight of damning evidence and a blizzard of accusations that were suddenly overwhelmingly plausible.

In one week seven detectives were sacked after Haken regaled the hearing with tales of coppers helping criminals and stealing drugs and cash from criminals.

The blame moved vertically as well. The contract of then assistant commissioner Ray Donaldson was not re-newed. The chief of staff to the police commissioner, Bob Lysaught, also went. Police Commissioner Tony Lauer, al-though not linked to any corruption or criminal behaviour, resigned amid suggestions he was inept.

Haken says his health was damaged by the tension of playing a double agent, of knowing one slip could have got him killed by rogue cops or criminals seeking revenge.

'I was a wreck, an absolute wreck,' he would say. 'Sick in the pit of my stomach, my nerves shot to bits. But what do you do? I had engaged to do a job and I did the job.'

FROM outside, the Hakens looked the suburban family from Central Casting. So much so, in fact, that they were cast as the ideal family by McDonalds, which used a picture of the couple and their children on restaurant placemats and advertisements.

The placemats caused hilarity at Kings Cross, Haken said. 'They were always all over the place. The junkies used to burn the eyes out of my picture.'

Haken was ruggedly handsome with a persuasive personality and his wife, Jayne, was good-looking enough to do part-time modelling work.

'To some people we must have looked like a model family,' he would muse. But there was plenty of trouble below the surface.

Attractive on the outside, dysfunctional behind closed doors, the Haken family was swept into a maelstrom of publicity before going into hiding.

Their troubles had started years before the Royal Commission, Jayne Haken would say, when her husband embraced the heavy drinking culture adopted by so many police at the time. They had met when she was a waitress at the Double Bay Steak House – in Lane Cove national park – where Haken and his mates at nearby Chatswood police station would often have their evening meal.

'They were easy going but they never left a tip,' she told *Australian Story*, in a telling aside about the selfishness, greed and suspicion of corrupt cops.

They married when Jayne was 20. Haken's taste for alcohol, police camaraderie and scoring easy money from criminals seemed as important to him as his growing family.

'His hours would get longer and longer and there were times when he didn't come home at all,' Jayne Haken said.

'I would sit in the backyard and cry because I was newly

married with two young ones. I guess they were drinking if they were not working. Trevor always had a drink.'

She realised how warped her husband's priorities were when she was almost due to have their second child.

'I was eight months pregnant ... and he didn't even come home on New Year's Eve. When work finished at 10 pm they decided to go and party.'

Another night an intoxicated Haken came home with two equally drunken police colleagues and continued drinking.

'They were both drunk as skunks and I had a new baby. I was suddenly awoken by a shotgun noise,' Jayne would tell *60 Minutes*.

'They had fired at the rooster down the back (of the yard).'

The couple had marriage counselling once but it was useless because, Jayne says, 'We would discuss it over dinner – and then he had to go and have a drink with the boys.'

But Haken's regard for 'the brotherhood' soured suddenly when he caught his wife in an intimate embrace with a colleague who had brought him home drunk and thought he had passed out on a couch.

'What really shattered me was when another detective I was working with made a move on her (Jayne),' Haken would reveal in a gruelling interview.

'That really broke my belief in the brotherhood. The relationship between another detective and my wife made me realise that I'd taken my eye off the ball completely by excessive drinking. I gave it up.'

The episode might well have been an underlying motive

for Haken to turn on his crooked mates. But, once he had betrayed them, like many protected witnesses he became disillusioned. He felt discarded and used by the authorities.

Haken's biography makes it clear he felt cheated by the system. In it, his analyst is quoted describing poor accommodation in a cheap motel, bad meals and problems created by his mother-in-law and wife.

The federal agents assigned to protect Haken were 'more interested in racking up all of the overtime and meal allowances they could,' the analyst said. 'They fed him crap. He couldn't go out to get his own food so they would cook cheap and nasty food and Trevor would have to eat it.'

But the analyst did not altogether paint Jayne Haken as a victim. 'His wife is quite beautiful. She would spend a lot of the money that he would make illegally on things like cosmetics and clothes. And she had a ball on all of this money but she claimed she never knew anything about what he was doing.

'She slept with a colleague of Trevor's and he caught them at it. He went a bit crazy about this and then gave up the drink.'

Haken's mother-in-law also caused problems for the family and the Royal Commission, the analyst said. 'She would often threaten to go to the Press, which threatened the security of the whole thing.'

In one terrifying episode, Haken felt as if he were being encouraged to commit suicide by those being paid to protect him – two officers from the witness security unit, known as WITSEC.

'Imagine if you can, driving in a car with two WITSEC officers, when for no reason they turn off onto a dirt road in a country area,' he writes.

He claims that one of the officers took out his police-issue handgun and said: 'What information did you give to the Royal Commission about (a Federal officer)? He's a mate of mine.' The officer allegedly handed the gun to Haken, who claims he promptly handed it back, believing it was an invitation to take his own life.

In the end, the Wood Royal Commission's success rested on Haken's decision to become a whistleblower – and on his remarkable recall of specific events.

Without Haken's detailed description of his own corruption and the involvement of so many others, counsels assisting like John Agius, Virginia Bell, James Black and Paddy Bergin would not have had the ammunition to destroy the wall of lies that had hidden bent police for decades. And Justice Wood would not have been able to pursue an inquiry that cast a long shadow over Australian police for many years. But as subsequent events in Sydney would prove, Wood's probe did not uproot police corruption altogether: it simply pruned it so that it flourished again when conditions suited.

– WITH RAY CHESTERTON

8

DEBBIE DOES DETECTIVES

Deborah realised that most of
them were wearing chunky gold
rings ... suspiciously similar.
It dawned on her they were
probably stolen: taken as a job
lot orchestrated by bent cops.

THE moment of truth hit Deborah Locke late at night sitting in an undercover police car in a lane behind a brothel in Sydney's west. Among the crackle and chatter of the routine police messages was a strange series of calls for a particular cop, stating that his wife had been 'abducted'.

She wondered why the older detective with her ignored what sounded like an horrific crime: one that should have enraged every serving police officer. Then he explained. The calls were bogus – a warning to a 'troublesome' cop to make him fear what could happen if he 'put them in' – meaning, if he reported his colleagues' corrupt activities to the authorities. The detective explaining this to Locke didn't realise that a far bigger threat to his crooked career was sitting right next to him.

'I felt like I was going to vomit,' Locke later told journalists while promoting her book, *Watching The Detectives*, ostensibly 'fictionalised' to head off defamation suits but clearly a version of her experiences in the New South Wales force. The fact was, she was poised to 'rat out' her colleagues at Parramatta Detectives by reporting corruption, discrimination and harassment.

At 24, she was wiser – and sadder – than the wide-eyed recruit who had joined up four years before. Long before she became Deborah Locke the hated whistleblower, the rookie Debbie Webb had twigged it was safer to go along with the bent cops than to cross them. When she first hit the streets of Kings Cross soon after the police academy, she'd sensed the danger of coming across as too honest. So far, she had been savvy enough to keep her hands clean and her eyes averted – but the time had come when she had to make a choice.

The veiled threats brazenly broadcast on the police radio confirmed what she already knew – that the bent cops played rough. And they kept bad company. A few days earlier, she had realised how difficult it would be not to be compromised. Her senior 'partner', given the alias 'Ron Marowitz' in the book, had gone to a long lunch at the Park Royal pub in Parramatta, leaving her in the detectives' office. After a few hours he called and asked her to come down.

She found Ron with two of Sydney's most notorious figures. One was Louie Bayeh, reputedly mixed up in prostitution, gaming and drugs. The other was 'Mr Big' himself, Lennie McPherson, whose interests intersected with Bayeh's but also extended to murder, robbery and large-scale theft. She smiled uneasily at the men, wondering what Ron wanted her for. When she found out, she was horrified.

Ron took her outside and produced a folded piece of paper. It was an application for a gun licence in the name of one of McPherson's close relatives. Locke didn't know what to say. Was it a trap? 'I fell back on my usual response and just laughed,' she would later write. When Ron pressed her she said, 'You have got to be joking'. When she refused again, he pulled out a wad of cash and offered her $150 – a lot for a five-minute job in 1988 – but no amount would have tempted her. Later, she claims, she kicked herself that she didn't take the gun licence application 'for evidence'. But she didn't. She handed it back to her bent partner with her fingerprints all over it. She had no doubt they were trying the routine ruse of implicating a newcomer in dodgy dealings, compromising her so she could not act against them.

'I just wanted to be a cop and do my job properly,' She would later tell journalist Maree Curtis. By attempting to compromise me, the bastards weren't letting me do that.'

She had to make a decision. She wasn't going to go over to the dark side, which left her with a tough choice. Should she 'rat'? Or do what hundreds of other anxious cops had done: pretend it wasn't happening and sit it out until she could escape with a pension, superannuation or extended sick leave.

'I honestly couldn't believe what was going on,' she

would tell Curtis. 'I was a young girl and I was shocked at what I saw. We were supposed to be the good guys. It was surreal. Everyone had a racket going and most of them had a sheila on the side – that was a status symbol.'

Apart from the casual and constant sexual harassment, abuse and discrimination, she was shocked at how willing her brother officers were to consort with crooks, milking them for favours while tipping them off about police operations. She wanted no part of it.

For a while she toyed with calling Detective Sergeant Kimbal Cook for advice. Cook had been her boss, briefly, at the Gaming Squad, and he was the only honest cop she felt sure of. She knew first hand what he had done – and how he had suffered for it.

Cook had worked in Internal Affairs and had been switched to Gaming to clean up its surveillance unit, where Locke worked. He seemed the sort of cop she had always wanted to work for. At one of his first morning briefings, she recalled, he had told the plain clothes members words to the effect, 'If you make a mistake I will go all out to help you. But if anyone ... does anything dishonest, corrupt, I will go out of my way to crucify you.'

Around the same time, the unit took on Frank Deak, another sergeant who had worked in Internal Affairs with Cook, and Gene Zubrecky. To Locke, they seemed excellent undercover officers. For a while. Then she noticed they had secretive conversations that stopped when she came within earshot. But Zubrecky's wife worked on the intelligence desk at the squad and seemed nice. 'They seemed like the perfect police couple'.

But although they were working under a boss that was

straight, 'It was uncanny that as hard as we tried, every time we attempted surveillance on a gaming establishment, the bastards knew we were there,' she would write. Once, when Gene Zubrecky had taken a 'sickie' at short notice, Cook had himself posed as a taxi driver to gain entry to an illegal gaming venue in a shed behind the Lane Cove National Park. When he got there, driving a borrowed cab, the organisers walked straight up and dragged him out of the car and started to beat him up. They knew he was a cop.

Another night, Cook led his team into a lane behind a suspect address in Surry Hills where, he had been told, an illegal game was being run. They broke open the back door with a sledgehammer – but inside, instead of illegal gamblers caught red-handed, was an unworried group of people that included a well-known and popular criminal lawyer. They were next to a long table covered with food under a large painted 'welcome' banner. It was clearly another tip-off, but at least this time no one was hurt. Standing next to the smiling lawyer was a man with a video camera, obviously hired to record the police's entry. The search produced nothing, of course. 'Our video guy videoed their guy videoing him. It was all a bit embarrassing,' notes Locke drily.

Later, the unit built a case against a big-time SP bookmaker who operated near the Victorian border and went on to make multi-millions in Vanuatu. After the bookie's arrest, Gene Zubrecky and Frank Deak asked their boss, Kimbal Cook, if he were interested in splitting the $10,000 bribe the bookie had offered them. He was interested – but not in taking the bribe. He was interested in nailing his crooked men. Next time they met, he secretly taped them, and arranged for their arrest after they picked up the bribe money from the bookie at a McDonalds car park in Goulburn.

Deborah was sitting an exam while this happened. When she went back to the office she found Gene Zubrecky's wife in tears. 'Between sobs she told me what had happened. "Kim set them up," she growled. "The bastard". I thought, Well, they have been warned. They knew the rules of the game. Frank must have thought he could trust Kim, as they had worked together at Internal Affairs years earlier.'

She asked Cook about it when he got back from Goulburn and got an answer that summed up the dilemma of the honest cop surrounded by the dishonest and the apathetic in an organisation that breeds paranoia. 'Well, what could I do?' he asked. 'How did I know it wasn't a setup? I have a wife and kids, a mortgage. What were they thinking? What choice did I have?'

The two cops were sent to jail. And Kimbal Cook's working life was never the same again. Nailing the two officers made him the natural enemy of almost every member of the Gaming Squad, not to mention most of the force. Once, as Deborah walked into the office, she overheard a group of angry cops muttering threats against their boss, Cook, hatred in their faces. Many of them had crossed the line themselves, she knew, and had it been slightly different, they might have ended up behind bars with Zubrecky and Deak.

The way she tells the story, the mutinous cops were discussing 'loading up' Cook with drugs or money – or bashing or even killing him 'to make an example' of him. This was how warped it had got. Up to and including the early

1990s, Sydney police ran 'red hot'. Bent cops ran the force, honest ones were ostracised and the ones in the middle mostly turned a blind eye because it was safer that way. For a long time, Deb Locke was one of those in the middle. Just supporting Kim was a social death sentence,' she wrote.

Later, she would do something about it. In the meantime, she just wanted to get away from the scary people in the Gaming Squad. Six weeks later she scored a transfer to Parramatta Detectives. Which was where she was teamed up with the senior detective she would call Ron Marowitz. It was a case of out of the frying pan, into the fire.

Marowitz was, she would write, 'a slimy, pock-faced little weasel' but he took a shine to her because she had been in the Gaming Squad and, luckily, the grapevine hadn't yet poisoned her reputation by painting her as a closet sympathiser of honest police who 'dogged' on 'good blokes' for 'copping a quid'. Ron's brother, Jim, had been in the Gamers and so he had assumed Debbie was staunch because, 'The Gamers was a tough squad to get into; you had to be invited to join the club, so the blokes at Parramatta thought I was cool.' She didn't bother correcting the impression that she jumped ship because of the arrest and jailing of her former colleagues, when in fact she just wasn't interested in getting bribes from crooks. The truth was she was worried about being put into a situation where she had to reject a bribe offered by a fellow cop.

All of which meant she had to put up with Ron duchessing her around the streets of Parramatta as a sort of trophy: the young, blonde detective who acted like one of the blokes. A dangerous role, and yet the only option seemed almost unthinkable at the time. It made such an impression that she opens her book by describing a lunch that made her guts churn. Not because of the food but the company.

'Ron was as flash as a rat with a gold tooth,' she wrote. 'It was a morning late in 1988. I came into the office to find Ron jumping out of his skin with excitement. "It's the big time today," he said, smiling. "I'll show you what it's all about, being a detective. We have a big lunch on today, and if you're a good little girl I'll let you come".'

It seemed like the usual patronising crap she copped from the men, who hustled free meals every other day on their 'patch'. She didn't realise it was a special day. At midday sharp, Ron grabbed the unmarked car keys and said they were going. The destination: a local Chinese restaurant that had been an illegal gaming den. There were already other unmarked cop cars in the restaurant car park, and more to come.

Inside, another detective already seated at a big table at the back of the room scowled when he saw Deborah. 'What did you bring her for?' he hissed at Ron, who assured him with words to the effect of: 'You can trust her. She'll be all right. I'm training her.'

As the other guests rolled in, she began to feel uneasy. There were two wealthy used-car dealers in expensive suits, four city detectives from one of the squads, casually dressed. Then came the heavy division: Louie Bayeh, one of Sydney's biggest 'colourful identities' – and a celebrity in Parramatta. And the cherry on top was Roger Rogerson, the most notorious detective sergeant in Australia.

'I started to feel as if I was well and truly in the wrong place. I had thought the cops were just pretending to be mates with these guys to get a brief on them ... It was beginning to dawn on me that the relationship here between cops and crims was different.'

She was caught. Every instinct told her to get out but she didn't want to draw attention to herself by leaving before Ron. And he was in no hurry: happy as a pig in shit.

Thoughts raced through her mind. She was the only woman present, and young and attractive. Would they all get violently drunk and hand her over to someone as a sexual offering? Or because of her Gaming Squad background, would they assume they could recruit her to be in on the giggle, as the saying went. She knew that being with drunken coppers was not safe, either way. If nothing else, if Internal Affairs were filming the lunch, her career could be ruined.

Despite her nerves, and the free gins she drank to calm them, she noticed that 'Louie' and 'Roger' were the ones holding court, regularly moving to a table to talk quietly with whichever of the guests wanted an audience.

Rogerson's reputation preceded him. The boy from Bankstown who had once looked like commissioner material was by 1988 probably the sharpest black knight in The Job. And he wasn't happy to see a 'front bum' or a 'dickless Tracy', as older cops called policewomen. His instincts were high. He glared at her.

Rogerson, Bayeh and the car dealers stayed cool and relatively sober. For them, business was business. But by the time genuine paying customers started coming in for dinner, the rest of the crew had drunk themselves stupid. Deborah realised that most of them were wearing chunky gold rings with rows of diamonds, suspiciously similar. It dawned on her that the rings were probably stolen: taken as a job lot in one heist orchestrated by the bent cops. Those wearing them should have been arrested for bad taste let alone anything else. But that wasn't all. Late in the afternoon, one of the detectives fell off his chair and went to sleep under the table. Then they smelt him. He had fouled himself. Worse, he was wearing white jeans.

Deborah Locke had grown up with alcoholic parents and gave the bottle a nudge herself. But this was a club she did not want to be in. Problem was: how was she going to extricate herself?

When the bill came around those still standing looked at each other and shuffled their feet. Paying was the one thing they feared. But it was all right ... Bayeh picked up the bill. And Locke drove all the way home to her parents' sorry farmhouse at Glenorie, northwest of Sydney. After what she'd seen that day, drink-driving was the least of her worries. Besides, detectives didn't often have to blow in the bag in those days. And if they did, it would be 'accidentally' dropped on the ground and go nowhere.

She was caught at a crossroads – with headlights coming at her from both directions. She would later write what it felt like.

'I had entered dangerous territory. Here I was with a bunch of crooks ... Just by being there I was afraid I might be implicated in their activities. I was also frightened that if they found out I had supported the arrest of two cops at the Gaming Squad they might kill me because I might have too much information about them. I was being drawn into the dark circle of police connections with Sydney's under-world ...'

DEBORAH Webb had joined the New South Wales Police in February 1984, the month that another feisty female destined to cause trouble, Kim Hollingsworth, was starting her final year of school at Wodonga. When Deborah walked into the old Redfern Police Academy, she was twenty years old, size ten, with long blonde hair. She was one of the token women in Class 201, second last to go through at Redfern before the new academy opened at Goulburn.

After twelve tough weeks of marching, running, shooting and other training, she graduated. 'I was given a silver badge, a notebook and a Bible. I also received a Model 10 Smith & Wesson six-shot revolver, twelve shiny bullets and a set of handcuffs.'

The graduation was the only thing her parents had been proud of in all their lives, she would write. They were both alcoholics, both the children of Gallipoli veterans who had come back from the battlefields as abusive, aggressive men who drank hard and blighted the lives of the next generation. So much so that their only daughter considered herself a survivor trying to escape a 'white trash' upbringing of which she was ashamed. She had one brother who was much older and played no part in her upbringing.

'My childhood,' she would write, 'consisted of people drinking, smoking and sitting around talking rubbish. I have few, if any, childhood memories.'

She grew up on an impoverished poultry farm at Glenorie, north-west of Sydney. Like many children of abusive alcoholic parents, she cared for them more than they did for her. She even called them by their first names, Irene and John, as if they were the children. It made her determined to escape through hard work. She could hardly read or write until she was nine but when she was eleven, her natural intelligence and drive asserted itself. She took to reading – and was a bright and willing student, motivated by watching the slow-motion wreck of her parents' wasted lives. Ironically, it was her mother's hunger for some sort of second hand respectability that pushed the young Deborah towards joining the police.

'With my family, I should have ended up a crook, not a copper,' she would say. But, from the time she was a little girl, her mother 'had always told me I was going to be a policewoman. So many members of our family had been arrested over the years, she wanted to add some respectability. She also had a list of people she wanted to get and she thought if I was in the police, I could get them for her. She held a grudge, did Irene.'

As she grew up, ashamed of her family, she never questioned that she was heading for the blue uniform. 'Coming from the family I did, I wanted some respectability, too. And I wanted to do the right thing. I wanted to make a difference. I wanted to go into the force and be a good honest person, a good police officer.'

But none of this, by her own account, stopped her having her own battle with the bottle. Grog was in the blood, usually literally. And she soon found that police work encouraged that. It was part of the culture.

First she was sent to North Sydney, which wasn't as violent or as seedy as the inner city stations, but it had its own hazards. There were twenty women at the station and a lot of casual sex among the police. But she was struck by how badly women were treated in the force.

'I couldn't understand the derogatory way I was spoken

to by the male police officers,' she would tell reporters. 'The women were told that we were lower than police dogs. The females were called "police mattresses".' This made a bad joke of the force's moves to recruit more women, she says. 'On paper, we were being accepted into the folds of police culture, but we weren't really. I had worked so hard to get there and I was so proud and so determined to be a policewoman. I was the first one in my family to do HSC and then to become a policewoman. I was breaking new ground. (But) I was copping all this abuse ...We were nothing more than tokens.'

Perhaps as a backhanded means of protecting her from unwanted sexual attention, the sergeant at North Sydney assigned Deborah to a woman-hating senior constable who made her six weeks with him a misery – but he could be relied on not to put the hard word on her for sex.

It was during her first six weeks of probation, on 28 July 1984, that she showed her capacity for bravery – and learned a lesson in backroom police politics. It happened when she and the senior constable were called to the Harbour Bridge, where a man had climbed over the safety barrier and was standing on a platform, threatening to jump.

Police were standing around, wondering what to do, so Deborah spoke to the man. He told her he hated women. It was a recent development: he'd formed the opinion they were 'all sluts' because he had woken up to find his best man screwing his bride-to-be at a roadside stop while they were travelling to Sydney to get married. The scene had upset him. But before he jumped, he fancied a cigarette. Deborah offered to take it to him and the would-be jumper agreed that she was the one he wanted to bring it to him.

She was heaved over the barrier onto the platform with the 'jumper', with nothing but a borrowed packet of cigarettes and a breezy line of chat to protect her – a fact that later led to trouble.

'We smoked several more cigarettes, which I felt was more likely to kill me than being pushed from the bridge. I gained his confidence, I think, because we spoke the same language and both came from a farming background.'

To the shock of the other police, whose plan had been to wait for the bloke either to jump or get sick of it, she talked him back over the safety rail. So far, so good. But the story wasn't over.

Back at North Sydney station, the broken-hearted bridegroom was stuck in a cell while they wondered what to do with him. Half an hour later, Deborah peered through the flap on the cell door ... and saw him hanging by the neck by his belt.

By the time they got the door open and cut him down, he looked dead. But he was only unconscious and came around. The grumpy senior constable gave him coffee and a sympathetic ear. He felt sorry for him.

'Perhaps,' noted Deborah deadpan, 'this was why he wasn't charged with trespass on the Harbour Bridge. Or perhaps it's because he was a suicidal male placed in a cell, unsupervised and with his belt and shoelaces.'

So the jumper lived to love another day. And probationary constable Deborah Webb was the heroine of the moment. Or should have been...

A few weeks later, an inspector broke the news that she wouldn't be officially acknowledged for her actions on the bridge. Why? Because they didn't want to get the Cliff

Rescue unit into trouble for allowing her over the rail without a safety harness on. The logic was twisted but unassailable: for her bravery to be recognised, it would be for risking her life by going onto the platform without safety harness, which in turn was a clear breach of correct procedure. Catch 22.

There was no way around it. If she had been shoved off the edge and died, everyone would have been in huge trouble. The way it had turned out, it was better to let sleeping dogs lie. When bravery meets bureaucracy, bravery loses.

Apart from the break-up of her first police romance – with a handsome cop who decided he was a woman trapped in a man's body – there was another reason to remember her time at North Sydney. It was the early morning prison van run.

She and a senior constable would regularly go to Long Bay prison to pick up prisoners for court appearances. Deborah would have to search each prisoner for hidden weapons before they got in the van. Then she would have to sit in a separate locked section at the back of the van to guard the prisoners in transit, an ordeal as they dragged to courts all over Sydney.

On one particular day, she was feeling carsick after dropping off prisoners at three courts when the van suddenly stopped in the street. She opened the door and saw two detectives and four uniforms, guns drawn and looking worried. They hurried her out of the way and then one of the detectives jumped into the van and dragged out a prisoner by the hair and belted him.

She asked the driver what it was all about. She would recall his answer in *Watching The Detectives*.

"'It's your lucky day," he told me. "The bloke we dropped off last ratted on that piece of shit. He was charged with killing his wife and two other people. You were going to be next. He's got a replica gun down his pants. You mustn't have found it. He had pulled it out back at the District Court and was going to use it on you when we stopped again.'"

Deborah didn't catch on. Then the old cop explained that the killer had planned to menace her with the replica pistol to force her to hand over her service revolver. And then, he told the other prisoners, he was going to shoot her in the head. Anyone who has shot three people has nothing to lose by shooting another one.

What saved her was that one of the other prisoners had taken pity on her and decided to break the criminal code by dobbing in the would-be killer as soon as he was unloaded back at the previous court, which had prompted the posse to come to the rescue before the van got to the next court.

Deb knew that having a gun pulled on her would have worked. She would have handed over her revolver. It was a lesson – but a confusing one. On one hand she'd learned how dangerous and unpredictable prisoners could be. On the other, she'd learned that treating them like human beings, not garbage, had made one of them take pity on her – and save her life.

She also learned to search people properly. Not that she was ever rostered back on prison van security. She was going to the Cross.

THE Kings Cross Drug Squad office in the mid-1980s was a rat's nest in the station basement. 'It was a small, underground concrete bunker with no natural light and the musty smell of damp carpet,' was the way Locke put it later, writing about her first experience of plain clothes work.

In the mornings she walked to work early along Darlinghurst Road, the hardened artery leading to the heart of Kings Cross. The last few hookers still on the street would say 'I've already paid sergeant (name) today'. Sure enough, as she later wrote, 'the roster confirmed every time that the bloke they had mentioned had started at seven that morning.'

The old hands at the station had a word for young officers on rotation, gaining experience: 'woodchucks'. Like many others, Deborah Webb went there because it would look good on her service register. The first thing she noticed was that the older detectives did a lot of whispering and treated the youngsters like rubbish.

The young policewoman found the Cross exciting at night, when it blazed with neon and noise. But the cold light of each new day fell harshly on the Cross. Young girls high on drugs or shaking and shivering as they came down, leaned on walls as the sun rose, waiting for one more 'mug' to score a few more dollars to buy more drugs: a pitiless and pitiful cycle that all too often ended in premature death.

Most street prostitutes were junkies in 1985 but there were still some old-school professionals ... pro pros. Deborah got to know and like two of them, who called themselves Betty and Chantal. Unusually, they didn't touch drugs, which was why they were still functioning – and still fit – in their late 30s. They both wore big, teased-up hair, lots of make up and tight, bright clothes in slinky material. They looked more like actors playing 1960s prostitutes as they stood in their usual pitches outside the Pink Pussy

Cat or Porky's. And they would always be pleased to have a rest from propositioning the passing punters to have a chat with the friendly young policewoman with the reassuring down-home twang of rural Australia in her voice. Deborah's slant on it was that they took a shine to her because she didn't treat them like garbage.

Chantal told her she had three kids in boarding school in Melbourne, and showed her photographs of them. One thing that Chantal told her stuck in her mind – and would figure on the back cover of her book. 'You're too nice to be a cop, Deb. You speak to us like we're humans, not like the other bastards. When you've been in this job as long as I have you see a lot of pigs come and go. Be careful of the blokes you are working with, they are not nice.'

The Kings Cross detectives took her to a strip club run by a Greek who called himself Stevie Stardust and who looked the part of the shady nightclub owner: shaven head, hairy chest, gold chains and sunglasses. He warned her about a particular detective and then said something that she later recalled as: 'Get out of here while the going is good, Deb. This is no place for a young girl like you.'

In the mornings, the young cops would walk around stamping on syringes in the gutters to break them so passing schoolchildren would be less inclined to pick them up or re-use them. AIDS was starting to take hold. One morning a teenage hooker told Deb she had the disease. 'The fear and hopelessness were in her eyes.'

On evening shifts the woodchucks would walk around in small groups. Deb was better at spotting trouble – and offenders – than most of the others, because she was more street smart. She had been a barmaid, her parents were alcoholics, and some of her cousins were bikies and had been in trouble with the law, so she had a fair idea of what low life was.

One day, a sergeant chipped her for having a long conversation in the street with a bikie parked outside one of the local tattoo parlours. What the sergeant didn't know was that the bikie was her cousin, 'Hairy Mick'.

Towards the end of her three months at the Cross, she was in the office finishing paperwork while most of the shift were up at the (famous bar) Bourbon and Beefsteak, where the management put on free seafood and drinks for the cops. The phone went. It was the inquiry counter upstairs: there was a young woman there wanting to see a detective.

'When I walked upstairs I saw the young woman, blonde hair hanging straight down, wearing blue jeans and T-shirt, and with a big gap between her front teeth. Having briefly spoken to her a few times on street patrols, I knew who she was.'

Debbie asked if she could help but the blonde woman dismissed her as 'just a woodchuck.' She was agitated and distressed and hurried out.

Next day she was found face down in a pond in Centennial Park. Her name was Sallie-Anne Huckstepp and her tragic story – of the well-educated, beautiful and doomed girl – would become part of Sydney crime folklore. Her death was blamed on notoriously violent criminal Neddy Smith and his bent police connections, namely Roger Rogerson, the central figures in the memorable Blue Murder television series.

Debbie later heard that she had been given 'a speedball that would have killed a horse' but that her tolerance to

Beach boys: 'Teflon John' Ibrahim (right), Adam Freeman and a young friend. DAVID FREEMAN: MYSPACE

Tough love: John Ibrahim clowns with David Freeman and a mate.

Tough tummy: Fadi Ibrahim, who survived being shot five times.

Tough head: 'Sam' Ibrahim, a bouncer, biker and big brother.

Posers: Adam Sonny Freeman, Paris Hilton and David George
Freeman, doing what they do best. DAVID FREEMAN: MYSPACE

Happy days: John Ibrahim (left), David Freeman and Todd O'Connor,
who died in 2008. DAVID FREEMAN: MYSPACE

At the funeral: John Ibrahim (second left) with mourners and minders. COURTESY *THE DAILY TELEGRAPH*

Missed: Louie Bayeh shows off bullet holes made by people who don't like him. BEN RUSHTON: FAIRFAX

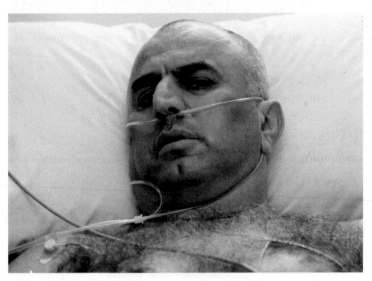

Gotcha: Bayeh holed up in hospital after being shot several times.
BRENDAN ESPOSITO: FAIRFAX

Louie: more minders than Madonna but it didn't block the bullets.
BEN RUSHTON: FAIRFAX

Last laugh: stripper turned police whistleblower Kim Hollingsworth wows another audience. ANDREW TAYLOR: FAIRFAX

A class of her own: schoolgirl Kim (third row from top, second from right) in Year 12 at Wodonga West High School, 1984. *BORDER MAIL*

Daddy's girl: the policeman's daughter who became a stripper, hooker and attention seeker. Go figure. ANDREW TAYLOR: FAIRFAX

Ratty: Hollingsworth with best mate Caspar, one of many rats at the Wood inquiry – but the only one with a tail. PAUL MILLER: FAIRFAX

Sleeping with the enemy: police poster girl Wendy Hatfield before being exposed as a gangster's girlfriend. DEAN SEWELL: FAIRFAX

Mad as a Hatfield: Wild Wendy seconds before assaulting the photographer. Who could blame her? NICK MOIR: FAIRFAX

Fouling the nest: 'Chook' Fowler leaves the Wood inquiry after telling more porkies. JESSICA HROMAS: FAIRFAX

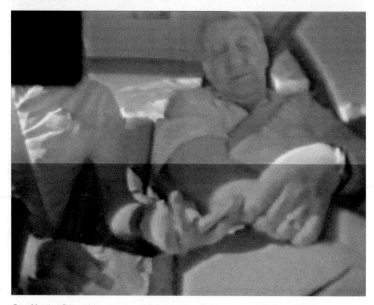

Stuffed: 'Chook' cops a quid on candid camera and stuffs his career. ROYAL COMMISSION SURVEILLANCE

Dud: even among bent police, Fowler had a reputation as a 'dudder'.
ADAM PRETTY: FAIRFAX

Colourful racing identity George Freeman, 50, marries third wife Georgina, 24. Enough said. FAIRFAX

Regrets: a heavily-disguised Trevor Haken reflects on the role reversal of the rolled-over cop. ABC TELEVISION

Braces and belts: a young John Ibrahim and friend practise casting long shadows at the Cross in 1991. *PEOPLE OF THE CROSS*

Gangster glamour: John Ibrahim and two new best friends, Tahnya
Tozzi and Tallie Nagel, at Bondi Icebergs on New Years Day, 2007.
KRISTJAN PORM: FAIRFAX

Multicultural: Ibrahim and David Freeman on holidays
together. DAVID FREEMAN: MYSPACE

drugs was so high the killers had to hold her under water to kill her. The consensus is that it was all to silence her over her willingness to speak out over what she called a police conspiracy to cover up the details of the death of her boyfriend Warren Lanfranchi, shot dead by Rogerson four years earlier.

Huckstepp had blown the whistle by going to media, insisting Lanfranchi had been deliberately murdered by corrupt police. In the end, all it got her was the early grave she'd enlisted for by turning her back on her middle-class life in favour of drugs and prostitution. Her looks and her intelligence meant that her story gained traction where others wouldn't. Her monument is a fine book written by an admirer, John Dale. He called it *Huckstepp: A dangerous life*.

BE careful what you wish for, goes the saying. Deborah Locke wanted to be a detective.

It was the appeal of working in plain clothes that led her to the Gaming Squad. It wasn't much of a reason, looking back on it, but she was young and still relatively innocent about the secret ways of the New South Wales police. Besides, she had worked with the son of the Gamers' commanding officer at the Cross, and he put in a good word for her.

During the interview for the job, a senior officer suggested she try the Highway Patrol on the grounds that, 'They're starting to let women in there.' It might have been good advice from someone with her best interests at heart, but how could she know that? She was only 21 and she wanted to be a detective.

The senior officer urged her to think about the

environment she would be going into with the Gaming Squad, and suggested it was no place for a woman. She would recall and record, with uncanny precision, his exact words: 'You would be the odd female in a squad of hard-working, hard-playing blokes. The language around here gets pretty rough.'

But if she wanted to follow her ambition, that's the way it was. Already, she had tried to do something about the treatment women received in the force. Inspired by a talk by the head of the Equal Employment Opportunities branch towards the end of her stint at North Sydney, she had spoken up. She approached the officer to complain about sexual harassment and discrimination but was 'basically told to shut up and that was just the way it was and that I should consider myself lucky to be there.'

Despite her growing disenchantment, she was still keen for the excitement of detective work that had led to doing the undercover work at Kings Cross.

'There's the police force and then there's the rest of society. Being a cop is exciting. The other day I saw a car go past doing a high-speed chase with lights and sirens and I was so envious,' she would tell Maree Curtis, long after leaving the force.

'It's the adrenaline rush. I was a detective. It's like a secret club that you had to be invited into and I had broken through the glass ceiling.'

The Gaming Squad branch of 'the club' had 60 members. Locke was the only woman, as the one before her had left days before after receiving a hard time. She was an Italian girl called Claudia, and Deborah heard she was 'too much of a nice girl' to handle the brutally sexist behaviour.

'The guys made disgusting comments about her being Italian and what they would like to do with her. No wonder she ran. I began to wonder what I had walked into.'

The sexual harassment started as soon as she walked in the door. That did not surprise her – but she would soon become uncomfortable about the more secretive goings on.

'Very little police work was done,' she would say later. 'There would be days when some officers wouldn't turn up at all and other days when we might only work for two hours. It was not very productive.'

It was at the Gamers that she would win two Commissioner's Commendations for police work. But it came at a cost. The job inevitably involved drinking in bars and clubs and it took its toll. On race days, Wednesdays and Saturday, detectives would visit pubs and drink, supposedly looking for SP bookies. Her social drinking would turn into a drinking problem in the two years she was there.

'It was a great job if you were an alcoholic,' she writes. They were given tax-free cash from a slush fund to pay for drinks and then do the round of the pubs, driving unmarked cars. Race days were better than a day off for the drinkers in the crew. The funny thing was, she notes, not many SP bookies were being arrested as a result of the supposed surveillance. And although the 'gamers' constantly drank and drove, it was never an issue. They were above the law but didn't enforce much of it.

She gradually realised that each ethnic community that ran illicit gaming had a police 'protector' in the squad. Her crew looked after Chinatown, another seemed to have an understanding with the Lebanese and another with the Greeks. One day a sergeant angrily remonstrated with her boss, saying he was sick of approaching Chinese involved in illegal gaming and having them yell, 'You can't touch us!' But after her sergeant took the other one away and talked to him he calmed down. It didn't stop the regular meals in Chinatown – almost always at restaurants that ran big games upstairs. And it was nothing but the best – usually the biggest live lobster in the tank was sacrificed to keep the detectives well fed.

But there is no such thing as a free lunch. Her sergeant, a big sporting man almost old enough to be her father, took her under his wing. One night after another Chinatown dinner he drove her to his home on the pretext of picking up something he needed. In the driveway, she would write later, was a silver Mercedes with deep circular scratches on the bonnet and roof. He said the vandalism had been caused by 'a woman scorned'.

Inside, he offered her a gin and tonic. She liked a drink and accepted, despite the fact she did not feel comfortable looking at family photographs – including adult children older than she was herself. He told her his children had left home and he had no one to share the house with. As she looked politely through a picture album, he sat beside her.

She jumped up, making excuses for not being interested in his advances. She told him about having to look after her alcoholic parents. She hoped that would be the end of it, but she would find out it wouldn't be quite so easy to fight off unwanted attention.

About a week later, she got to work to find two strange detectives waiting for her. They were from Internal Affairs – as opposed to the sort the sergeant had tried to embark on. This pair was investigating everyone in the office who'd helped raid a Greek card game at Marrickville a few days earlier. She had to go with them and answer a few questions.

A complaint had been laid that police had stolen money, gold rings, and a bracelet from the Greek card players. The investigators were not interested in her version of events. One typed her statement while the other dictated it. It said she had seen nothing untoward while searching the premises and that no one had complained to her there, and that she had mostly been out in the car. This was basically true, but she was unhappy about being told what to say and what to sign. It was, of course, the same feeling that countless offenders had complained of after being interviewed.

Meanwhile, it was back to the hard-living, hard-drinking life of the squad. One night, described in *Watching the Detectives*, her amorous sergeant got drunk, produced a bundle of fireworks from his locker and got Deborah to drive to each of the venues where they knew there were card games in progress. At each one, he would light a big bunger and toss it through the door, where terrified patrons would hit the floor when it exploded.

But 'Sarge' had more than fireworks in mind. He made another pitch for her to live with him, arguing that the age difference wouldn't matter and that he had plenty of money to keep her 'happy'. When she resisted, she writes, 'He pushed me up against the wall of an elevator, trying to kiss me as we were coming up from the basement to the office.'

Fighting him off, she bolted from the lift to the women's room. Inside was a policewoman she names as Mandy Price, from the Surveillance Unit, who asked what was wrong.

Deborah would recall replying she was 'sick of fighting these bastards off'. To which Mandy Price had answered: 'They're all dumb pricks' and offered to talk to a senior officer about moving to the Surveillance Unit. 'I had to go there because the same shit was happening to me.' She said the gaming squad office was a 'zoo ... full of animals'.

Within a week, she was doing surveillance.

FOR someone who was starting to feel persecuted, Locke was going pretty well for a while. The surveillance gig meant wearing casual street clothes, driving a new sports car supplied by the office, and being issued with slush fund cash to splash around to help develop a cover – which was pretty well all the time. Surveillance detectives worked from home, to avoid being seen coming out of police buildings. They would meet at a coffee shop or McDonalds that was close to that day's target, then split up. Overtime was virtually unlimited. One of her new colleagues regularly filled his car from the police bowser, and found enough spare time to run his DJ business after hours.

There were funny jobs. Sometimes, female undercovers would go to male strip shows to ensure that no pubic hair was revealed. On another job, Deborah's friend Mandy was sent to a brothel to apply for work. During the interview, Mandy agreed to a request to strip and pose for some erotic photographs. After she revealed this at the debriefing later, the boss ordered the crew to raid the brothel to recover the photographs in case they ended up in court – or in the newspapers.

For a while, it seemed better than working for a living. But, as usual, there was a catch.

In late 1986, Mandy and Deborah moved into a motel room at Bondi as cover to infiltrate an illegal gaming house at Kings Cross. They chatted up an 'old guy' called Ernie who ran the front counter of the gaming house, called the Barclay Club. He gave them the job of minding the security system designed to keep police out while illegal games were on. It was putting the foxes in charge of the henhouse.

Ernie liked the girls. They must have seemed more trustworthy than most he met. Unwisely, as it turned out, he showed them his collection of stolen jewellery in a small chest under his bed. He had been a 'fence' for years, and had picked over the best gear stolen from luxury houses around Double Bay. To Deborah's untrained eye, a lot of the jewellery seemed old enough and valuable enough to be family heirlooms, which could never be replaced. 'My family's home had been broken into and I knew what it felt like to lose irreplaceable family things,' she would write. 'I was more interested in getting this stuff back to its owners than in a bunch of Lebs playing cards.'

A few nights later, she was working the counter when who should walk through the door but 'Grimy Graham', a heroin addict and one of her street contacts when she had worked at Kings Cross the previous year. He laughed to see a cop working security for the gaming house. She was terrified he would sell her out, as he always needed money for heroin. She called her boss to say she had been 'burnt' and didn't feel safe. He said too much money had been spent on the operation to abort it, and to finish the shift and to call him next day. She was scared that if the crooks were tipped off, she would be dragged out the back door and made to disappear. But 'Grimy Graham' must have remembered how she had treated him kindly, and kept his information to himself.

Next night Deborah called in sick and Mandy took over the spot. When the police raided, she opened the door for them and then ran off, making it look as if she were frightened and had left the door open accidentally.

The raid was a success. The club was closed down. The detectives searched Ernie's room for the jewellery Deborah told them about. But when they came back they said that the chest was empty. She never knew whether to believe it or not.

It was back to the Gaming Squad. That's when she met the honest boss she would always admire, Kimbal Cook. The man who knocked back a bribe and then nailed his bent colleagues for taking it. And had to live with the fallout. She believed in him and his code but she knew he was hopelessly outnumbered. She did not want to work in a squad so dominated by corruption and went to Parramatta and found out that corruption was everywhere. By that night in April 1988, listening to veiled threats to an honest cop being broadcast on the police radio, she was screwing up her courage to break ranks and tell the truth.

THE longest journey starts with one short step, the saying goes. For Deborah Locke that step was a telephone call to the home of her former Gaming Squad boss, honest Kim Cook. There were good reasons to think twice about making this move. An officer called Phil Arantz had been thrown in a mental institution after speaking out about falsified police statistics. And, more notoriously, a detective called Michael Drury had been shot as he stood washing dishes in his kitchen in front of his wife and two small children. Although no one has ever been charged with Drury's shooting, the consensus is that former Melbourne hit man Christopher Dale Flannery pulled the trigger on the orders of corrupt police – not long before Flannery himself disappeared because of his potential to turn on his Sydney 'patron' George Freeman.

As Locke would tell reporters, she called Cook at home and asked to meet him. She poured out her story to him in an Oxford Street coffee shop. He told her she had no choice but to go to the Internal Police Security Unit and offered to make the arrangements and accompany her. Days later she found herself, heart pounding and palms sweaty, in a small office with two senior officers from the internal security unit. To her surprise, after introducing her to the officers, Kim Cook left. She was on her own.

Again she told her story. None of it surprised them. They seemed to know every character she mentioned but they seemed uninterested. One of the stories she told them was about being tricked by 'Ron' the dodgy detective into filing a report for a supposed break and enter at the house of a man who turned out to be Ron's brother. The report, almost certainly the basis of a bogus insurance claim, was filed in triplicate. Yet the internal security officers wanted her to retrieve a copy of it from the busy Parramatta Detectives' office, where she risked falling immediately under suspicion. It was downright dangerous – but that didn't worry the men from headquarters. A whistleblower's lot is not an easy one. Which is exactly what she found out when she returned to Parramatta and waited for a chance to raid the records to get a copy of the dodgy report. One of the detectives saw her and asked her, point blank, if she were waiting around to 'get a copy of your report'. They knew. She couldn't believe it. Later in the shift two detectives told her they had a source at the Internal Security Unit ... and the source had leaked about her interview there. It had taken less than a week. The boss of the office warned everyone that the phones were tapped and glared at her as he said it. And another detective told her she was 'a silly little girl'.

Locke was terrified, with good reason. Her life could have been in danger. She called the senior officer at internal security. He made soothing noises but when she said she'd been told 'they' had an informer in the security unit, he went quiet. Then he offered her a transfer to the Commissioner's Policy Unit at police headquarters – starting 36 hours later.

When she started the new job, a superintendent told her that 'we' should not bother the Commissioner, John Avery, with her problem. Instead of seeing Avery, who was soon to retire, she would talk to the assistant commissioner in line for the top job, Tony Lauer. It was the first Locke knew that Avery was going and Lauer was taking over. Suddenly, she was at a high altitude – but not enjoying the view.

She waited for what seemed like a long time for the interview with Lauer. When it came, she blurted out her whole story of corrupt activities with names, places and dates. His reaction, she would later write, was mainly what to do with her. After she again attempted to tell him how bad things were, he told her that police 'don't like whistleblowers', which was true.

It was the first time she'd heard the term 'whistleblower'. It would soon become part of her everyday vocabulary.

By the end of the interview she was quietly convinced that Lauer thought she was – if not exactly at fault – then certainly taking a risk by dobbing in other cops.

'I felt like a silly little girl who had done something that everyone else knew not to do,' she would write of the scene in the office high in the sky. Finally, Lauer told her she would be put with Michael Drury, the other 'outcast' who had been shot in 1984, apparently for his refusal to bend to bent police. Together, they ran Task Force Wave, a faintly bizarre scheme to trap car thieves by setting up cars fitted with sophisticated thief-catching gear. The electronic gear was worth a huge amount of money but the 'bait' cars were old bombs no self-respecting thief would want to pinch from a supermarket or railway car park. It was a miserable time for Locke. Because Drury had his office in another building and was preoccupied writing a book, *In the Line of Fire*, with Darren Goodsir, she spent much of it working alone from a desk in an old hat factory in Surry Hills. At home, meanwhile, she started to drink with her parents. She was only 25, and felt as if her life was over.

It wasn't. After swinging a transfer to the comparative normality of the Fraud Squad, she met the man who would change her life – and her surname – Greg Locke. She took notice when a detective warned her not to trust him because 'if there's money to be found, he won't take any.' A backhanded compliment that first aroused her interest, then her feelings. She started a relationship with him a month later but was still a long way from being saved from the dark hole in which the police force – and her alcoholic parents' dependence on her – had left her. First she attended meetings of Alanon, a group for relatives of alcoholics.

It was good, but it wasn't enough. That didn't happen until a little old lady at one meeting told her she had to give up drinking completely or she would end up a hopeless alcoholic like the rest of her family.

She gave up drinking, one day at a time. And she married Greg and had her first baby.

She had tried to clean up her troubled life. But there was still the small matter of cleaning up the police force.

SIX years is a long time. World War II lasted for six years. That is how long it took from when Deb Locke first went to the Internal Security police in 1988 to when the Independent MP John Hatton aired her damning evidence in State Parliament in 1994. The New South Wales Premier of the day, John Fahey, apologised for the treatment she'd suffered at the hands of other police.

It was this, more than anything else, that forced the Wood Royal Commission, which exposed entrenched police corruption as well as organised paedophile activity. It was in its way a great victory against overwhelming odds. But nothing could repay her for what she had sacrificed. As Maree Curtis would write much later, Locke's career was in tatters: 'She had endured 10 years of emotional and verbal abuse and sexual harassment; had suffered a miscarriage; been treated for depression; was a recovering alcoholic; and she was struggling to hold on to her physical and mental health.'

There was good reason for the fears playing on her mind: speaking up had put her life at risk. Once, while at the Fraud Squad, she was called to an interview with the Independent Commission Against Corruption when a disturbing thing happened.

'As I was putting things in my handbag ready to leave, one of my colleagues strolled up and said "Have you got your gun with you?" When I asked him why, he said, "You better take it with you or someone here might use it on you".'

Was it a veiled threat – or a genuine warning from a colleague who sensed that something evil was in the wind? The fact is that if she had been found shot dead with her own gun, it would easily have been dismissed as a 'clear cut' case of suicide to fellow police investigating the death of someone easily painted as an alcoholic, prone to depression and obviously under great strain. In fact, a senior New South Wales police officer had been found in just such circumstances some years earlier. Officially, he shot himself – but the rumour is that bent police lent him a hand.

By the time Locke wrote *Watching the Detectives*, published in 2003, she was 39, had left the force well behind and had two more children. She and her husband were surviving on police pensions after taking medical discharges from the job that had turned them into pariahs. Despite everything, she told Curtis, she had no regrets about what she had done.

'If you decide to take a stand, you can't stop,' she said. 'You just have to keep going and see it through.' Of her book, since republished to catch the wave of publicity surrounding the *Underbelly* drama series, she said: 'In a way, it's closure. Those bastards did a lot of bad things to me.

'If I found myself in the same situation, I would do it all again. It has taken a huge toll – on my life and on my health and on my family – but at least I feel as if I've done my bit.'

The Wood Royal Commission started on 24 November 1994, and sat for 365 days. It adversely named 200 police officers, among others. At least ten people committed suicide, including police members, school principals and paedophiles. Three people were arrested for failing to answer questions. The Commissioner's main recommendations were the setting up of a Police Integrity Commission, random drug and integrity testing and the abolition of the New South Wales Police Board. The Police Commissioner was given increased powers to hire and fire.

9

THE CHRISTMAS CLUB

```
      There was enough money
hidden in the garage to buy a
 family size house — and the
      police were going to
  steal every dollar of it.
```

BENT cops, crooked lawyers and crims have a saying: 'It's only a rort if you're not in on it.' This explains why the police that missed out on a 'whack' of $200,000 lifted from a cocaine dealer in an operation codenamed Pickup were jealous of those who split up the cash.

The cops with empty pockets called their bent brothers 'the Christmas Club.' It had nothing to do with Santa Claus, reindeer or carol-singing, and any goodwill between the bent officers who shared the money would prove short-lived.

The theft – brazen enough to impress career criminals – would bring nothing but trouble to those who pulled it off. Trevor Haken was one of them and it is his inside account that exposed the anatomy of a classic police scam.

'The name (Christmas Club) was because it all (happened) around Christmas and was a nice little present,' Haken writes in his biography *Sympathy for the Devil*.

It happened in 1983. Despite (or because of) the massive amount of money involved – the equivalent of a million dollars in today's currency – splitting the take sparked much bitterness among corrupt police. Only a dozen or so got a cut. Those actively involved in the sting – plus Haken – got $13,000 each. Others in on the joke got $1000 each. But plenty who knew about it didn't get any.

Among those who got payouts was a future assistant police commissioner, Ray Donaldson, who would later be forced to resign when faced with evidence of his 20 years of corruption. But he wasn't alone.

Sharing top billing with Donaldson as the most senior policeman to leave the job in disgrace was the police commissioner's chief of staff, Bob Lysaught, whose career was wrecked by the tears of a colleague's distraught teenage daughter.

For Donaldson, Lysaught and the rest, Operation Pickup was the beginning of the end. It all started with the Joint Task Force, known as the JTF. It was supposed to be the most elite crime-fighting force Australia had ever known. But it had a hard core of arrogant opportunists who grew bloated with corruption until the group was disbanded after five years. And of the scams they pulled, Operation Pickup looked the easiest score of all.

It centred on two Sydney drug dealers named Salisbury and Powley, targeted by the task force and under close scrutiny.

Coincidentally, Victorian police contacted the task force to say a man they had under surveillance in Melbourne was coming to Sydney to buy drugs from Salisbury and Powley, (later code-named JTF2 and JTF3 when they appeared at the Royal Commission.)

It seemed a win-win situation for everyone except the two drug dealers. The buyer from Victoria, unknowingly purchasing drugs for the undercover policeman who recruited him, did not suspect that the serial numbers of the cash he was carrying had been recorded by Melbourne police, nor that he was under constant surveillance by the Joint Task Force in Sydney.

He completed his drug deal at Sydney airport and returned to Melbourne, where he was immediately arrested. Back in Sydney, JTF2 and JTF3 were delighted with their quick and profitable transaction – but not for long. They were arrested before they got out of the airport car park.

A search of their car produced two kilos of cocaine and a slab of hash, as well as two bags of cash – one holding $27,000, the other $14,400. It was enough to send the task force officers to look for more money and drugs at a Manly garage that JTF2 and JTF3 were known to use.

When the police got to the garage, according to later testimony, their faces lit up. They had stumbled over Aladdin's Cave. As the search began, one of the two arrested men knew exactly what would happen. 'Someone will get a nice new brick veneer tonight,' he predicted. Meaning, there was enough money hidden in the garage to buy a family size house – and the police were going to steal every dollar of it.

He didn't have to be Nostradamus. As well as cocaine and the usual drug paraphernalia, police found a briefcase they later said contained around $200,000. JTF2 would tell the Royal Commission it was actually closer to $280,000.

The real figure could be either or neither of the above: it's hard to pick a winner in any dispute about the relative truthfulness of crooked police and drug dealers. But there is no doubt it was $200,000 or more.

Haken says the cash was brought to the task force headquarters in William Street, Kings Cross, where the marked money from Victorian police was isolated.

The drugs and money from JTF2 and JTF3's car were faithfully recorded as evidence. But the cash stolen from the Manly garage was given to Haken, who acted as paymaster and bundled it into individual packages with the recipient's name on the front of each.

Police who took part in the raid got $13,000. Others who had the night off got $1000. Haken said that included Detective Ray Donaldson, who would rise to be head of the squad before it was disbanded five years later. Although Haken was not physically involved in the raid, he also took $13,000.

Unbeknown to other police and confirming the adage about not trusting a thief, two officers who drove the two drug dealers' car from the airport to Manly found $6000 hidden under a seat and decided to split it on the quiet.

Then a new problem emerged. The money designated for return to Victorian police was several thousand dollars short. Somehow, someone had double-dipped in the corruption payments.

Haken says in *Sympathy for the Devil* that it took a frantic round of phone calls before the missing money was allegedly returned to the task force's Dennis Pattle by JTF 16, Alan Taciak. Haken took no more chances. He drove to Pattle's home to collect the cash.

Haken says that as well as taking his $13,000 share, he gave similar amounts to Detective Sergeant Harry Bendt and detectives Taciak, Pattle, Terry Kilpatrick, Michael Tracey, Glenn Matinca, Frank Gillies, Chris Dent, Ian Lloyd and two detectives from other agencies.

There was a nice touch of irony, according to JTF10, a rollover officer. He said the appropriately-named Bendt, the senior officer, tried to persuade three corrupt officers to give him their $13,000 cut for a share in a real estate deal he was organising. All three declined. 'He would have ripped them off,' JTF10 said.

Haken says that Donaldson, Detective Inspector Ray Southwell, Detective Inspector Brian Meredith and former Australian Federal Police officer Richard Paynter were among those who took $1000.

Police who thought they were entitled to a share of the money were unhappy with the distribution organised by Haken and they had a supporter in Donaldson, even though he got $1000.

He would call Haken a 'horrible, lashing (which means 'ripping off') little cunt' when he learned years later of Haken again short changing colleagues with money stolen from a drug dealer.

More than any other evidence of endemic corruption in the police service, the Joint Task Force disgrace made the biggest impact with the public.

'We were worse than the criminals,' one corrupt officer would admit – and no one disagreed.

The Joint Task Force combined elite officers of the Australian Federal Police and the New South Wales police in a squad supposed to be the best of the best. It wasn't. It was the worst. Not all police working in the squad were corrupt but there was a hard core of intractable officers out for what they could steal – from the minor to the massive.

One officer in the 'Christmas Club' even staged a fake stab wound in his arm to collect as much as $10,000 of taxpayers' money as compensation. And Haken organised for a new carpet in the Westfield Towers building (where the task force headquarters was) to be stolen and laid in his own home.

Haken knew instantly he was with birds of a feather when, soon after arriving at the task force, he overheard Southwell telling colleague Richard Paynter about a sweet deal he had engineered: he had accepted $8000 from a drug dealer named David Kelleher to strip his name from a brief. Haken realised it did not matter where you served in the police, there was corruption to be found.

The Royal Commission hearings would shred the JTF's reputation, with revelations of lying, extortion, fraud, assault, theft, perjury, selling information about police investigations and 'loading up' people with drugs before charging them.

In theory, the task force was a timely move to counter the flow of drugs being funnelled through Sydney to the rest of Australia. It supposedly recruited the brightest and best officers into an independent body with generous funding and high expectations.

Instead, many officers simply merged their flair for criminal behaviour into an organised powerhouse of corruption.

Their methods of raising illegal payments from criminals or just generating advantages for themselves were varied and ingenious. At one stage Haken sold Donaldson, the eventual boss of the unit, a stolen outboard motor for $100 after telling him it had been taken during a raid on an eastern suburbs house.

Another time, Southwell damaged the suspension of his own sedan and simply swapped the damaged part with one from the police car driven by the unsuspecting Donaldson, who took the vehicle to a government garage where it was repaired at taxpayers' expense.

The brazen $200,000 Christmas Club sting was crude but it reflected the red-hot opportunism of corrupt officers inside the task force who would stoop to anything from extortion to perjury and straight-out theft to make money. Worst of all, they would sell out police investigations.

The corruption network came crashing down after selected officers were confronted with evidence of their corruption, gathered through electronic surveillance and telephone taps. Their choice was to become undercover double agents for the commission to avoid charges themselves. A case of setting a thief to catch a thief.

And no matter where the Commission headed in its inquiry into the JTF, the signposts of corruption invariably seemed to point at Donaldson and Lysaught, who were close friends and had followed tandem career paths.

Donaldson, called the 'Smiling Assassin' by his troops, proved a man of hugely contrasting opinions. He privately attacked the Royal Commission while publicly endorsing it, then went running to the Supreme Court on a failed mission to suppress his name and the allegations against him.

He denied all knowledge of any officers being corrupt then resigned (before he was pushed), claiming his reputation had been butchered beyond belief.

Arrogant and derisive about the Commission when it was first announced, Donaldson showed his true colours in a conversation with a colleague who had 'rolled over' and was wearing a recording device.

'The whole fucking thing's frog shit,' Donaldson ranted. 'This is a hundred million (dollars to run). It's the WOFTAM Commission (Waste of fucking time and money). Any team of fucking galoots could have gone up to the Cross. It's been going on for 100 years.'

To the delight of the public gallery at the Royal Commission, Donaldson's WOFTAM tirade came immediately after he had been in the witness box under oath.

He was asked: 'And there's never been an occasion when you've done anything that a fellow policeman would take as a want of support for the Royal Commission by way of word or deed. Is that correct?'

Donaldson: 'Correct.'

Counsel for the Commission: 'Would you listen to this tape?'

Donaldson could blink and swallow but he couldn't run and he couldn't hide. But he lied. A diehard believer in the quaint idea of the 'big blue gang' being invulnerable to any investigation if police remained staunchly united, he repeatedly denied everything. But it was too late.

The gallows for Donaldson and Lysaught, the police commissioner's chief of staff, was built on the plea of former officer Paul Deaves, who rolled over to become JTF7.

Deaves broke down in the witness box as he shamefacedly detailed his corrupt behaviour, including a massive $100,000 scam on a drug dealer. He wasn't alone in reaching for the tissues.

By the time he had finished detailing the widespread corruption in the task force, the sixteen colleagues he'd implicated were in tears as well as they saw their careers crash and burn.

Deaves became a weapon of mass destruction for the Commission, unhesitatingly naming fellow officers that he said acted corruptly, including Donaldson and Lysaught.

He came into the hearing through the 'roll-over' door reserved for officers who had changed sides and his testimony burned holes in his previous dodgy evidence.

He admitted he was corrupt, had accepted bribes in the past and had direct evidence linking other police with bribes from criminals. And he was willing to tell all.

Deaves said his teenage daughter had begged him to tell the truth in the witness box, whatever the consequences.

'You're a policeman, dad,' she had said. 'You've sworn to tell the truth.' So he did. His colleagues, facing the sack over charges ranging from theft to intimidating witnesses to perjury and drug dealing, thought he should have stuck to the adage that children should be seen but not heard.

Deaves' testimony was poignant, partly because it had to be so personally treacherous. He was a long-time personal friend of Donaldson and Lysaught, who was godfather to Deaves' son. JTF6, another officer who rolled over, was also a close friend of all three men.

That intimacy turned to ashes as the pair saved their own hides by switching sides and working undercover for the Commission. Deaves recalled the past and JTF6 captured the present on a recording device he wore into Lysaught's office to tape conversations.

Deaves revealed his and Lysaught's involvement in a scam that extracted $100,000 from a slow-thinking cocaine dealer and a midnight rendezvous on a winter's night to distribute the spoils.

The pay-off came when two police cars driven by officers with no known interest in nature study pulled into Koala Park, a deserted tourist attraction at Castle Hill in outer Sydney. With only gum trees as witnesses, a white cloth bag containing $44,000 in bundles of $50, $20 and $10 notes was tossed from one car to Deaves in the other with the message: 'Here's your Christmas present.'

It was actually mid-1987, not Christmas time, but the police calendar is elastic about such things.

Deaves' first reaction to the windfall was to phone Lysaught from a public phone and say: 'Everything is sweet.'

The police in Koala Park and the dozen or so others in on the rort were the dark side of Santa Claus. They were splitting $100,000 in cash they had conned out of a drug importer called John Murphy.

Murphy, big in cocaine, thought he was buying his way out of being charged over millions of dollars worth of drug importations. He was a little optimistic. As Deaves would later reveal in the witness box, the task force had no brief on Murphy and could do nothing to help him – but the temptation to relieve him of $100,000 was too much to ignore.

Murphy's $100,000 offer was relayed to New South Wales drug officers Peter George and Chris Hannay who in turn, the Commission was told, passed it along to Lysaught and other senior police. Lysaught was named as the mastermind of the extortion scheme and a corruption conduit to his friend Donaldson. They even set up 'think tanks' to find a way to make it work.

'During the course of discussions with Mr Lysaught it was decided that, as we didn't have a brief on Murphy anyway, we were not in a position to charge him,' Deaves said. 'There was a discussion about basically distancing ourselves from the money and Murphy. I have a recollection Mr Lysaught and myself also spoke to Dick Paynter and Brian Meredith.'

Paynter and Meredith allegedly drove the police car that arrived at the Koala Park and threw the money to Deaves – a charge they denied, along with other allegations of corrupt behaviour.

Lysaught was the bagman. He took $17,000 of Murphy's bribe for himself and another $5000 he said was for Donaldson. A total of $44,000 went to four officers with the remaining $56,000 divided between other police in the rort.

With the ghosts of his past threatening him, Lysaught decided attack was the best defence at his first appearance before the Commission. It didn't last. He had come into the hearing like a brass band. He went out like a tin whistle.

He castigated the media for pursuing him and protested his innocence until counsel assisting, John Agius, dropped the stunning news that Lysaught's office had been infiltrated and recording devices planted in it.

'Mr Lysaught, I tell you now so that you may know and think about this,' Agius said. 'For quite some long time now (JTF6) has been assisting the Royal Commission by having meetings with people, including yourself, at a time when he was wearing a listening device.

'The Royal Commission has those holdings and there are a large number of them and your voice features prominently. The Commission would like you to think about your position between now and the time you return to the witness box.'

The realisation hit Lysaught like a bucket of iced water. He had been sold out by a man he trusted implicitly.

Agius demanded an answer. Did Lysaught understand the situation?

It was a bitter moment for Lysaught as he whispered, 'Yes'. Having headed down a dead end by initially denying ever seeing or hearing of any corruption during their time in the force and sticking to their story, Lysaught and Donaldson had to sit like condemned men waiting for the trapdoor to drop as a black cloud of allegations burst over them.

Surveillance and bugging, modern policing's best tools, were being used to rid the modern force of some of its dinosaurs. Other tapes recorded secretly in Lysaught's office and played for Justice Wood revealed officers pledging to hold their ranks at the Royal Commission.

Deaves also said Lysaught had shared a $10,000 bribe with other corrupt police for not opposing a bail application by a Central Coast heroin seller.

'Rollover' officers told of Lysaught instigating an aggressive twelve- hour interrogation of a woman at Sydney airport and bullying her into signing a partly false statement he had compiled about her conspiring to import drugs even though none had been found on her person or in her luggage.

Deaves said other officers involved in the case had met to go over the details to ensure 'their statements dovetailed to make it look like it had actually happened.' The woman was subsequently jailed.

The allegations against Donaldson mounted until they were a noose around his neck. Being fingered for receiving money from the drug raid was just the start of his problems. Eye witnesses said he had also assaulted a man involved in heroin trafficking and then colluded with other officers to lie about the case in court.

By this stage the supposedly rock-solid task force that Donaldson was relying on for support was fracturing fast. Realising their past sins were surfacing and confronted by Haken's forensic memory and recorded evidence, guilty officers rushed to 'roll over' and tell their stories to the Commission to reduce the looming penalties.

At one stage former squad members JTF1, JTF6, JTF7, JTF8 and JTF 9 were lining up behind Haken to give evidence. Then came J10 and J11. In poker it was a straight.

It was JTF8 who revealed that Donaldson had assaulted an Asian cocaine dealer during a raid on a house in

Kirrawee in Sydney's south. It happened after police tracked imported heroin (packed into a car axle) to the house.

JTF8 said the raid was more violent than he'd expected despite the fact the suspects found living at the house had shown little resistance.

'It was a hard entry. The Asians living there were secured violently and pushed and thrown to the ground,' JTF8 said. He admitted grabbing a man named Truang and slapping him before dragging him into the yard, where other police converged on him.

'I recall the man (Truang) being hit across the face two or three times by another police officer,' JTF8 said. 'Hard-handed slaps to the side of the face. The man (a Vietnamese) was screaming and wailing as he was being bashed in the backyard.'

Asked which officer had hit the man JTF8 replied: 'Detective Sergeant Ray Donaldson.'

The assault had also been witnessed by people next door. Unluckily for the cops, one of the witnesses was a retired fireman and lay preacher with an irresistible urge to tell the truth. 'We didn't know he was watching what went on,' JTF8 said feelingly.

The people in the Kirrawee house were charged with conspiracy to supply heroin. But the neighbour willingly gave evidence of having seen Truang assaulted. To overcome the problem the police involved had a 'scrum down' and decided to deny the allegations en masse.

'Under oath I denied these allegations as did the other police involved,' JTF8 admitted.

Royal Commissioner: *What other police denied those allegations?*

JTF8: *Mr Donaldson was among them.*

RC: *Did you speak to your police colleagues about what evidence you would give about the matter in court?*

JTF8: *Yes. We decided that the assault would be denied.*

JTF8 said Donaldson agreed with the decision to lie to the court. Other former colleagues also rushed to kick Donaldson's battered reputation to death.

Evidence was given that he had once helped dispose of a police car severely damaged when Lysaught hit a parked vehicle while trying to change lanes after a drinking session in inner Sydney. Lysaught had called Donaldson, who told him to hide the vehicle until morning. Donaldson would later decide the car was so damaged it should be dumped so JTF6 reported it stolen.

As the allegations mounted, an increasingly jittery Donaldson verged on a state of shock. He knew there was plenty more where that came from. For instance, the Commission heard that Donaldson had illegally intervened in a case being heard by Royal Commissioner James Wood when he was a trial judge.

It revolved around a raid on a Five Dock home in Sydney's inner-west and the arrest of two heroin dealers whose names were suppressed. The raid, Operation Bing, was so farcically handled it could have been a script for a comic book.

Even though cocaine was genuinely found on the premises, the raid was 'chaotic', according to Deaves. He said the male heroin dealer had been assaulted and police were swearing and screaming at the top of their voices and using language like 'sit down, you fucking moll' to the man's partner. Unfortunately for them, the house was being bugged – and the tapes hadn't been turned off. The rogue cops realised too late that all their swearing, bullying and violence was on tape.

Deaves said he had taken this problem to Detective Sergeant Rob Milner, the JFT deputy leader, but Milner refused to help and wanted the tapes played in their entirety in court. In other words, he seemed to be the only character in the pantomime with any idea of what proper policing was about.

Donaldson was next on Deaves' list to ask for help. 'He told me we would have to get rid of the tape because it could not be played,' Deaves recalled.

After waiting until Milner went on holidays, Deaves and JTF 20 stole the tape and edited out the troublesome words. JTF 20 burnt the original. But in court the two dealers complained about being assaulted and queried the authenticity of the modified tape played in the trial.

Justice Wood, then the trial judge, ordered that the tapes be tested by experts for authenticity and that Legal Aid provide enough money for ten hours of examination.

Deaves, embarrassed at giving evidence to a Royal Commissioner about the way he had been duped as judge, admitted they had thwarted Woods' plan by putting the doctored tape at the bottom of the pile to be tested.

They then diverted the expert's attention by continually talking about his electronic equipment until the Legal Aid funds were exhausted. 'He only got through about seven tapes before the cash ran out,' Deaves said.

Commissioner Wood said from the bench that the evidence against the couple had been very powerful.

'Roll over' witness and former officer JTF16 proved full of malice and without any morality. A search of his home by Royal Commission officers found pipes stuffed with money buried in his back yard, along with a .38 Smith & Wesson service revolver issued to another officer.

The two men had argued so JTF16 stole the other officer's pistol because he knew that losing your weapon was a serious breach for a police officer. JTF 16 was eventually sacked from the force and was last known to be selling cars for a living.

Another example of the task force members' insatiable appetite for corruption also came in Operation Bing, again involving drugs.

Deaves, seconded to the task force from the Australian Federal Police, was part of a surveillance team watching the Five Dock house, where suspected heroin importers Pat and Elizabeth Curry were living.

The couple were being watched when they went to Bangkok. Pat Curry owned a Sydney taxi school and was eventually convicted after heroin was found hidden in the panelling of one of his cabs.

He was interviewed by Haken and Deaves and while he was in custody, all his furniture was stolen, including a refrigerator. 'We received a note from Curry's solicitor saying there was no furniture in the house,' Deaves told the

Commission. 'Everything had been taken from the house. Just about everything that wasn't nailed down was gone.'

Deaves said Donaldson, by then the commanding officer in the JTF, had been angry about the theft, insisting the stolen furniture be returned.

'He (Donaldson) basically said: "I don't care who took it. I want it put back straight away".' Deaves denied that he or Haken were behind the theft and blamed an officer called John Cushion.

Police also raided the home of an associate of the Currys in the mistaken belief they would find drugs and money. 'Mr Donaldson blued about nothing being found,' Deaves said.

The task force got its own back for missing out on finding any easy money. When Curry's associate was later arrested on an unrelated matter, JTF6 and Deaves 'verballed' him.

THE officer codenamed JTF14 was one of the many police – those who appeared before the Commission and those who did not – who had regarded the police brotherhood as invincible. Sticking together in adversity was their mantra – but it didn't last when the rats started to rat on each other.

Corrupt police were uncovered in all sorts of places, and JTF14 was one of them. He was recalled from working on assignment in Great Britain for the Australian Federal Police. He arrived back in Australia to admit he had framed a suspected drug dealer out of misguided loyalty to other corrupt police.

It was a long way to come to be sacked from a cushy overseas posting. At that stage JTF14, a detective superintendent in the Australian Federal Police, was the most senior officer to appear before the inquiry.

He said Ray Donaldson had driven him to a house in inner-city Alexandria to plant a knife near where a drug dealer had earlier been arrested. It was part of a subterfuge to provide a corrupt financial windfall for another officer, Detective Sergeant Richard Paynter, who retired from the force in 1986 medically unfit.

Paynter had cut his arm climbing a corrugated fence during a raid on the Erskineville Hotel to capture a man named Eric John Honeysett in1983 but he wanted to turn the injury into something more lucrative. So he claimed he had been stabbed by a knife supposedly wielded by Honeysett during a scuffle.

There was no scuffle and no knife. An unarmed Honeysett ran out of the hotel into a lane and despite 'almost everyone from the task force being there' he managed to climb a fence and get onto a roof while being shot at by police, who luckily all missed him. They could steal a barn door but they couldn't hit one.

Honeysett jumped into a backyard and was captured only because he tried to run through the house and stumbled over two large Greek men sleeping in the hall trying to catch a breeze on a hot day. The Greeks fell on top of him as he shouted, 'You fat bastards.'

Then Honeysett's day rapidly got worse. He was fitted up with a charge of attempted murder of Paynter with police falsely claiming he was carrying a knife. Honeysett being 'armed' was necessary, of course, because it justified police shooting at him. The fact that it would mean a man would serve a huge jail sentence for something he hadn't done didn't matter to them.

Haken's account was: 'There was no knife so we had to put a knife into the scenario somewhere. So the Fed (JTF14) took a knife and threw it back over the fence.

'Of course, when the scientific guy was photographing the scene the next day he found the knife.' Naturally. Planting a 'throwaway' for honest colleagues to find is one of the oldest tricks in the bent cop rulebook because the innocent dupe gives flawlessly sincere evidence.

JTF14 corroborated Haken's evidence, saying Paynter told him he was going to claim he was stabbed by Honeysett and asked him to go back to the scene in a car driven by Donaldson and plant a knife.

Two more protected witnesses, JTF 15 and JTF16, said their statements – used to support the case against Honeysett – were false and had been compiled only after police rehearsed their story.

Honeysett, trapped in a web of lies, had done the best deal he could. Finally accepting that the odds of him beating the manufactured evidence and a conspiracy were astronomical, he pleaded guilty to both a drug charge and using an offensive weapon. 'It was me against the task force,' he told the Commission in explanation of his guilty plea.

The whole charade was a disgraceful example of how far bent police would go to fit someone up with a false charge to suit their own selfish purposes. Morality was discarded as casually as a 'throwaway' knife.

Even a doctor, who initially said the gash on Paynter's arm did not look as if it was caused by a knife, was pushed towards a conveniently vague conclusion. Police had commented that her 'failure' to recognise the injury as a knife cut was a 'pity' because it was crucial evidence against a criminal who had 63 convictions for rape and assault on women.

She said: 'Where do I sign?'

The fit-up was an almost sadistic act by the police involved. Honeysett faced a possible twenty years in jail for attempted murder of a policeman had he not pleaded guilty to the manufactured charge.

Paynter, who had retired from the force on medical grounds, denied the allegations. But the combined evidence of the guilty Federal policeman, Haken and Honeysett, who emphatically denied he had ever attempted to stab anyone, finally carried the day.

JTF14 paid a high price, despite regaining some integrity by telling the truth about the Paynter sham.

'It was misguided loyalty,' he said of his involvement, adding his name to the list of police who felt compelled to be corrupt to stay in line with senior officers who had control over their future. '(What I did) was utterly inexcusable and impermissible.'

But apparent remorse wasn't enough to atone for his sins. Commissioner Wood killed JTF14's future as a policeman.

'Do you think you could stay a day longer in the Federal Police?' Wood asked. It was a rhetorical question. The only anwer was 'No'.

While JTF14's support strengthened Haken's version of what happened, his recall from overseas to testify was puzzling because no incentives seemed to be on offer except being sacked instead of being prosecuted. There was no prosecution of anyone else involved in the scam.

'I don't know quite what happened,' Haken would write. 'Someone must have convinced him (JTF14) to say "Well, this happened" and then he'd be okay to go back to England and live happily ever after.

'You've got a Federal Police superintendent coming back from England saying: "Yeah. Righto. That's what we did."

'And there's all these other people saying that's what happened but no prosecutions.

'I believe Paynter received a $2500 payment as a result of a criminal compensation payment for the (cut arm).

'If you look at his history, he's claimed for injuries in motor vehicles and other things. Mate, he's the most injured man in history. He shouldn't be able to walk. He should be like Raymond Burr (from the TV crime series *Ironside*) ripping around in a wheelchair.

'The DPP (Department of Public Prosecutions) hasn't prosecuted the majority of people who ought to have been prosecuted out of the Royal Commission. People haven't asked why. The DPP should be asked to explain this.'

The failure of the DPP to pursue obvious – and in many cases admitted – guilt was disappointing, especially after the stern warning about penalties facing corrupt police issued by the Royal Commissioner at the start of the hearings.

He said police and criminals who were later shown to have lied to the Commission 'must expect significant penal sentences – that is, significant periods in jail. It was wishful thinking.

LYSAUGHT and Donaldson were linked by a mutually beneficial friendship. So strong was the link that counsel assisting the Royal Commission, John Agius, accused them of being the most prominent links in a chain of corruption stretching from working police almost to the doorstep of Police Commissioner Tony Lauer.

While there was no suggestion of impropriety about Lauer, he emerged from the imbroglio as an administrator of stunning naivety.

Writing in the *Weekend Australian*, ABC commentator Quentin Dempster nailed Lauer's inability to survive the overwhelming evidence of his ineptitude.

'A revolver in the library appears to be the only honourable course open to Tony Lauer: pre-emptive resignation,' he wrote.

'He could jump before he is pushed, admit failure and declare his wish to allow the rebuilding of public confidence in the police force through Wood's pursuit of the truth.

'At the moment, Lauer's tactics are to maintain a low profile. The silence is deafening.'

Former Independent Member of Parliament, John Hatton, a long time campaigner for the Royal Commission to be set up, called for Lauer to be sacked. 'The failure of his administration warrants his sacking now,' Hatton said.

In the end, Lauer did resign, perhaps avoiding a more dramatic end to his career. A huge hurdle for him was his support for Donaldson's integrity despite rapidly mounting suspicion to the contrary.

Lauer said he had no doubt about Donaldson's ability to continue in his role in the force. 'Assistant Commissioner Donaldson has sought and should be granted the opportunity to respond as soon as possible to these allegations,' Lauer said. 'These allegations stem from some years back when Mr Donaldson was not assistant commissioner.

'I hope eventually the Royal Commission will start to deal with more contemporary policing rather than these incidents of some time ago.'

Allegations about the $100,000 bribe extracted from Murphy and the role of Lysaught and Donaldson in the corruption had surfaced previously and led to a 1990 Crime Commission inquiry by a judge.

But the police involved put their heads together, as usual, and told concurrent lies, claiming it had never happened. Lysaught and Donaldson were both exonerated.

Without the incriminating eavesdropping from other corrupt officers wearing recording devices, the Royal Commission's inquiry a decade later and subsequent exposure of the corruption might have gone the same way.

This time Lysaught was unceremoniously sacked. Donaldson was told his contract would not be renewed and resigned immediately. But he didn't go quietly.

'I don't think I will ever recover,' he whined, saying the media scrutiny of his 35-year police career had 'destroyed my character and reputation.' He said one true thing: that his entire career had 'been in vain'. No one argued with that.

And in a bizarre reminder that no power in Sydney is mighty enough to change the thinking of established police about supporting a colleague, no matter how circumstances may taint him, Lysaught got a new job.

A newspaper reported that Lysaught became manager of a block of units in Queensland – the sort of job that usually commands a good salary because it requires supervising the renting of units to holiday-makers. When Lysaught's dodgy background was raised, who came to his rescue? Senior New South Wales police, of course.

The *Sun-Herald* commented: 'They like a certain kind of policeman up there in the deep north.

'Disgraced former New South Wales chief superintendent Bob Lysaught's foray into management at Broadbeach's new Capricornia high-rise unit block per the use of laudatory references from senior police, who should have known better, has been given the thumbs up.

'Capricornia's Body Corporate has approved Lysaught continuing in the new role.'

Those who had suffered because of the actions of bent police did not end up with such a comfortable life.

– WITH RAY CHESTERTON

10

BILLY, NOT SILLY

'What Bayeh did was to do what
Woolworths did - put people out
of business. Not by cutting
the prices, just cutting
their legs off.'

BILLY Bayeh tried to pass himself off as a modern-day
Rumplestiltskin, the magical gnome who could spin straw
into gold.

No one believed him. They knew the real source of his
chunky 'junkie' gold jewellery and his money was drug
dealing: cocaine and heroin, mainly.

Billy's declared taxable income was $35,000 a year as
part-owner of a suburban shoe shop. He claimed that somehow he was able to spin that minor wage into a lifestyle that
embraced losing millions of dollars in betting, lavish holidays and meeting the mortgage on a million-dollar house.

Even his international honeymoon with his wife Tanya was Bollywood lavish, incorporating a stopover in Singapore for an $800 dinner at the legendary Raffles Hotel, where a round of pink gin slings costs the average weekly wage.

That was the glittering and glamorous side of Billy's life. The dark side was the dealing of slow death through the drugs he sold to addicts in Kings Cross alleys and nightclubs, bribing police, threatening to kill anyone who got in his way and profiteering from sleaze, lies and thuggery.

A trusted Bayeh lieutenant who rolled over to become a protected Wood Royal Commission witness, code-named KX14 (KX denoted Kings Cross, 14 the number given each witness), gave an insight into King Billy's empire. In six months, the informer said, he had helped cut heroin and cocaine worth $2.5 million. Some shoe shop.

Bill Bayeh and his older brother, the renowned standover man Louie, used intimidation and police protection to get their turn at controlling Kings Cross vice in the 1980s and 1990s.

Billy started small, competing with a dozen or more dealers of equal status. But he had an entrepreneurial flair for using modern corporate methods and violence to get ahead of the pack.

'What Bayeh did down the track was to try and do what Woolworths did – that is put people out of business,' notes self-confessed crooked cop Trevor Haken in his biography, *Sympathy for the Devil.* 'Not by cutting the prices or anything, just cutting their legs off.'

The Bayeh brothers arrived at the Cross at a pivotal moment in Sydney's drug-dealing scene, where nothing is constant except change. The population, the dealers, the nationalities and police attitudes revolve as predictably as a carousel.

'One mob moves out and another moves in within minutes, like blow flies to a dead carcass,' Haken explains.

The Lebanese took over from the Romanians, but then an attempted invasion by Vietnamese criminals hoping to replicate their dominance at Cabramatta in Sydney's outer west was quickly squashed by police. A Russian group also pushed into the scene for a while.

The Cross was a no man's land for any sensible member of the public wanting the protection of law and order. The area's shabby chic status as a bohemian hangout for the artistic, literary and musical had long crumbled – invaded by the godless and lawless as drugs and vice took over the 'night time' economy. A raffish young lady had degenerated into a seedy, broken-down whore.

Senior police had given up and there were no resources to fight crime. While stationed at the Cross, Haken once took $200 out of petty cash to buy a beaten-up Datsun 180B. It needed two milk crates to prop up a broken driver's seat, reducing its capacity to just three people.

For a while, he claimed, the Datsun provided the only transport police had to take arrested people to Kings Cross Station to be charged. It was bizarre that a jalopy was being used as a de facto cop car but it fitted in with the madness of the red light district on the edge of one of the world's great western cities.

'You got off the train (at Kings Cross Station) and it was wall-to-wall junkies and crooks from all over the place. If someone got out of jail anywhere you knew they'd end up here,' Haken says. By the 1980s, the bohemian days when the Cross featured characters like the white witch Roslyn Norton were long gone.

In their place, accelerated by the arrival of US troops in the 1960s on R & R from Vietnam wanting drugs and sex, came the heavy drug dealers and flesh peddlers. They got a tight grip on Kings Cross that hasn't been loosened in almost 50 years.

Mostly, things were good for the drug sellers. Addicts are permanent customers and corrupt police are compliant. But sometimes, even at the Cross, the black market in sex and drugs got a little tight when the economy dived.

Neil Chenoweth wrote in his book about the 1992 recession, *Packer's Lunch*: 'The Cross was doing it tough as well, though on the surface little seemed to have changed.

'As the Wood Royal Commission would reveal, the area was dominated by four major heroin and cocaine distributors, eight major drug outlets, seven strip clubs running prostitution and a solid phalanx of standover men.

'Victims disappeared, killers beat murder changes, police officers stole drugs and money from dealers, ran protection rackets, made up evidence and threatened witnesses. Business as usual, it seemed.

'At one point in the early 1990s an axe murderer was thinning out the tourist population at the Cross on a random basis but it rated barely more than a mention in the Press. But behind the happy facade even the Cross was feeling the recession.

'Bill Bayeh, brother of that well-known friend of the City, Louie, who would feature prominently in the Wood Royal Commission, was said to be so down on his luck in 1991 that his onetime protégé Danny Karam lent him $50.'

Karam was obviously travelling a little better than Bayeh but the money drought hurt everyone, even the sensitive souls who ran protection rackets. Standover man Anton Skoro would later testify that the drug dealer who paid him $2500 a week to operate in the Cosmopolitan cafe regularly resorted to paying him with caps of heroin rather than the folding stuff, Chenoweth wrote.

'They were always running out of money,' the standover man complained. 'They were the poorest drug dealers I've ever known.'

Two years after having to snip $50 from Karam to keep body and soul together, Billy Bayeh was back and making a fortune running four heroin and cocaine outlets at the Cross – Laser's fun parlour (reportedly turning over $20,000 a night), the Penthouse billiard room, the Down Under Hostel and the Cosmo.

When Bayeh eventually copped fifteen years jail for drug offences in 1996, Danny Karam was one of the princes in waiting to take over the drug throne. Unfortunately for the callous Karam, he was gunned down by his own gang – called Danny's Boys – before he could steal the crown.

It is not known if Bayeh ever repaid Karam the $50 loan.

MOST people are insulted when they are called an idiot. Not Billy Bayeh, he was delighted. In fact, he went to extraordinary lengths to have sessions with a forensic psychologist to get official endorsement of his simplicity – and not just verbally. He needed it in writing. He wanted an official diploma 'proving' his supposed feeble mindedness to hang on his wall, the way graduates hang their degrees.

It was, of course, a ruse to attempt to escape drug charges. It exposed the extent to which the New South Wales legal system could be exploited and manipulated in imaginative and daring ways by various criminals and their associates.

Bayeh was arrested in a Bondi motel room in November 1990, a week after Kingston Rule won the Melbourne Cup for Bart Cummings at 7/1. He was charged with being knowingly involved in the supply of cocaine. At first, he claimed that police stole $2000 of the cash and cocaine they found under his pillow in his room before 'booking' him for $4640.

He said the money had come from backing Kingston Rule but later he dropped his claim to the missing cash. Police said Bayeh had known cocaine was in the room and that it belonged to Thierry Boetel, who'd been mentioned in evidence as a drug dealer and who had access to the room.

It was a tough situation for Bayeh, one that required great finesse to keep him out of prison. So, with considerable help from unidentified friends, he constructed an elaborate ruse that involved forged letters saying he was of good character but virtually moronic. He manipulated a forensic psychologist into classifying him as 'borderline intellectually handicapped' with an IQ of 75.

Meanwhile, Boetel conveniently provided a written confession to Bayeh's legal team saying the cocaine was his and went to the Gold Coast to evade a police hunt. If there was one.

It worked. Billy got off with 300 hours of community service on a charge that would usually bring time in jail. The aftermath came two years later when the Wood inquiry started turning over the mulch that had hidden much of the real story.

It turned out Bayeh's solicitors had arranged for him to be psychologically tested before his drug trial in the District Court in March 1994. The report from a forensic psychologist assessed Bayeh as barely smart enough to tie his own shoe laces, stating that his IQ of 75 put him in the lowest five percent of the population.

There were no encouraging points for Billy in the report but that didn't matter: according to it, he was hardly smart enough to read it.

He was assessed as immature – and illiterate in both English and Arabic. Two years later, in the Commission witness box, the psychological expert for hire said he was stunned to hear of Billy's extensive business interests and his criminal history involving drugs and violence dating back to 1975. In fact, the boffin raised a vital question: could he be certain that the man he had examined was the real Billy Bayeh? Accusations were made that the man he examined might well have been a slow-thinking 'stooge' pretending to be Bayeh.

Asked to identify Bayeh from a photograph and asked if he had met him before, the 'trick cyclist' was undecided.

'I don't believe I have but I can't state categorically that I haven't,' he replied. 'That person (indicating the photograph of Bayeh) doesn't look familiar to me. I have a shocking memory for names but not usually faces.'

Unfortunately, his assessment had been unchallenged as evidence used to support Bayeh's legal battle. The same applied to three references from people attesting to Bayeh's good character. Former detective Charlie Staunton – Bayeh's right hand man – would later go to jail for contempt for refusing to answer questions about corruption, including what he knew about the source of the references.

They were later proved to be forgeries. After a lifetime of working within a judiciary system he strongly supported, Royal Commissioner Justice Wood was visibly shaken by any suggestion it could be manipulated so easily to help criminals dodge jail. As the evidence mounted, he threatened to track down not just corrupt police but also lawyers, expert witnesses and private investigators operating on the shady side of the law.

Wood ended up admitting he had changed his mind and realised systemic corruption could occur in many ways, such as by weakening a prosecution case by withholding evidence or witnesses – or by shrinking the amount of drugs or money allegedly involved.

Both defence and prosecution teams could also be involved with presenting untrue or slanted evidence and withholding criminal antecedents.

None of that especially worried Bayeh, who was free to continue a spending spree that would make most millionaires envious. But trying to follow his mental state was a trial in itself. On any given day, a little like Alan Bond, he apparently veered from being a village idiot to a financial wizard in control of three profitable businesses. Amazing.

Billy's petite and pretty young wife Tanya told the Royal Commission her husband was so mentally defective, he initially confused the IQ test with contraception. This caused great hilarity among reporters covering the Commission.

Ray Chesterton wrote in the *Daily Telegraph*: 'Wouldn't that have been a honeymoon from hell until order was restored? "No Billy. It's not a balloon. Try again".'

Tanya held a Bachelor of Arts with a major in psychology. She said she had taken Billy for the test in which her husband's IQ was rated at 75. Presumably, she stayed around to lead him home otherwise he might have had trouble crossing the road.

Despite her own qualifications, Tanya robustly denied that her own knowledge of psychology had led to a few trial runs at home to acquaint Billy with what questions might be asked.

Tanya told the Commission that despite the psychologist's misgivings, she was certain the man she took for the test was her husband. She spent a total of six hours in the Commission witness box but she didn't win many fans. She was repeatedly told she was a liar, a perjurer and had signed legal documents she knew to be false.

'You've come here today looking as sweet as a picture and told every lie in the world,' said the Police Service's legal representative. 'Who told you to come here with your cock and bull story, your husband?'

She answered quietly: 'No'.

Tanya was compromised by application forms she had filled out for bank housing loans listing their annual income as $400,000 plus. Like so much of the paperwork in Billy's life, the income on the application and its sources were false.

Meanwhile, Billy had other big problems of his own. Acknowledged as the drug czar of Kings Cross and turning over an estimated $20,000 a week from just one outlet, he was trying to find an identity that would cover all of his 'personalities.'

He was acknowledged as smart enough to run a drug empire and launder money through horse racing but stupid enough to be classified as having an IQ of 75. Third, and most importantly, he was also a police informer like his brother Louie. So he was an idiot savant – and a dirty rotten rat.

Billy had rolled under pressure and changed sides to help the Royal Commission by dobbing in every bent copper he could remember bribing. But Slick Willy soon became Silly Billy as he struggled to stay in touch with reality as all his crude cover-ups and masquerades to avoid detection fell apart.

The evidence was overwhelming and included tape recordings made by confessed corrupt detective Haken exposing Bayeh's payoffs to police, often at Birkenhead Point, a retail shopping complex at inner-suburban Drummoyne. But there were dozens of other places where money changed hands as well.

During one three-day period Haken collected more than $8000 from Bayeh to split with other corrupt police, then another $8000 a month or so later. Bayeh also gave a former Kings Cross detective called Stephen Pentland $150 towards the cost of his 30th birthday party at The Tunnel nightclub, which happened to be a notorious drug selling outlet.

A former employee of Billy's who turned police informer (codename KX1) during the Royal Commission, organised the party. Pentland said that during the festivities Bayeh shook his hand and gave him $150, saying put it 'on the bar for your friends.'

Pentland said he understood that Bayeh and one of his employees – soon-to-be famous John Ibrahim – had paid for the food and drink. Billy also provided finance when Pentland went broke at the races trying to raise money to pay back a student loan.

'I spent a lot of time at Canterbury race track,' Pentland admitted later. 'If Bill ever had a good win out there and he was quite happy, he would slip me $200 and tell me to have a bet on him in the next race. I just lost the plot and took the money.'

Pentland left the police service after eight years on medical grounds but he didn't go quietly. His farewell party at the West End Hotel in the Sydney CBD was memorable.

His police mates, with Constable Gary Leach in the vanguard, inflicted serious injuries on a drinker at the hotel before throwing him into the street and kicking him unconscious. The man allegedly provoked the fracas by laughing at a policeman's moustache. Or possibly it was a policewoman's moustache. Steroid abuse was not unknown.

Unfortunately for the police involved, the entire episode

was caught on film by the Professional Integrity Branch who, co-incidentally, was investigating several officers at the party.

After police predictably denied any involvement in the fracas they were forced to watch tape of the incident showing the victim exploding out of the hotel doors and Leach and a Constable Peter Kelly kicking him as he lay on the footpath.

But such high jinks were trifles compared with the main game: Billy Bayeh was trying to hammer round blocks into square holes to explain his millions of dollars in unaccounted wealth. He was struggling with arithmetic.

The Commission showed him spending $278,300 from a salary of $35,000 in 1993-94. Outgoings included $120,000 towards buying a $500,000 luxury home, $18,000 to service a $400,000 mortgage, $50,000 in cash to a barrister who represented him in March 1994 in the District Court over cocaine charges, $32,000 to lease the Penthouse pool room at Kings Cross, $20,000 to Diners Club, $17,000 to establish a shoe shop at Bankstown, $16,000 cash to honeymoon in Lebanon and $6400 to a TAB phone account.

There were also spontaneous trips twice a month to Gold Coast luxury hotels and restaurants with his wife and friends and $10,000 gambling losses at Jupiter's Casino.

In desperation, Bayeh claimed the balance of the money had come from successful betting on racehorses. This brought guffaws from the crowd, as he had already been established as the world's worst punter. Counsel assisting, John Agius, said Billy owed more than $784,000 to bookmaker Jeff Pendlebury.

In nine months Bayeh had turned over $3.6 million with Pendlebury – and lost most of it. Betting transaction sheets obtained by the inquiry showed he rarely had a winning day.

'You must think you have won the lottery today if you think we will believe that (the success at punting)' said Agius.

Bayeh's betting exploits and Pendlebury's reaction to the non-payment of such a massive debt were the subject of much perusal. Agius suggested Pendlebury was involved in a money-laundering scheme with Bayeh. Or that Pendlebury, because of the debt, could lay claim to Bayeh's estate and hold it for him until any jail sentence was completed.

The bookmaker denied both suggestions, saying he had thought Bayeh was a coffee shop owner and became 'frightened when told he was a big noise at the Cross.'

There is no doubt Bayeh was using one of the oldest dodges of all to launder black money. A criminal would wait at the races or at a TAB outlet until he saw a punter with a big winning ticket lining up to collect.

If the winning ticket was for $10,000, the criminal would offer the punter $11,000 for it and everyone was happy. The punter is $1000 better off and the criminal gets a TAB cheque for $10,000 of freshly laundered money.

The *Daily Telegraph's* Ray Chesterton found Pendlebury's patience in waiting for repayment of such a big debt extraordinarily heart-warming.

'Remarkable? Well, astonishing really for those who never suspected the flinty hearts of bookies overflowed with such a passionate need to do deeds for needy punters,' he wrote.

'There was no push for settlement, which should ensure Pendlebury is knocked off his stand at the next meeting by punters anxious to share the experience of such generosity.

'Pendlebury thought Billy owned a coffee shop. Billy would have needed to be the sole outlet for Brazil's entire coffee crop to bet the way he did.'

Asked why he had a reputation as a drug dealer, Bayeh stumbled for an answer.

'I just ... people are jealous,' he muttered.

Three taped telephone calls added to intriguing evidence about Bayeh. He says in Arabic to one caller: 'There is nothing good for cooking; it is only good for smoking or injections. If you bear with me for a few days I will get something for you.'

Bayeh conceded he was talking about cocaine but continued to deny he was a dealer. His stupidity and arrogance in believing he could live so lavishly without any visible legal means of support would be his undoing.

For all the amusement provided by squirming under questioning and offering bizarre explanations for his wealth, at times Bayeh showed himself as ruthless as any dealer on the streets.

He once told corrupt cop Trevor Haken he would kill anyone who got in his way or exposed his drug dealing. Then he would kill their families.

He used threats, renowned hard man Danny Karam and gun play to get rid of opposition dealers and would buy off police who posed interference.

To the end, though, Billy Bayeh remained mystifying. Despite having no defence against charges of bribing police and drug dealing earning him millions, Billy had trouble grasping the seriousness of the situation. Even when he was caught on a secret camera cutting up drugs with KX11, he thought it might all go away.

Billy said all he wanted to do was sell his Cosmopolitan coffee shop at Kings Cross and leave Sydney to begin a new life with his pregnant wife when the Commission ended.

Counsel assisting the Commission John Agius confronted him, asking: 'Has the reality of your situation dawned on you? When you woke up this morning and saw the sun did it also dawn on you that you would be in jail before this year is out.'

Puzzled, Bayeh replied: 'I don't see why.'

Perhaps it finally dawned when he was arrested outside the Commission rooms and subsequently jailed for twelve years.

– WITH RAY CHESTERTON

11

GET LOUIE

Hearing whispers on the street
that he shouldn't be buying
any green bananas, Louie
started asking well-informed
people's opinions about his life
expectancy. The answers
weren't reassuring.

LIKE his namesake Louie the Fly, Louie Bayeh was bad and mean and mighty unclean but at the end of the day, he was just a crook who got lucky ... for a while. For a long time, he was worried there was trouble ahead and he was right.

The notorious criminal and standover man had more minders than Madonna for his rare public appearances because of death threats he claimed corrupt New South Wales police officers had made against him. He said the threats had been confirmed by a senior policeman – and by the infamously psychotic and violent Lennie McPherson, Sydney's Mr Big.

Corrupt police wanted Louie dead because, like other allegedly tough guys on the streets – including his brother, the drug czar Billy Bayeh – he had cracked under pressure, telling an Independent Commission Against Corruption (ICAC) hearing in the early 1990s the names of officers he paid and how much he paid them.

Hearing whispers on the street that he shouldn't be buying any green bananas, Louie started asking well-informed people's opinions about his life expectancy. The answers weren't reassuring. McPherson, his former partner in crime, sent a chill down his spine by telling him he was the target of a proposed assassination attempt by a drug dealer named Tony Zizza.

McPherson said the deal bent police were offering was that in return for killing Bayeh they would drop drug charges against Zizza. It was a 'win-win' for everyone in the game – except for the now rather rattled Louie. The planned hit was confirmed by senior policeman Merv Schloeffel, who was then working in internal security. Zizza was again named as the likely assassin.

Bayeh contacted Zizza to get it from the horse's mouth. Zizza confirmed the deal. His reward for knocking Bayeh, he explained, would be to walk away from drug charges scot free. Bayeh didn't like the answer but couldn't fault the logic. He'd do exactly the same thing if the boot were on the other foot.

It was a stunning turnabout for Bayeh: to go from being predator to being the prey, a reversal of the role he had made for himself since arriving in Australia from Lebanon in 1953, aged fourteen. He'd been in trouble ever since as he worked his way up the criminal career ladder.

An ICAC report from the mid-1990s said Bayeh had been convicted of five offences, mostly involving violence, but had never been sent to jail. Probably the closest he came to imprisonment was being found guilty of malicious wounding in 1980. He was ordered to pay fines and compensation of $3000 and put on a good behaviour bond for four years.

In 1990 he was ordered to perform 300 hours of community service for discharging a firearm near a public place. They were minor offences compared to the criminal heights he would reach as he created an empire built on selling violence and brutality to protect drug dealers, sleaze merchants, brothels, strip joints and pornography outlets.

Louie was also treacherous, manipulative and self-serving. Attempted murder and using guns, violence and bashing to maintain control were routine for him.

Trevor Haken, the self-confessed corrupt detective, never denied his hunger for graft from any source but made an exception for Bayeh. Haken says he never took slings from Bayeh because he despised him, saying he acted like a cartoon replica of a tough guy. Whenever possible, notably at a well-regarded Kings Cross restaurant called Pinocchio's, Haken went out of his way to make Louie's life miserable.

Bayeh would park his Mercedes with its blacked-out windows in the no-standing zone in front of the restaurant to emphasise his importance and contempt for the law. This was too tempting for Haken.

'He acted like some Mafioso boss wanting everyone to see him so I'd wait until his food was served and then tell him to piss off out of there,' Haken says in his biography.

'He didn't like it. It was a like a contest of importance. He was showing everyone how important he was so I'd show him he wasn't. I couldn't do business with him. He was so heavily involved with others I thought he was dangerous and that proved to be the case.'

During the 1980s Louie Bayeh discovered the real relationship between criminals and coppers at the Cross. He claimed he was framed by then detective Nelson Chad on a stealing charge and had asked what could be 'done about it'. What would it cost to make it go away?

Chad asked for $200 a week and got it. Bayeh continued to pay Chad's replacement, John Brown – and paid more and more money to more and more police after that. When his business partner, Con Kontorinakis, complained that two police – Paul Brown and Ian Wally – had closed down the Love Machine drug outlet, Bayeh rang Chad.

A meeting was arranged in a restaurant and the two policemen said the place could re-open if weekly payments were made. 'It all started from there,' Bayeh said.

The cosy arrangements came drastically unstuck when Bayeh was charged with drug offences in 1990. After years of watching the law enforced only against other people, Louie suddenly found himself arrested on drug charges that he naturally claimed were false. For once he might have been telling the truth.

Given the extensive police contacts he had bought and paid for, Bayeh was furious that he had been loaded up without warning. He wanted answers. Every businessman wants a return on investment.

He claimed he'd paid a total of $12,000 to officers Ken McKnight (in two exchanges), $500 to Arnie Tees and another $500 to a third policeman to find out what was behind the frame-up. He never did find out – and retaliated by going to the ICAC in 1990 to complain about what had happened to him. After that, he claimed, he feared angry police would try to kill him in revenge.

At a meeting with Inspector Arnie Tees, Louie wore a wire to get evidence and told the ICAC that corrupt officers had offered him the names of the police responsible for the set-up – and the reason for it. This information would cost him $10,000.

He told the Commission the police who made the offer could be set up for a raid by anti-corruption forces at a lunch he would organise. Under surveillance, Bayeh was seen lunching with half a dozen men known to be police. He was also seen leaving the restaurant to withdraw $12,000 from a nearby bank and then returning to the restaurant. Then it all got murky, in typical Bayeh double-dealing style.

He claimed he passed the $10,000 to a policeman or police in the restaurant toilet. The surveillance crew outside said they saw nothing. An account of the stake-out was passed to the Department of Public Prosecutions, who ruled there was not enough evidence for criminal proceedings.

And the original charges against Bayeh that started the interest in corrupt police allegations? They were part heard at the time of Bayeh's $10,000 bribe revelation. And they were subsequently dismissed.

The ICAC, which had to explain its performance to a Parliamentary Joint Committee, refused to have any further dealings with Bayeh after he demanded, in addition to the usual protection arrangements, payment of three million dollars if he gave further evidence.

That was part of the intriguing backdrop to Bayeh's appearance before the Royal Commission in 1995. Although Bayeh claimed he no longer paid protection money, he said he still feared for his life because of his revelations about police corruption to the ICAC.

He also had grave concerns about the attitude and unpredictability of Lennie McPherson, whose reputation as a standover man, thief, armed gangster and robber, drug dealer and killer – and 'fixer' – was unmatched in the Australian underworld.

At one stage McPherson and Louie Bayeh were partners in selling their protection services to brothels, strip joints, massage parlours and night clubs, forming as intimidating an association as the Sydney underworld had ever known.

McPherson, who died in 1996 in jail, was a psychopath linked to at least half a dozen murders. His brutality and sadism were almost beyond belief.

Author Tony Reeves recounts in his biography of McPherson that he had been estranged from his mother for some years but decided to pay an unannounced visit on the day of her 70th birthday, carrying a white rabbit.

McPherson demanded to know why he had not been invited to the party the rest of the family had held for her earlier that day. When his mother admitted it was because of his criminal activities, McPherson ripped off the rabbit's head and threw its twitching body at her feet before storming off. In fact, at her foot – the mother-of-ten had had one leg amputated.

With a partner like McPherson it was no wonder Bayeh would tell the Royal Commission that he suffered from depression and chronic intestinal problems.

'I have been to see at least 50 doctors,' he said.

With two giant bodyguards flanking him and a third leading the way, Bayeh's protection detail looked like a scene from a B-grade Hollywood gangster movie as they walked through Sydney's business district toward the Royal Commission hearing. The only interest Bayeh and his minders generated – the media aside – was from impatient pedestrians on their way to work.

In the witness box, Louie did a Bradman. He became the first crim turned police informer ever to score a century of corrupt police on his pay roll. Having rolled over and agreed to the novel concept of telling the truth, Bayeh admitted publicly to bribing 'at least' 100 police over a couple of decades, paying hundreds of thousands of dollars to protect his brothels and strip clubs from raids.

As a kingpin of the slimy flesh peddling industry centred in Kings Cross and extending to Parramatta in the west, Louie was earning millions of dollars. With his younger brother Billy set up as the heroin and cocaine king of the same area, the Bayehs were pulling in money like Saudi Arabian oil princes.

At one stage Louie was asked to explain the origin of more than a million dollars that Royal Commission investigators found hidden in various bank accounts while claiming his taxable income was $347,000.

'I don't recall whether I put money in bank. I can't explain that. I don't know,' he stumbled, bunging on a thick accent.

Louie did admit to having a financial interest in the Love Machine club at Kings Cross and being paid $2500 a week from its profits and for looking after two other drug dealing nightclubs Stripperama and Porky's.

With his brother Billy living a millionaire-lifestyle from drug sales while offering a taxable income of only $35,000 a year, the money overflowed for everyone.

The obese Pandelis Karipis, alias 'Fat George', had a brothel called The Pink Flamingo. It and another business, called the Battlers Inn, were both drug-dealing outlets raking in the cash and providing a genuine insight into the riches available peddling heroin and cocaine to desperate people.

A former barrister down on his luck and in the grip of a self-inflicted nightmare ended up working for Fat George. He told the Royal Commission that on New Year's Eve 1993 around 150 hits of heroin were sold at $80 each and 300 deals of cocaine at $300 each – around $42,000 on the night. And that was just a couple of outlets.

Billy Bayeh told Haken on a secretly-recorded tape that feared muscle man Russell Townsend was making $100,000 a week selling drugs in Kings Cross, including 250 half caps of rock heroin a day at various venues. Townsend was said to be acting on behalf of McPherson, who was in jail.

It was massive money and dealers and sellers, especially in Chinatown, must have been delighted to buy drugs cheaply from bent police with limited foresight and imagination. A free feed, a few bottles of scotch or a few dollars was enough to turn most police into drooling poodles.

Selling their integrity was inexcusable but selling it so cheaply was just plain stupid. Police were too dense to see they were risking their entire careers and reputations for chicken feed while the criminals were making millions.

It was not without risks. Occupations like Louie's in areas like Kings Cross are always volatile. Challenges come from other ambitious employees and rival gangs. Only the police can be neutered by paying bribes. Other problem people were not so docile.

No one was better at buying his way out of trouble than Louie Bayeh. But he wasn't sure if the vendetta waged by police he had exposed to ICAC two years earlier had ended when he got his summons to appear before the Wood Royal Commission.

Bayeh, like his little brother Billy, had initially been sparing in his public statements about police corruption and the officers involved. Then they both rolled over. After giving his evidence privately, Louie worked feverishly with his legal advisers to stop it ever becoming public.

But Justice James Wood ruled that while Louie might have fears for his safety as a consequence, the tapes should be released as a way to keep the public informed about the Commission's progress and entice more people to come forward with evidence.

So into the witness box went Louie, saying in English so heavily accented that Merrylands (the Sydney suburb) was taken down as 'ambulance', that he could not understand why police were so keen to see him dead that they were prepared to use a hired killer. In this he was ignoring the incriminating evidence he'd given in private to ICAC investigators, naming dozens of police to whom he had paid bribes.

'Still up to today I got no idea why New South Wales police they want me killed and I know I'll be killed anyhow,' he said haltingly. 'If what I said in public, if what I said in court now...if all these guys know I named these names ... if I go outside I don't believe I'll last a week.'

To make his point about the uncertainty of his life, Bayeh brought up the fate of former Melbourne hit man Christopher Dale Flannery, who had come to Sydney in the 1980s and launched a murderous wave of terror and panic among the criminal set before disappearing in circumstances suggesting he'd been murdered by corrupt police.

'I believe what is going to happen to Chris is going to happen to me,' he said. It was garbled but everyone knew what he meant. 'One day the police will pick me up, I will never come back, same thing happened, you know nobody will find my body – same as what happened to Chris.'

Asked how many police he'd paid off over the years, he played a numbers game with the Commission.

'Was the number twenty?' asked the Commission counsel.

'More,' Louie said.

'How many more?'

'Up to 100.'

His business principle 'number one' was to pay police 'money to stay away from my places,' he said. He could even rattle off the names and positions of officers he paid, including squad commanders.

'I was paying $300 to the consorting squad, $300 to the armed hold-up, $300 to Kings Cross station,' he said. Sometimes there would be $400 for 'police bosses' as well.

Louie at least seemed convinced that Flannery was shot dead on 9 May 1985. All anyone else unconnected to Flannery's disappearance knows is that the hit man went to his car in the garage of his apartment block, the Connaught, near CIB headquarters in Sydney and found it would not start.

It is said that when Flannery went outside to hail a cab to take him to George Freeman's house, two policemen he knew stopped and offered him a lift. He was never seen again.

One rumour is that two more policemen got in – one on either side of Flannery – when the car stopped at traffic lights. Before he could react, and with his arms pinned to his side by the bulky police on either side, an officer in the front seat turned and shot him, the story goes. Flannery's body has never been found and no one has ever been charged.

In 1997 New South Wales coroner Greg Glass gave a finding that Flannery was murdered, probably on 9 May 1985. Glass also found that the secret to what happened rests with disgraced former detective Roger Rogerson.

Rogerson denies any knowledge but conceded on the *Sunday* television program that: 'Flannery was a complete pest. The guys up here in Sydney tried to settle him down.

They tried to look after him as best they could, but he was, I believe, out of control.

'Maybe it was the Melbourne instinct coming out of him. He didn't want to do what he was told, he was out of control. Having overstepped the line, well I suppose they said he had to go. But I can assure you I had nothing to do with it.'

Rogerson offered one other insight on Flannery on a newspaper blog when he questioned the hit man's supposed prowess with a pistol.

'Neddy Smith (a notorious gangster doing life for murder) called Flannery Mr Rent-A-Kill. He was laughing at him because he was such a crook shot.'

Wayward shooting certainly featured in one of Flannery's earlier hits in Melbourne. He missed his target at his first attempt, with a non-lethal head shot. In a frenzy, he then emptied his gun into the head and back of the escaping man.

Death interfered with Flannery's ambitions to be a heavyweight figure in the Sydney underworld as rival forces lined up violently against each other in the 1980s to decide who would control the lucrative crime scene.

On one side was Tom Domican, who arrived in Sydney from the United Kingdom where he had served time in jail on two occasions for ten months and then eighteen months for offences ranging from theft of motor cars, burglaries, break and enters, driving without a licence, having an unlicensed pistol and being in breach of a probation order. He also did time for theft of a motor vehicle.

In Australia he was convicted of minor breaches before

being jailed for fourteen years for crimes of violence. The conviction was overturned on appeal.

Then chief superintendent Ken Moroney told the ICAC that Domican had been of considerable interest to police in relation to serious matters for a number of years.

'It is my understanding, and I'm sure the understanding of my senior colleagues, that his associations extended to and within the criminal underworld, particularly within the Sydney metropolitan area.' Moroney said.

The drug dealing, intimidation and general race to get the next dollar eventually became so intense at the Cross that egos and ambitions of various people collided and things became threatening.

It started with the emergence of a new drug dealer on the scene, Robert Daher, who rose suddenly from being a doorman at the Love Machine nightclub to running the Pink Panther and its drug distribution network with a few known Kings Cross faces.

Haken says he was approached by another officer, Malcolm Bigg, with an offer to share $300 a week from Daher as protection money for his new operation. Already being paid by Billy Bayeh to overlook his drug-selling operations, Haken accepted the new deal after assurances the two deals were mutually exclusive.

Assurances are a fragile currency at the Cross. Daher's people took over the Budget Inn above the Pink Panther nightclub and started their racket. The supposedly harmonious blending of two drug selling outlets did not last long.

Despite Daher's agreement with corrupt Kings Cross police, his premises were raided by officers from a drug unit outside the Kings Cross region – a drug unit that alleg-edly had a close relationship with Billie Bayeh.

The payback came when Daher had a man plant drugs in Bayeh's nightclub, Lasers, on a night when co-inciden-tally Haken and Bigg were both off duty. With the drugs planted, Daher arranged a phone call to Kings Cross sta-tion with a tip about where the stash could be found. With Haken and Bigg not around to run interference and no chance of diverting the hastily-arranged raid, the drugs were discovered.

Reactions were predictable. Louie Bayeh, as the prin-cipal standover man in the Cross, was responsible for the protection of his little brother Billy's nightclubs and drug centres and was incensed by Daher's audacity. So he gave Daher the mother of all hidings outside the Majestic Coffee Lounge to publicly avenge the loss of face the drug raid had caused him. Commission witness KX11, who went on to serve a jail sentence on a drug charge, would give evidence that Louie pulled a gun at one stage.

The fracas resulted from increasing tension as weekly turnover from Daher's drug-selling outlet at the Budget Hotel grew to $40,000, rivalling the figures Billy Bayeh was generating at his nearby outlet.

KX11 said that before the shooting Billy Bayeh's guard dog Sam Ibrahim had warned him that the Budget Hotel turnover was getting too big. 'He said Billy's getting a bit upset,' KX11 testified.

'I was up at the Pink Pussy Cat (another drug selling nightclub which KX11 also ran) and he (Ibrahim) said: "You and your boys fuck off from the Cross. You're not wanted here no more."

'I said: "I'm not going anywhere."'

'Then all of the people started crowding around us and Assif Dib started swearing at Louie and Louie pulled a gun out on him. Assif took off through the back door.'

Gunplay in the Cross raised the stakes dramatically. The same day, Louie's home in peaceful Ermington in western Sydney was sprayed with bullets in a drive-by shooting. Louie's wife and children were in the house at the time. Bullets tore through the walls and windows but no one was hurt.

The attack was poorly received by police and other gangsters as it broke the previously observed tradition of families being sacrosanct no matter how fierce battles between criminals became. Strangely, Bayeh went public with the dispute, claiming police had done the shooting. But the police already had their suspects and the Royal Commission was told the men responsible were Daher's men, Norman Korbage and Assif Dib.

Peace talks were arranged as both sides started to worry about what might happen next. Dib and Korbage, who is now dead, refused a suggestion to meet with Louie Bayeh at his house for fear they would be shot dead by either henchmen or by police, who had the house under surveillance. Daher finally approached Haken and Bigg, offering $5000 to have his men Korbage and Dib arrested to ensure they stayed alive and were not loaded up with false evidence.

The two officers carried out their part of the bargain, arresting the two shooters at Bankstown Police station to avoid any prying police inquiries. Haken and Bigg then set about the next stage of the job with gusto. Pockets full of bribe money, they concocted a far-fetched story to explain how Dib and Korbage could be on the scene of the shooting but not be involved.

The manufactured story was that a third person was with them in the car when the bullets started flying. The mystery 'third man' had fired the gun, of course. And even though the shooter had been sitting with them at the time, neither Dib nor Korbage could recall his name or identify him. They got off.

Haken told KX11 that 'all your dreams have come true – the boys are going to be no-billed.' A no-bill is an instruction not to continue a case because there is insufficient evidence to proceed to trial.

The *Daily Telegraph* said KX11 expressed the general sense of gratitude that the problems had been bribed out of existence by taking a key detective to a Sydney massage parlour for an all expenses-paid night.

The epilogue to the saga came when the Royal Commission was told Korbage had called Bayeh and begged forgiveness for shooting up his home and endangering his wife and children. Bayeh accepted the apology – provided Daher also coughed up $50,000 in cash to underline his contrition. Proof of the power Kings Cross police could exert without consulting higher authorities or worrying about legalities, Haken sent word to Daher to get out of the Cross and not come back. He went, and a fragile peace was re-established.

Drug dealers and criminals generally thought they were paying for police protection. Corrupt police said that wasn't correct, but they were splitting hairs. The criminals were actually paying to be left alone while police concentrated on prosecuting other criminals who did not pay. That way arrest figures stayed healthy, senior command had no reason to complain and money continued to flow into the pockets of corrupt police.

The shooting up of his home and the lingering threat from corrupt police whose careers he had ruined would not be the first time Louie's life was endangered by would-be assassins. First, though, there were gang wars in which police and criminals did not know who to trust or how to stop the carnage. For Louie it was a rare chance to play a role as peacemaker.

Meanwhile, business continued as usual at the Cross. Louie acted as a bagman for payments between a Chinese brothel owner and corrupt police – a senior sergeant called Kim Thompson and a sergeant, Neville Scullion. Both later admitted taking bribes and were sacked from the force.

Thompson and Scullion had approached Bayeh saying they wanted $20,000 to quash a murder charge against a man named Steve Sui or 'Karate Steve' after a man named Kato Mo had been killed in a fight between Chinese gangs outside Sui's brothel in Kellett Street.

After interviewing Sui several times, Scullion and Thompson allegedly told Bayeh: 'We have enough evidence to charge Steve with murder but if he gives us $20,000 he will not be charged.'

At first, Sui refused to pay the money but changed his mind when Bayeh emphasised the seriousness of the situation. Bayeh then told the detective that Sui would pay but in instalments because he was broke. Sui made a down payment of $5000 which, Bayeh says, he passed on to the two policemen. He also passed on another $5000 but Sui refused to pay any more, saying he had no money.

When the police persisted, Bayeh says he walked away. 'I said: "You've got his address and phone number. You see him yourself. I don't want to get involved any more".'

Intriguingly, Bayeh played his unlikely role as a peacemaker in a notionally unlikely venue: Sydney police headquarters. There, the leaders of the warring factions, hard man Tom Domican and the equally aggressive Lennie McPherson, met for an uneasy conference.

It was a desperate and hasty strategy to calm an explosive situation that had the potential for bloodshed and bodies in the streets.

Battle lines were drawn over the ownership and distribution of illegal poker machines after McPherson thought he had been dudded by gaming club boss Fayez (Frank) Hakim, who had come a long way in Australia after migrating in 1952. Starting as the owner of a delicatessen in Cleveland Street, Redfern, and supplying rissoles to the canteen of the old New South Wales Police Academy nearby, gave Hakim a chance to make friends with police of all ranks. He also befriended illegal gambling identities like Graham 'Croc' Palmer and Louie Bayeh.

Respected investigative journalist Bob Bottom wrote in 1991 that Hakim had been recorded telling Lennie McPherson: 'You are a flag and should be obeyed and should be respected.' *Sydney Morning Herald* crime reporter Malcolm Brown wrote that Hakim became an unofficial 'godfather' in the Lebanese community until the twists and turns in his personal dealings caught up with him. Hakim was a Mr

Fixit who moved in a shadowy world between crooks, police and politicians, he wrote.

'Hakim's office was raided in 1985 and he was found to be in possession of 11.1 grams of heroin and with money suspected of being illegally obtained. He was fined $1000. That year Hakim became involved with a solicitor, Howard Hilton, and two other people over a conspiracy to bribe the New South Wales Minister for Corrective Services, Rex Jackson, over the early-release scheme. His job was to procure prisoners who were willing to pay for getting out of jail early.

'For that, Hilton, Jackson and Hakim all received jail sentences. A trembling Hakim was given a six-year sentence. He was released from jail in 1989 but his career was in tatters.' He died in 2005.

But that was later. In late 1984 Hakim was alive and kicking goals. He created a deep division in criminal ranks by allowing Domican and Bill El Azzi to set up illegal poker machines in a Marrickville club.

McPherson was enraged by the decision and arranged a meeting with Domican at the club to vent his displeasure. Domican didn't turn up, which inflamed McPherson's explosive rage.

Bayeh said McPherson then rang Domican to say: 'If you don't come back here, I'm going to come to your place and fuck you, fuck your wife up, blow all of you away.'

Bayeh added that McPherson then sent Snowy Rayner to pump bullets into Domican's house. Although no one was hurt, it was an insult that could not be overlooked.

On 27 January 1985, Domican sent a gunman to shoot

up Christopher Dale Flannery's house, mistakenly blaming him for the McPherson-ordered shooting. Flannery, psychotic with a need for revenge, went looking for a gun to shoot Domican. He found one and claimed to have shot at Domican outside Kingsgrove Police Station on 12 April 1985 – but missed, adding to the theory that for a gunman he was a lousy shot.

A poor workman blames his tools, which was a fatal mistake on Flannery's part. He blamed the gun and was on his way to Freeman's house to get a machine gun to have another go when he reportedly took his fateful lift in a police car and disappeared.

Significantly, Domican was pondering the fact he had been at Kingsgrove police station following a request from Arnie Tees to come in and make a statement. Meanwhile, rumours flew like bullets. Sydney's underworld figures trod nervously and looked over their shoulders, fearful of being a target or becoming collateral damage. It was no time to be making new enemies.

Bayeh said he was told by Detective Keith Conwell to stay away from Lennie McPherson. 'Tom Domican's going to shoot Lennie McPherson,' Conwell allegedly said.

This was the background of the secret peace meeting convened by police, Bayeh claims, on the top floor of their building in College Street. Bayeh says he wanted the meeting to go ahead and that Inspector David Leach arranged it.

Watching each other as carefully as a mongoose and a cobra would, McPherson and Domican sat and talked in a glass office for more than an hour with Bayeh, Leach and

Conwell watching anxiously, out of earshot.

McPherson seemed to be optimistic about peace being restored but it was a fantasy. Bayeh admitted making his home available to McPherson for a meeting with disgraced detective Roger Rogerson, Arnie Tees and another detective to work out how to kill Domican.

'They talk about shooting Chris Flannery's house and all of that,' Bayeh told the Commission. 'And Lennie McPherson says tell Arnie Tees if he shoots Tom (Domican) he'll give him $200,000.'

McPherson indicated at the meeting that George Freeman, Frank Yates, Les Jones, Greg Melides and 'Croc' Palmer had all thrown money into the pot to raise $200,000 for the hit. A similar offer was made at the meeting to the other detective, whose name was never divulged.

Bayeh said he also hosted another meeting at his home attended by McPherson, Flannery and Neddy Smith. A month later, Flannery was dead. In 1987, another raging hot head, Barry McCann, was shot dead in Marrickville.

In a sub-plot to the original dispute over illegal poker machines, McCann and Neddy Smith also fell out with fatal consequences in the mid-1980s.

Sydney Morning Herald journalist Steve Gibbs wrote that the bad blood between the two men came to a head the night Smith knocked out McCann's eldest son in the family hotel, The Landsdowne, on Broadway.

'Once outside, Smith's companion lined up five or six of McCann's bouncers at gunpoint against a wall, while Smith took a baseball bat from his car and flogged each one till he fell,' Gibbs wrote.

'A fortnight later, Smith was leaving the Quarryman's Hotel at Pyrmont when one of three men in a parked car opened up on him, Jimmy Traynor and Tex Moran. Traynor was seriously wounded by two blasts.'

Smith's associate in carnage, 'Abo' Henry, joined in by shooting McCann gang member Terry Ball in the head. Ball survived and in April 1986 ran down Smith outside the Iron Duke Hotel.

Smith and Henry survived the 1980s but did jail time, a drunken Henry for stabbing police prosecutor Mal Spence, a berserk Smith for stabbing tow-truck driver Ron Flavell to death in a fit of stupid road rage.

Earlier, drug dealer Tony Eustace had been shot dead in a killing Flannery claimed he did, an event described in detail in *Underbelly: A Tale of Two Cities*.

To add to the simmering drama at the Royal Commission over Bayeh's explosive evidence, who should turn up but McPherson? He was driven in from Cessnock Jail where he was serving time for assault, to deny everything during one of the most bizarre appearances ever recorded in an Australian court.

In an outburst in which he painted himself as a character with the qualities of Mother Teresa, McPherson unblushingly claimed he had never collected money from illegal gambling clubs or from Louie Bayeh.

He also denied ever having paid police for anything and certainly had never arranged with police to murder Tom Domican for $200,000. 'Never once have I got a dollar off a single person in my life and here I am a standover man?' McPherson roared. 'Who am I standing over?'

Bayeh's links to drug controversy and violence continued well after the Royal Commission. On 12 July 2000, Bayeh was half-way through a meal at the El Bardowny restaurant in Narwee in outer Sydney with a trusted underling named Sam. He was somehow lured outside about 2am – two hours after arriving.

Witnesses said when Bayeh left the restaurant, Sam was already engaged in pushing and shoving with some Lebanese men who leapt out of a black BMW. Bayeh joined in the scramble when one of the participants shouted at him: 'You're not working my ...'. That was when Bayeh's legs were shot from under him.

At least seven bullets were fired from as many as three guns during the shooting. No one was killed but a teenage youth taking a cigarette break from a mate's birthday party inside the restaurant was wounded.

Bayeh obeyed the code of the west and refused to comment on the incident when interrogated by police. So did Sam, who claimed he was around the corner having a smoke and had missed the fire fight.

A bloodied 9mm automatic handgun along with 50 bullets and three magazines was found by detectives near a garbage bin. Four bullets had been fired from the gun with another in the chamber ready to go. The pistol belonged to Bayeh.

Bayeh was struck in the groin and the legs by slugs from high-powered handguns. Detectives called the attack a 'deliberate hit'. The gunman and his colleagues raced away from the scene in the BMW.

'Obviously this was not over something minor,' said Crime Agency Detective Superintendent Bob Inkster.

A month later, widespread and co-ordinated police raids to execute search warrants led to seven arrests, including one of three men wanted over the Bayeh attack.

Police also found heroin, other drugs, weapons and more than a million dollars in cash during the raids. Police said one of the men arrested had recently lost several hundred thousand dollars at Melbourne's Crown Casino. He was initially identified as the principal in a heavy cocaine and heroin syndicate in Sydney, operating out of a Kings Cross hotel.

Security guard Helal Safi, 25, doorman Noureddine 'Tiger' Laa Laa, 32, and Elie Geadah were charged with shooting Bayeh with intent to cause grievous bodily harm. But there was a twist. Bayeh, too, was charged with discharging a firearm with intent to inflict grievous bodily harm. He was released on bail. There wasn't much risk he would abscond, as he was stuck in a wheelchair.

But he recovered well enough to go back to his old ways. In 1993 he pleaded guilty in the District Court to demanding money with menaces. Police say he collected as much as $180,000 in protection fees from Parramatta brothel keepers between 1988 and 1992. He was also given jail time in 1997 for perverting the course of justice.

At the time of writing he is still in prison, where his best friends are the flies.

– WITH RAY CHESTERTON

12

ROGER THE DODGER

If Roger Rogerson was directing
the traffic, I wouldn't leave
the kerb.
Sydney Queen's Counsel, 1986

THERE are a lot of stories about Roger Rogerson, some of them true. Depending on who's telling the tale, he is (or was) good or evil, charming or chilling, ace detective or baddest apple in the barrel.

The prosecution says he gunned down a robber as cold-bloodedly as he once allegedly connived to get a fellow policeman shot. But the defence has witnesses that Rogerson once rescued several children from drowning – as fearlessly as the night he disarmed a vicious killer, winning another bravery award to add to his collection.

He was also chivalrous – maybe even sexy. There is the Shirley Bassey story, which goes like this: as a young detective, Rogerson was walking in downtown Sydney when a man carrying a woman's handbag ran past. Quick on the uptake and on his feet, Rogerson chased and caught the thief and took the handbag from him. When he opened it, he realised it belonged to Bassey, who was appearing at a nearby theatre at the time.

After booking the thief, Rogerson took the handbag to the theatre and was shown to the singer's dressing room. In the ensuing conversation he mentioned he was half Welsh himself – related, in fact, to the famous privateer Sir Henry Morgan, the pirate who became Governor of Jamaica. The grateful Bassey took him for a drink – and the rest, as they say, is history. What happens in the dressing room stays in the dressing room. Suffice to say that whenever she came to Sydney after that, the sultry songstress caught up with her favourite Aussie cop.

Rogerson is not only descended from the pirate Morgan but from an English family involved in establishing the Salvation Army, so he has links with both piracy and the pulpit – the good and bad angels of his nature.

A story he tells reveals the ambiguous moral code of a man who had the nerve to play both good cop and bad cop until the rules changed and he was left out of the game. Not that he would admit to any of that: he pleads good cop to every charge.

It happened in 1994, when he was half way through his three-year jail sentence for perverting the course of justice. One day, two neatly-dressed strangers turned up to see him at Berrima prison ('a dogs' jail' as Rogerson calls it in prison slang, 'full of paedophiles and ex-police').

Sombre and earnest in their dark suits and ties, the visitors looked a little like Mormons, he recalls mischievously.

They reminded him of Senator Bob Brown, whose father had been a tough old sergeant with Rogerson in happier days. They were on a mission, but it wasn't from God or the Greens; they were from the Wood Royal Commission into the New South Wales police force.

After introductions, they outlined the deal: if Rogerson would testify about the 'police culture' of the previous 30 years, he could walk free the same day on a special licence. Helpfully, they just happened to have the form ready for him to fill in.

Rogerson asked exactly what they expected for the get-out-of-jail card. They said they wanted him to tell the commission all about a group of 'old school' senior police. They listed several names well-known to him, including one man he regarded as a mentor.

'They told me I was a conduit between what they called old "corrupt detective sergeants" and younger officers,' snorts Rogerson, ridiculing the prim legalese of the men in suits.

'The blokes they wanted me to tip a bucket of shit on, they were great Australians,' he says indignantly. 'One fought on the Kokoda trail; another was a tail gunner in the war, for God's sake. But that didn't matter. If I was willing to bag them, all I had to do was sign up and I'd be straight out.'

One of the men slid the form across the table. Rogerson calmly picked it up, tore it into pieces and dropped them in the bin. It was his way of saying the interview was over. He went back to his cell to face another eighteen months behind bars.

Meanwhile, the men from the Royal Commission faced the trip back to Sydney with the interesting news that the most infamous bent cop in Australia couldn't be bought.

For Rogerson, that's where the story ends. But it poses questions: did his defiance that day show fierce loyalty, high principles and absence of guilt? Or was it a calculated ploy because he knew he stood a better chance of living a long and relatively peaceful life if he quietly did his time and didn't 'roll over' on his old crew, some of them hard men with too much to lose. Maybe it was a bit of both.

When Rogerson reads this he will no doubt swear. 'I had nothing to roll over about!' he has told the authors several times. That's his story and he's sticking to it. No-one does it better.

You have to watch Rogerson ... if I was to ask him: 'Why did you handcuff my client?' he would answer 'Well, sir, I knew he was wanted interstate on three armed hold-ups and I was concerned for the public's safety'. The judge would direct the jury to ignore the remark, but the damage would be done.
– Sydney barrister, 1986

BEFORE Roger Rogerson went to jail again in early 2005 – after pleading guilty to lying to the Police Integrity Commission to protect a friend – he appeared to be in a bad way. So bad that two days before he was due to face the New South Wales District Court in December, his solicitor took him to his psychiatrist, one Thomas Clark, who said later he was shocked by the rapid change in the patient.

A few months before, Dr Clark had assessed Rogerson as 'stoic' and with 'a new resolve to shape his life' – but now the former policeman seemed incoherent, depressed, and even suicidal. He could not instruct his solicitor sensibly because he could not follow logic. He showed signs of paranoia, possibly even 'creeping dementia', according to the good doctor.

'He has been neglecting himself. He's usually such a dapper sort of person. He was actually in tears. He broke out quite inappropriately,' Dr Clark told the court. The breakdown was such that Rogerson had been admitted voluntarily to a psychiatric hospital for ten days, which had prevented him from attending court.

Unmoved by expert evidence, the Crown prosecutor asked: 'Could this all be an act by him, a ploy, to avoid being sentenced?'

'It could be,' the 'shrink' admitted – an answer that must have deepened Rogerson's depression symptoms immediately.

At least his solicitor, Paul Kenny, stayed on message. When Rogerson came out of hospital some weeks later to be sentenced to a minimum of one year's jail, Kenny sadly told reporters: 'Roger used to be a tough guy – these days he's just a broken-down old man ... a hard man completely broken by the system.'

Rogerson's physical courage, like his intelligence, has never been in doubt, even among his detractors. He must also be a fine actor. For, only weeks before his harrowing court hearing, he had put on a convincingly brave front to speak at the 50th birthday of retired standover man Mark 'Chopper' Read in Melbourne. Ignoring his own troubles, he spoke warmly and well to what he calls 'a small but eclectic' group of well-wishers gathered at a pub in inner-suburban Collingwood.

He told funny stories, joked and had a few drinks with people he once would have taken pleasure in locking up. Had there been a piano in the place he might have knocked out a few tunes the way he used to at police functions. But, apparently, this was all a false front. Because when he returned to Sydney to face his demons, his cheery façade allegedly crumbled.

But it's amazing what a little quiet reflection in jail can do. Three months later, locked in Kirkconnell Correctional Centre in rural New South Wales, Rogerson pulled back from the brink of what his defence counsel had painted as imminent mental collapse.

During his first jail sentence, at Berrima Prison in the early 1990s, he had made clocks and dining tables to sell to an eager outside market. This time he concentrated more on matters of the mind during what he now chirpily calls 'my 12-month sabbatical.'

As well as reading a bible sent by an anonymous well wisher – not his clergyman son-in-law, he says – he took on sudoku puzzles. He soon became the jail champion, a remarkable achievement for a 64-year-old man so recently threatened by mental decay. He even noted solutions in an exercise book so he could memorise winning patterns.

By the time he was paroled in February, Rogerson had recovered so well he seemed almost as sharp as a psychiatrist, barrister or journalist – probably sharper than some. In fact, when the authors of this book called him he recalled precise details of a conversation we'd had two years earlier. It is amazing what twelve months of rehabilitation can do for a prisoner willing to put in the effort.

Either that or the prosecutor was right all along, and his 'breakdown' wasn't an excusable lapse but a lapsed excuse.

Before Avery, they used to make heroes of people like Rogerson ... His greatest mistake was being born 20 years too late.
– Andrew Keenan, journalist,1986

ROGERSON was a good shot – a bit too quick on the draw, some say – but drawing a bead on the man himself is not easy. He seems open and disarmingly friendly, with the knockabout Paul Hogan charm that served him so well as a policeman, partly because it contrasted with the 'beige in colour, decamping in a northerly direction' style so many of his colleagues put on with the uniform. Mostly, it's a routine.

But, like Hogan the bridge rigger, Rogerson the colourful cop was smarter than he let on. At work he mastered guns, handcuffs, cars, typewriters, cameras and all the other tools of trade. After hours, he was a handy engineer and builder – his boilermaker father and others had taught him to weld and to make things.

But go into his home and the most striking thing you notice is the number of books there. Hundreds of them line the shelves – and many are biographies, memoirs and histories. This, in a way, is the most surprising thing about him – that he is an intelligent, self-taught man who has acted a part most of his adult life.

There are other surprises. Where a stranger might expect Rogerson to be careful about security, he is nonchalant about it. He and his (second wife) Anne have dogs – but they are little friendly terriers, not savage guard dogs. One of the worst things about being jailed in 2005, he says in a revealing moment, was that one of the little dogs, Mitzi, died of a tumour while he was away. Anne was distraught and he was powerless to help or comfort her. That's when a note of bitterness creeps into his voice. It is never far away.

The trouble with being Roger Rogerson, he concedes, is that the man gets buried under the myth – beneath the stories, the jokes, the lies, the exaggerations, the colour and entertainment of it all.

He blames *Blue Murder* for this. People think they know all about him because they have seen the compelling 1995 television series based on events in the early 1980s Sydney underworld. A 'docudrama' that became cult viewing, it blends the marketing appeal of perceived fact with the narrative drive of fiction. Young people who were barely born when Rogerson was a policeman take 'Blue Murder' tours of the real-life pubs, restaurants and streets where the series was shot.

Rogerson thinks *Blue Murder* was brilliant entertainment. But he also thinks it was murder on any chance he had of salvaging his tattered reputation. He argues that to see it as a balanced study of police corruption in Sydney is like mistaking *Saving Private Ryan* for a history of World War 2, or Heath Ledger for the real Ned Kelly. Compression, dramatisation and the legal necessity to fictionalise, exaggerate or delete characters and events inevitably skews the story – in ways not always obvious to the audience.

The fact that the series was suppressed in New South Wales for several years because of ongoing trials gave it the cachet of being 'banned' – and a quasi-judicial credibility. If it might sway a jury in a real-life trial then it must be right, mustn't it?

Rogerson argues – unsurprisingly – that the charismatic but undeniably bent cop bearing his name in the series is nothing like him. 'For a start they had him smoking – I've never smoked in my life,' he fumes. And? 'They had him inviting Neddy Smith to barbecues at my house. I never let (Smith) near my house or told him where it was.'

Item by item, Rogerson picks holes in the treatment of 'his' character, using the lawyer's tactic of finding specific flaws in the opposing case to persuade a jury that the whole thing is suspect. He knows a thing or two about lawyers' tricks: unlike most police, he was never nervous of submitting himself to cross-examination in trials of those he had arrested, and was a dangerous witness that mostly acquitted himself well, boosting his status among other cops.

One of his pet stories underlines the dilemma of being portrayed as a handsome villain by a fine actor (Richard Roxburgh) who uncannily resembles Rogerson when he was younger.

'When *Blue Murder* came out I sat down to watch it with my wife Anne,' he says. 'After watching for a while she turned to me and said: "I didn't realise you were so good looking when you were young".'

It has become a stock joke, but he knows it is on him: behind the laughter is the fact the televised illusion will always outweigh what he says and does. He has been defamed and shamed and flattered at the same time and is powerless to stop it.

That *Blue Murder* is art rather than history gets lost in

the other media coverage of the last 25 years. What the film-makers did – for good legal and dramatic reasons – was put Rogerson (and his criminal associate and informer 'Neddy' Smith) front and centre of a sinister but generally plausible account of police corruption and criminal behaviour.

Potential defamation action (funded by the deep pockets of the police association) meant it would have been too risky for film-makers or reporters to highlight – or even question – the shadowy conduct of particular police who had not been successfully prosecuted, or at least named in Parliament. The few with convictions carry the can for the many to have avoided prosecution.

The result is that Rogerson is caught in a notoriety trap: people who have been convicted or jailed (or are dead) are repeatedly named and blamed in the media because they are safe targets. This emphasises their guilt – and, in the process, appears to diminish that of others.

Rogerson's name has become shorthand for 'bent cop', erasing the fact that many other police – and a few politicians – were just as guilty, but got away with it because they didn't risk 'sticking their head over the parapet', as one of Rogerson's former colleagues puts it.

The point is underlined by Darren Goodsir, the then investigative reporter whose book *Line of Fire* underpins much of *Blue Murder*, together with 'Neddy' Smith's memoirs. Goodsir is high on Rogerson's list of critics (and vice versa) but he says there were worse police than him – 'cops who did grubby deals with paedophiles and others who did hits.'

But you won't catch Rogerson complaining that he carries the can for the ones that got away. That would be an admission.

Unlike that other well-known Bankstown boy, Paul Keating, Rogerson still lives in the old neighbourhood and sticks to the street fighter code ...

If you get knocked down, get up. Keep punching. Don't dob anyone in. Keep smiling. Never admit pain, fear or guilt. Especially guilt.

Roger is a polite, courteous, gentlemanly old fellow these days ... but I'm never going fishing with him.
– Mark Brandon 'Chopper' Read

IT is close to quarter of a century since the then Detective Sergeant Rogerson was drummed out of what he routinely calls 'the best police force that money could buy' by a police tribunal he dismisses contemptuously as 'a kangaroo court'.

Being found guilty of internal discipline charges rubber stamped the end of a once-brilliant career that had already capsized nearly two years earlier. He was deeply disgraced well before he finally handed in his warrant card in late 1986.

Under the old New South Wales police regime that produced him, he might have stared down the allegations against him. But any chance he had of surviving the scandals that started to break in 1984 evaporated when John Avery become the state's new Police Commissioner that year.

Avery was a new broom set to sweep out what the media dubbed the force's 'black knights', and he tackled the job with missionary zeal. Rogerson was not the only name on Avery's hit list, but it was near the top. He was doomed when Avery took over.

Rogerson had been the New South Wales CIB's golden boy – a double-edged reputation. Among Sydney's colourful identities, he was an object of admiration, speculation and suspicion. His network included senior police and heavy criminals, groups that overlapped too brazenly, even by the standards of the day.

Headlining Rogerson's criminal contacts were 'Neddy' Smith, a violent armed robber and drug dealer, and Lennie McPherson, one of Australia's best-known organised crime figures. When the flamboyant Melbourne hit man Christopher Dale Flannery arrived in Sydney, Rogerson added him to his list of useful drinking buddies.

Rogerson argued that such strategic alliances kept his finger on the underworld's pulse. Another view is that it positioned him to direct the cross-traffic of bribes, inside information, and favours between key gangsters and the headquarters of a police force some rated among the most corrupt in the first world, just behind those of Hong Kong and New York. These two views of Rogerson's 'strategy' were not necessarily mutually exclusive: a shrewd operator might get both valuable information and bribes, often from the same sources.

In a sense, Rogerson and other 'black knights' were mercenaries – soldiers for hire. They worked 80 per cent for the community and 20 per cent for themselves. And for a long time they were good enough at their craft – and their graft – that 80 per cent efficiency was enough to keep the politicians and the people happy.

But as the nature of crime changed, the old checks and balances disappeared. While old-fashioned cops siphoned a 'tax' from ancient vices – prostitution, illegal gambling – things ran smoothly. Corruption, at a certain level, can be efficient.

No-one denies that Rogerson punched above his weight as a detective sergeant. Whatever his methods, he got results. He made many arrests, won more commendations for bravery and skill than his peers and, by the start of the 1980s, seemed set to crown a brilliant career by one day becoming a superintendent or even assistant commissioner. He certainly thought so, back when things were going well.

There was a precedent for this. In 1966 more than 800 well-wishers attended a farewell dinner for a legendary New South Wales detective, Ray 'Gunner' Kelly, at the Chevron Hotel.

It was an ecumenical gathering of criminals, racketeers, SP bookies, judges, politicians, doctors, publicans, horse trainers – and a handful of tame journalists who had puffed the Kelly legend. The then Premier, notorious 'rusty knight' Sir Robert Askin, addressed the crowd – calling Kelly his friend. Kelly, later awarded an MBE, had reputedly helped make Askin a wealthy man. The policeman and the premier retired with assets far outstripping their legitimate incomes. No-one thought to question it, at least publicly, until they died.

As young detectives, Rogerson and his mates worked with Kelly and other 'well-connected' police: Fred 'Froggy' Krahe, Don Fergusson, Bill Allen and more.

The story goes that Kelly would test young detectives by asking 'Would you load a criminal?'. If one answered 'Yes' he would be transferred into Kelly's squad, but if he said 'No' he would be sent elsewhere, out of harm's way, and often into a career dead-end.

It was a self-selecting process that meant entire CIB squads followed Kelly's methods of 'loading' people with incriminating evidence – usually weapons, but also drugs and any other evidence that might be useful in gaining a conviction against criminals who weren't 'on side' with the sharp operators in law enforcement.

Rogerson says 'friendly' magistrates trusted police and went along with the system because it kept criminals off the streets. Some, of course, might have been friendly for reasons other than preserving law and order. Such as the disgraced former chief magistrate Murray Farquhar, exposed after years of systematic corruption that involved not just police but politicians, lawyers and, possibly, even judges. From avoiding parking tickets and speeding fines right up to serious perversions of justice, they all thought they were above the law.

But times changed and those who did not change risked being exposed. By late 1984 Rogerson was in disgrace and was ordered back into uniform for the first time in 22 years. Instead, he took extended leave. By then he faced accusations that will dog him all his life – the worst being the shocking allegation he had conspired to have an undercover detective, Michael Drury, shot to help a drug pusher facing court.

He would eventually be acquitted of this (and of attempting to bribe Drury) but as long as the Drury shooting remains officially unsolved, it hangs over Rogerson.

It was an horrific crime against an apparently honest policeman for doing his duty. Drury was shot twice through the kitchen window of his home, standing near his young daughter. The .38 calibre hollow-point bullets inflicted massive internal wounds.

Drury survived but thought he wouldn't, making a 'dying deposition' in which he accused Rogerson of attempting to bribe him to 'run dead' in a big heroin-trafficking case against a then flourishing Melbourne drug dealer, Alan Williams.

Some thought he was delirious or affected by medication but Drury stuck to his guns despite pressure from at least one senior investigating policeman, the late Angus McDonald, who apparently could not or would not believe the monstrous allegation against one of their own.

But 'Roger' the golden boy was already a little tarnished. He had been under attack by sections of the media – notably well-known investigative reporter Wendy Bacon – and the family and friends of Warren Lanfranchi, a criminal Rogerson had shot dead in intriguing circumstances in 1981.

It is undisputed that Rogerson shot Lanfanchi twice, and that the shots were paced several seconds apart, for reasons that have never been fully determined to everyone's satisfaction. The shooting was ostensibly while police were trying to arrest Lanfranchi at a meeting set up by Rogerson's underworld contact 'Neddy' Smith.

Lanfranchi's family and his girlfriend, an articulate, attractive and media-savvy prostitute called Sallie-Anne Huckstepp, went public – accusing Rogerson of killing

Lanfranchi because he had robbed a heroin dealer friendly with bent police.

Huckstepp, too, would be killed – she was strangled and found floating in a pond in Centennial Park in early 1986. 'Neddy' Smith, who had set up the fatal meeting with Lanfranchi, was charged with her murder years later after boasting about it to a fellow prisoner.

Rogerson is not shy about the Lanfranchi shooting. He robustly defends it as a 'clean kill' of a violent gunman, sex offender and drug dealer wanted for several armed robberies – and attempting to shoot a traffic policeman. He says Lanfranchi was also the prime suspect for a murder in Wollongong: his fingerprints had been found on a baseball bat found near the body of a man who had been bashed to death.

None of this, of course, answers some lingering questions. Did Lanfranchi (as his girlfriend Huckstepp swore) have a $10,000 bribe on him ready to hand over? The police said he did not. Did Lanfranchi produce a handgun? The police said he did, and claimed that was why Rogerson was forced to shoot him – twice.

A coroner's jury subsequently found that Rogerson had killed Lanfranchi while trying 'to effect an arrest' but declined to find it was in self-defence or in execution of his duty. It was an interesting and perhaps even understandable each-way bet by the jury, though not altogether logical. This can happen with juries which are not convinced of someone's guilt or innocence and invent a middle path regardless of the evidence. It was the jury's way of showing it would not swallow the police version of events.

Despite longstanding media and public disquiet over

the Lanfranchi shooting, fuelled by the dead man's family and by Sallie-Anne Huckstepp's subsequent death, few police rank it as the blackest mark against Rogerson – mainly because Lanfranchi was considered a dangerous criminal who'd attempted to shoot a traffic policeman, an act considered suicidal by many. With good reason, judging from Lanfranchi's fate.

One respected Victorian detective who worked in Sydney in the 1980s, and who has no connection with Rogerson or his supporters, says the consensus is 'Lanfranchi had it coming – he goes in the stiff shit file.'

But the Drury case is different – although, astonishingly enough, it was not seen that way at first by some police. When Rogerson was initially acquitted, in separate trials, of attempting to bribe Drury, then of conspiring to kill him, other police congratulated him. Rogerson got a standing ovation at a CIB dinner after the acquittal, a show of unity and defiance by 'the brotherhood' that must have been disturbing for Drury and his family.

But when Rogerson was subsequently charged over holding $110,000 cash in bank accounts under false names, support for him withered – even among so-called 'Black Knights' in the force. When newspapers ran bank security photographs of an edgy Rogerson waiting to get the secret money, his former supporters knew he had lost the public relations war against Avery's 'God Squad.' The long-running 'joke' was finished, at least for the time being.

Rogerson's convoluted explanation of the cash's origins strained credibility – and would, in fact, eventually land him in jail for conspiring to pervert the course of justice. It seemed to some police who had supported him that while they were passing around the hat to bankroll his defence, he had been stashing cash that publicly implicated him in sinister deals, almost certainly with drug dealers and gangsters – but possibly with would-be cop killers. It looked bad for everyone. For self-preservation, if not moral pangs about Drury being shot, many distanced themselves.

All of which might explain why Rogerson is now far more quiet about the Drury shooting than about the Lanfranchi case. In the 1980s he claimed in court he had never met a corrupt policeman 'except Michael Drury', but that bravado later gave way to caution.

Now he calmly repeats his version of events. That on his way home on the night Drury was shot, 6 June 1984, he dropped in at the Arncliffe Scots Club to meet the hit man Chris Flannery. Flannery, he says, had called him earlier in the day about a suspect car he had seen in his street. Flannery thought he was a target, too – correctly, as it turned out, given that he disappeared later.

Rogerson says he had drinks with Flannery and left around 6.30pm. But Flannery's wife, Kathleen, later stated that Rogerson was still at the Scots Club when she turned up about 7.15pm. The time gap is crucial. Then again, the notorious Kath Flannery was not necessarily a reliable witness and might have her own motives for making life hard for Rogerson.

It was suggested, later, that the meeting was all too convenient because it smacked of an attempt to provide alibis. In his book about the shooting, *Line of Fire*, Darren Goodsir theorises Flannery had time to shoot Drury at 6.10pm and then hurry to meet Rogerson to build an alibi. Rogerson says he was with Flannery at the time of the shooting.

Doomed beauty: model and dancer Revelle Balmain before she vanished. COURTESY BALMAIN FAMILY

Innocence: teenage Revelle with her father Ivor.

Happy family: Revelle with her mother Jan and sister Suellen.
COURTESY BALMAIN FAMILY

Missing, believed dead: the studio shot released by police a week after Revelle disappeared. COURTESY BALMAIN FAMILY

A creep – but is he a killer? Gavin Owen Samer pawned his girlfriend's clarinet to pay a pimp but insists he did not harm Revelle Balmain. COURTESY *THE DAILY TELEGRAPH*

Mr Big Mouth: Lennie McPherson in the frame, talking. BRENDAN
ESPOSITO: FAIRFAX

Mr Fixit and Mr Big: George Freeman and Lennie McPherson at
Paddles Anderson's funeral. JACKIE HAYNES: FAIRFAX

Crocodile smile: charming, cunning and treacherous, Freeman knew bent cops who reputedly gave Christopher Dale Flannery his last lift. DAVID TROOD: FAIRFAX

Locked and loaded: a pregnant Deb Locke set to tip a bucket on fellow cops. ANDREW TAYLOR: FAIRFAX

Violent night: Barry Michael paid twice for his title win over Lester
Ellis. Once in the ring, later in a nightclub brawl.
COURTESY BARRY MICHAEL

Alphonse Gangitano: his
goons held down Barry
Michael while he bit and
bashed him. SLY INK ARCHIVES

Blood brothers: the veteran Michael consoles his young opponent
Ellis after taking his world title. Ellis forgave him. Gangitano didn't.
COURTESY BARRY MICHAEL

Wrong way: 'Big Bill' Waterhouse with trouble-prone son Robbie
and loyal daughter Louise at the height of the Fine Cotton debacle.
ANDREW TAYLOR: FAIRFAX

Guilty and innocent: Hayden
Haitana the fast talker with
Fine Cotton the slow galloper.
Haitana went to jail, Cotton to
greener fields. CHANNEL 9

Man in the middle: trainer
George Brown before he went to
Sydney, where he was tortured
and killed when a ring-in went
wrong. COURTESY BROWN FAMILY

Bold personalities: Bill and Robbie Waterhouse and their bag man before the Fine Cotton disgrace. FAIRFAX

Roger Rogerson: cocky, courageous and corrupt. Dangerous with a gun and in the witness box. RUSSELL McPHEDRAN: FAIRFAX

Dead beautiful: Sallie-Anne Huckstepp went to the Cross just before she was drugged, choked and drowned.
FAIRFAX

Making a point: an unrepentant Rogerson answers his critics. Lucky he didn't have a gun. RICK STEVENS: FAIRFAX

Fred Cook: big scorer on and off the ground; looked after bent cops as if his life depended on it. It probably did. COURTESY FRED COOK

Christopher Dale Flannery: when a Sydney police hit squad came south to get him, they missed. But his luck didn't hold. SLY INK ARCHIVES

Mr Sin a.k.a. Abraham Gilbert Saffron: died after trying to sue
the authors. Was it natural causes ... or the long-term effects of
unnatural acts? SLY INK ARCHIVES

David McMillan: escaped from the 'Bangkok Hilton' with a brolly
and a balsawood pistol. COURTESY DAVID McMILLAN

The silver fox: legendary criminal lawyer Chris Murphy taking care of business. DEAN SEWELL: FAIRFAX

So if it wasn't Flannery, who did shoot Drury?

Asked this question, Rogerson pauses and says he heard it might have been another Melbourne gunman, Laurie Prendergast. Then he changes the subject.

He did not become a rogue cop. He was never tempted from the path mapped out for him by his mentors and superiors ... It was the path that moved.
– journalist Andrew Keenan, 1986

THE man behind the Rogerson myth is almost 70 now. He is a husband twice over, father of two, grandfather of seven, devoted oldest son (of three siblings) of a sweet old lady who went to church every Sunday on her electric scooter until she was in her 90s. He doesn't wear jewellery and is partial to singlets and cardigans. He polishes his (plain black) shoes with military attention to detail before going out, as most older policeman do. He wouldn't look out of place at a bowls club, an Anzac march or a Rotary meeting. You just know he cuts the lawn dead straight.

He is smaller than a lot of policemen of his era; age and injury have eroded the hard physical presence he once had, though not the infectiously cheerful manner. But he still has the sort of combative confidence shared by top sportsmen and others used to imposing their will on others, which reminds you of what he must have been like as a younger man with a badge and a gun and formidable forces on both sides of the law at his fingertips.

He mentions that (the well-known journalist) Evan Whitton likened him to the young Don Bradman in a piece called 'Flight of Fear' published in 1970.

Whitton, in fact, credits the Bradman comparison to a co-author, but agrees it was accurate. He recalls the occasion well. In 1970 he and Hanford accompanied the anti-corruption campaigner Bertram Wainer to a tense meeting with senior New South Wales police to discuss abortion rackets. The acting head of the CIB, the ill-fated Don Fergusson (mysteriously found shot dead at police headquarters some years later) chose the junior Rogerson and his 'mentor' Noel Morey to front the corruption-busting Wainer.

Whitton recalls that Rogerson, though only 29, 'was the sharpest of the three' and did indeed look like Bradman: compact, gimlet-eyed, cool under pressure, self-contained and not fussy about who got bruised for him to get his way.

The resemblance between the bagman and the batsman was not only physical. Someone once wrote that Bradman combined 'poetry and murder' at the crease; in business, too, 'the Don' had a ruthless streak that made him unpopular with the genteel Adelaide business establishment. Rogerson reputedly also did some of his best work with a bat, usually of the baseball variety. But that's all a long time ago – he would consider it bad manners to bring it up.

He now lives in a neat house in a neat street in Padstow Heights, barely a postcode away from where he grew up in Bankstown in Sydney's west. Enterprising reporters have been known to peek over his fence then write stories transforming the unremarkable brick veneer into a 'mansion' with pool and luxury 'Daimler' sedan in the garage.

The facts, he says, are a little duller: the car is a 1980 Jaguar that his wife bought for $9000 many years ago from a workmate. Mostly, he drives a geriatric station wagon to carry tools to do manual work. He says he and his second wife took out a mortgage to buy the house for $365,000 in 1998 and have been paying it off.

He still has the weekender on the northern coast that he bought in 1979, and the five-metre fishing runabout he bought second-hand in 1978.

The fibro house he bought in Condell Park in 1965 went to his first wife, Joy, when their marriage collapsed in the early 1990s. The strain of court hearings and allegations must have been shattering for the quiet, church-going woman he had known since they met at Sunday school. Rogerson's two daughters – 'they call me a silly old dickhead' – are married with children. He has a sister from whom he is estranged and a much younger brother, Owen, who was also a policeman until Roger's reputation caused problems for him, through no fault of Owen's.

Like many men his age, Rogerson spends a lot of time in sheds – tinkering, building and repairing. He is a good mechanic and carpenter and can weld and turn metal. He works on cars and houses – and helps neighbours and friends with theirs. He once painted a house for a pensioner neighbour; an act of generosity that several people say is typical. Favours went both ways – a court was told a neighbour let the helpful detective keep a taped-up biscuit tin of 'documents' at his place. The prosecution suggested it was full of cash. Rogerson disagreed.

His work ethic is strong. When he was in jail the first time, 1993 to 1995, he made fine jarrah wall clocks and dining tables that sold for good money – the tables for up to $2500. It helped pay off his huge legal bills. Each piece had a Rogerson nameplate – apparently a good selling feature.

Especially among police, even interstate, who fancied the notoriety of a Rogerson-made original.

Manual work has been hard for him since he wrecked his shoulder a few years ago. A roof collapsed under him while he was helping a friend demolish a shed. He fell four metres, fearing that flying corrugated iron might kill him.

His left side, including his hand, will never be the same again. He carries his right shoulder cocked in the air and he limps. He still works 'on the tools' but has to swing a hammer with two hands. Worse, his balance has been affected. In early 2006, he fell while re-building his garden fence and cut his legs.

It's all a long way from the man portrayed in *Blue Murder*, a home-grown Dirty Harry with a taste for dirty money. But the reputation persists. He now plays along with it, propping up a maverick image born last century to turn an honest dollar out of the notoriety that dogs him. An irony not lost on him.

Well before 'going away on my fact-finding mission' – his description of jail – he started touring pubs and clubs with Mark 'Jacko' Jackson and Mark 'Chopper' Read, among other attractions. The enterprising Jackson – former AFL full forward, actor, battery marketer and novelty heavyweight boxer – had tracked him down and asked him to join the troupe.

They advertised him as Roger 'The Dodger' and called the show The Good, the Bad and the Ugly. Rogerson had been a regular speaker at friends' weddings and birthdays but this was different: somewhere between after-dinner speaking, sport club 'smoke nights' and vaudeville – with a touch of the old circus freak show.

He admits he used to get 'hot and bothered' and defend himself every time someone had a crack at him on talkback radio. Now he doesn't worry. Touring with a later version of the show, he flips the bird to the mainstream world that has all but turned its back on him. Besides, he needs the money.

He reckons his last court case cost him $200,000 and he is paying it off. There is nothing about his lifestyle to suggest otherwise. The fact that he would even go on the road like a sideshow act suggests he needs the money. It's physically easier than labouring, though not always more rewarding financially.

He did his first show at a Bondi pub in late 2003. It was a packed house – and more than half were police. Young constables that had been babies when he was in 'the job' lined up for his autograph. He could hardly believe it.

And they seemed happy to laugh at his tall tales and sarcastic digs at the modern police force that turned its back on him and some of his contemporaries.

'I used to be in the best police force that money could buy,' he begins, pausing for the laugh and then delivering the tag, 'but these days they're so bloody useless no-one wants to buy them.' Boom boom. He's been telling that one for a while. It's one of the lines he uses in between a few anecdotes that skate around the more boggy spots in his C.V.

Not that Rogerson has any illusions about what he's doing, or the crowd the travelling show attracts at clubs and pubs. Talking to a friend on the telephone before a 'gig' in Perth in early 2006, he said drily, 'We attract an ecumenical crowd, mate – but we're not keeping them from the ballet or the opera.' It's as funny as anything he said on stage later that night, and undoubtedly true.

His problem – not that he'd admit it – is that after two jail terms and two decades of being demonised as the most corrupt officer in what was arguably one of the most corrupt police forces in the western world, he is the odd man out in both mainstream society and its criminal underbelly.

Whereas an ordinary career criminal – thief, robber or drug dealer – would regard jail as an occupational hazard and feel no genuine shame, a policeman who has prosecuted and preyed on criminals is marooned between two worlds – and powerless – when convicted and stripped of his badge and gun. He loses respect in the reputable society he is part of, is an embarrassment to his family and friends, no longer has any power on the street and is unwelcome among most 'real' criminals. He is an embarrassment to the force – and a liability to corrupt associates who have avoided prosecution and are nervous of exposure. His contemporaries have nothing to gain by acknowledging him. For some, this could be suicide territory. But Rogerson is made of sterner stuff, it seems.

He might be slumming it a bit now, but the air of steely resolve is still close to the surface. The sense of self. When he turns up at the hotels to do the show, he is wearing neatly pressed slacks and button-up shirt, and his conservative black shoes have a parade ground shine. To look at him, he could be a recently retired inspector heading off to chair a Neighbourhood Watch meeting.

On one hand he is holding a mask of respectability to the world, sticking to his script that he is a wronged man sacrificed for political expediency in a war between old guard and new. But as the respectable world gradually turns its back, his old networks decay, and age and physical injuries curb his ability to work, he also exploits the myth that's grown around him. He doesn't have much choice.

Like old gunfighters, old boxers and old singers down on their luck, he has to play the only card left to him – turning a dollar from people's curiosity about the famous. Or, in his case, the infamous.

Buffalo Bill became a circus act, Joe Louis a 'greeter' at a Las Vegas casino, Leo Sayer played cheap clubs for 20 years. And Rogerson does the 'sportsmen's night' circuit, mining the myth that, in his heart, he knows is a fair stretch from the reality of a grandfather with a crook shoulder and a limp.

He's too smart to believe his own bullshit. Still, the work ethic beats strongly in him, and he has never dodged a quick 'earn'. And sometimes he gets a surprise at who turns up to see him.

Before a show at a pub in Sydney's west, a middle-aged man approached him in the car park and shook hands. His name was Brian Harland. Back in Novermber, 1980, Rogerson had arrested an armed jail escapee who shot dead Brian's young brother, Rick Harland.

Rick, a 21-year-old apprentice, was awarded a posthumous bravery medal for chasing the escapees after they robbed the hotel where he worked part-time. Hours later Rogerson cornered the armed killer, Gary Purdey, in a backyard garage. Rogerson could have shot him, but didn't. Brian Harland often wishes he had.

Every year until she died Rick and Brian Harland's mother sent Rogerson a Christmas card thanking him for treating her family so kindly during the murder trial.

Brian Harland is still grateful. 'Roger was the only one in court to say that Rick was a brave young fella. The others just called him "the body" and "the deceased" but he could see what it meant to Mum. He was at the top of the tree then and now he's doing it tough. I went to see him as a show of support.'

The police force awarded Rogerson its highest award in 1980 for arresting Purdey. Michael Drury won it the next year. Which proves the adage that it's a small world: just three years later, one police hero stood accused of taking blood money to have the other police hero shot.

Rogerson is a man of his word ... but he killed men in the line of duty, was very vicious and wouldn't hesitate to lock you up and flog you badly – with the help of other police, of course.
– Arthur 'Neddy' Smith, criminal

MABEL Rogerson was 90 at the time of writing but her mind, her voice and her personality were strong. After 81 years, she still had traces of her native Wales in her voice. The first thing she tells a stranger is about her family's 'pirate ancestor' – the privateer Sir Henry Morgan, knighted by Charles II for plundering Spanish ships and settlements in the Caribbean in the mid-17th century.

'Sir Henry was very clever. As long as he brought back booty for the monarch all was forgiven,' she says. 'He didn't end on a noose. He ended up a gentleman farmer and died a natural death.

'My mother's grandfather had his own sailing ships and worked from the Cardiff docks. He was descended from the Morgans. Our family moved to Pontypridd when my mother was a teenager. That's where Tom Jones comes from,' she adds helpfully.

Rogerson jokes that the old lady's story of the pirate relative is her oblique way of explaining – or even justifying – her rogue son, but she would never be so disloyal as to hint such a thing. She is touchingly staunch to her first-born despite the heartache he must have caused her for 20 years.

'Roger has had a raw deal, you know,' she says. 'He was taught the value of things and was determined to do the best at whatever he took on. He has always been straight in all his dealings and I don't think it's true the things they say about him. I think it's jealousy.'

Roger Caleb Rogerson was born in Sydney 3 January 1941, and spent his early childhood in Bondi before the family moved (with Mabel's parents) to a farmlet at Bankstown that they called, rather grandly, 'Castlefield'. Because, the old lady explains, 'our house was our castle and it was in the middle of a field'. They had a cow called Daisy, goats, hens and a horse – an old trotter – that Roger rode to Bankstown Central School, where he went with hundreds of other children whose parents were migrants. He learned piano and played the organ at the local Church of Christ. Later, when he married, he would buy a piano on time payment terms before he bought a television.

Roger was named after his father Owen's nickname, 'Rodgie'. The middle name 'Caleb' came from his maternal grandfather, Caleb Boxley, a former coalminer, who had migrated to Australia from Wales with his wife Gwendoline when Mabel was nine. The three generations lived happily together. 'We had the most precious thing a family can have – a home filled with love,' Mabel recalls.

Mabel was, and is, highly respectable and proud of her mother Gwendoline's ship-owning, landed ancestors – and of the fact that a great uncle on the Boxley side of the family was a prosperous English manufacturer of steel chains who helped set up the Salvation Army.

There is a touch of frustrated ambition about Mabel Rogerson that might explain why her oldest son grew up to be keen to prove himself by doing well financially. As a teenager in the depression, Mabel made do with a poorly-paid job as a dressmaker and machinist and her dream of going on to university withered. 'We'd not the means, dear' she sighs, all these years later.

If young Rogerson got a sense of frustrated entitlement and middle-class ambition from his ambitious mother, then he might have got a little working class grit and humour from his father. In some ways Owen Rogerson came from a harder place and worked all his life with his hands.

Owen was a Yorkshireman, born in 1901. Adventurous, bold and practical, he did his time as a boilermaker in the Hull shipyards before migrating to Australia in 1920. He went broke with a partner attempting to establish a peanut farm in the Northern Territory and then the Depression brought him to Sydney to work on building the Harbour Bridge. He was on the crew that heated and hammered the last rivets to finish the bridge. After the war broke out in 1939 he worked on the docks fitting ships with gun emplacements, and after the war worked in the railway workshops. Compared with the girl he would marry, he was a bit of a knockabout.

Owen had met Mabel at a dance in 1939 and they married later the same year, on the eve of war. She was 23. He was 38 but he looked young and had a silver tongue and told her he was 30. She did not uncover the deception for years and was not amused. According to Roger, 'Mum didn't talk to him for a while but they must have made up because my little brother was born later'. All the loyal Mabel will say now is that her Owen was a 'man's man' and a good talker.

The thing about Rogerson being descended from Sir Henry Morgan, pirate by royal appointment, is that in a sense history repeated itself.

Sir Henry, essentially a mercenary, was allowed rob Britain's Spanish enemies if he shared the loot with the king. This licensed piracy in the Caribbean was a forerunner of the system in Sydney before John Avery took over the police force in 1984. Police controlled crime on the tacit understanding some of them skimmed payment – for themselves and key politicians – from gambling, prostitution, abortion and drug rackets. Those who didn't like it kept quiet. It wasn't wise to buck a system that went right back to Sydney's corrupt and colourful origins under the 'Rum Corps' of early settlement days.

This was the system that the then unsuspecting Rogerson joined when he became a police cadet just after his seventeenth birthday in 1958.

It was a turning point, perhaps. His mother had wanted him to go on to university and study to be an engineer, and Rogerson himself had considered joining the air force. In fact, he said he'd 'try' the police first and could switch later if he felt like it. Had he done that, it could all have been so different. He succeeded at anything he took on. Had he gone into the services, he would have served during the Vietnam War period.

He had the brains, the ambition, the self-discipline and the cunning to play the game, the streak of ruthlessness shared by executives and sports coaches and successful officers. He could easily have ended up a senior officer. In which case, he would be likely to be in a reefer jacket with the other chaps at the Naval and Military Club instead of doing shows in beer barns with Jacko and Chopper and the rest.

As it happened, New South Wales had probably the best training for young police in Australia in the 1950s and 1960s. Rogerson and his young contemporaries were drilled in touch typing, shorthand and law and by the time they graduated three years later, the best of them were highly proficient in the practical skills of police work – writing reports, processing paper work and giving evidence in court. And Rogerson was one of the best and brightest of his year.

One of his classmates, Barry Leaney, was a high achiever and a good student. They shared the same birth date; they graduated four weeks apart and stayed in touch early in their careers. They both drove Volkswagens. When Leaney's broke down, the capable Rogerson fitted it with a new clutch for him. Later, they went on holiday to the Gold Coast together, where Leaney met the girl he would marry. Rogerson was best man at the wedding. The Leaneys went to Rogerson's first wedding in 1965 but they drifted apart later.

It wasn't until much later, Leaney says carefully, that he realised they had taken 'separate roads' – and that he had been lucky not to be recruited by the crime squads. Leaney worked in Special Branch, which monitored fringe political movements for potential threats – an important but relatively passive role. In contrast, Rogerson started with 21 Division, a 'flying squad' used to clean up trouble spots, and later moved to the armed hold-up squad, where he would make his name.

Leaney thinks he was insulated from corruption because he was in a branch that crime squad detectives sneered at because it was intelligence gathering rather than 'catching crooks'.

Once, late in the 1960s, the Leaneys visited the Rogersons at home. They noticed how many expensive electrical goods their hosts had. Leaney merely assumed Rogerson was getting more overtime than he did. His wife, however, doubted that. She was later proved right.

Two years ago Leaney was organising a 45th class reunion. He invited Rogerson but he said he wouldn't come. 'Roger has thick enough skin but he didn't want to embarrass anyone else in case some of them left when he turned up,' Leaney says.

'I feel sorry for the man. I would not turn my back on him if I saw him in the street. A lot has happened, but he still remains a good bloke.'

There was one prisoner telling everybody he'd been shot by me ... I said to him 'Look, mate, the people I've shot don't end up in the hospital, they go straight to the morgue,' and that quietened him down.
– Roger Rogerson, 1990

CALL any one of many of tough ex-Sydney cops – and some serving ones – and mention Rogerson's name and men whose sharp memories for names, dates and descriptions are their tools of trade suddenly go vague and selective. They recall Rogerson's achievements – the arrests, the commendations – but the rest is a blur. They can't wait to hang up. They are not rude or abusive but would obviously rather go to the dentist to have teeth drilled than talk about the man they knew so well.

'I'm nearly 81, you know' quavers Noel Morey, who led the feared armed hold-up squad when Rogerson was at his peak. 'My memory isn't too good.' He is distracted because his wife has heard the R-word and urges him to be quiet and get off the phone. Mrs Morey, a highly respectable woman, was once called as a witness – about Rogerson's alibi on the night of the Drury shooting – and it could be that she heard enough to cure her of singing the praises of her husband's keen young offsider, as Rogerson once was.

Call another ex-policeman, a senior security executive with a big firm, and it's as if his telephone has turned into a tiger snake. No names, he says warily, parrying questions about Rogerson until he steps outside his office so that none of his colleagues hear him raking over old scores.

He is guarded but explains the mixed feelings he and many other former police colleagues have about Rogerson.

He remembers a time when a crew of detectives were sent up the north coast on a job. They could have spent a day lazing around while they waited for something to happen but Rogerson wouldn't hear of wasting time.

It turned out that he had a distant relative, a reclusive older man who had fallen on hard times and was living in 'a pigsty' of a shack. Rogerson felt sorry for him, so he took the crew to the shack and they cleaned it up from top to bottom. Like painting his pensioner neighbour's house, it was beyond the call of duty, but that was typical of the good angels in his nature. He was officer material, a natural leader whose 'dash' could make him a hero in some circumstances and a villain in others. It takes nerve to break the rules that most people obey, which is why the law-abiding majority are fascinated by true crime.

The former colleague says: 'In ways he was fundamentally kind – and a pillar of courage and competence, with no reverse gear.'

He pauses. 'But I am a friend of Michael Drury, which makes it hard. All I can tell you is that Roger was a complex character.'

I like reading Jeffrey Archer. I'm reading his prison diaries at the moment. He's an ex-cop and an ex-con like I am – but I don't think I'll be getting a Lordship.
– Roger Rogerson, 2006

THERE is 'nobody more ex- than an ex-cop' the saying goes. When you get drummed out of the job and jailed that applies in spades. So what does the future hold for Rogerson?

If he ever did have black money stashed away – apart from the \$110,000 over which he was first prosecuted in 1990 – there is no sign of it now. Four trials and a divorce will do that.

Mostly, he is determined to keep up a brave front. He talks of leaving Sydney one day, perhaps when his wife finishes work. They dream of buying a little place in Tasmania. The way he describes it, he yearns to set up a few acres to recapture the innocence of childhood when the family – all three generations – had their farmlet at Bankstown in the 1950s, complete with chooks and ducks and goats and a cow and their beloved terriers. Another 'Castlefield', if not completely cut off from stares and whispers, then at least further away.

In hours of talking over several days, Rogerson is cheerful and friendly but it's clear he holds up a mask. He avoids any note of regret and pleads always that he's a good cop battered by forces beyond his control. That's his story and he's sticking to it. No-one does it better.

Despite the stoic shell, he sometimes sounds wistful about the family life wrecked by his fall. He says that after one of his daughters accidentally overheard a story about one of his transgressions, she said to him, 'Mum had some good reasons to leave you, didn't she?' and he had answered, 'She probably did.'

He jokes that he reads the death notices each day to see which of his enemies he has outlived – but the bitterness is real. He says he was made a scapegoat by senior officers currying favour with the new regime.

The question is not whether he was guilty but that others were, too – something he has never said, but which must bite deep. Especially when he was in jail and he knew that others – the ones that got away – were soaking up the sunshine in their weekenders up the coast, or retired in Queensland on the proceeds of their ill-gotten gains.

Only once is he truly angry. 'They want to see me in the gutter, a broken-down drunk,' he grates. 'But I won't let it happen. I'm too proud.'

Then he recovers and makes a joke of infamy. 'I've got broad shoulders,' he says, 'even if one of them is stuffed.'

13

SMOKING OUT MR SIN

In the Saffron years where
there was smoke there was fire
and where there was fire
there was Abe.

PLENTY of pretenders have fought and plotted to be King of the Cross, but Abe Saffron stayed on the throne longer than all of them.

By the end of the 1980s, the old reptile had made so much money he could fake going legit and pass himself off as the prosperous entrepreneur and philanthropist he'd always claimed to be. As if no one knew he had enough hookers and dodgy clubs to service the entire US Navy if it had sailed through the Heads one day.

No matter what the racket, if it was illegal and mugs would pay over the odds for it then Abe peddled it: from sex and porn to sly grog and drugs. He was up to his elbows in companies with shares in other companies that controlled so many bent businesses probably only he knew exactly what he did and didn't control – a puppet master jerking the strings of a heap of patsies and proxies.

Certainly no one in authority seemed to want to know more about Abe than Abe was willing to share. Between bribery and blackmail of police, public servants, politicians and the odd wayward judge – Abe's brothels and clubs catered for sexual fetishes and had hidden cameras and one-way mirrors – he had authority exactly where he wanted it. That is, doing him favours and harassing his business competition.

After decades of collecting the wages of sin around Sydney (and Adelaide and Perth) he could afford to stand back a little. There was still plenty of money to be milked from the Cross, from the oldest profession and its near relatives.

The only thing that had changed since he'd got his start after the war were the faces on the street. They came and went, the mugs and those who preyed on them, but Abe endured, seemingly above it all. A protected species.

In 2004 the Sydney City Council installed 115 brass plaques in the footpaths of Kings Cross to mark the characters that have played a part in its raffish history. There were to have been 116 plaques but the one dedicated to Saffron was shelved ostensibly because the old man's lawyers threatened legal action on grounds that the plaque inscription was defamatory. This was a pity because the terse lines were a masterpiece of understatement – and absolutely true:

Abe Saffron. Publican and nightclub owner from 1946. Convictions and court appearances from 1938. Friends in high places.

Even after Saffron died in 2006, the authorities were nervous about green-lighting the plaque. The problem, as ever, was the friends in high places. Connections of one ex-Premier and a former Prime Minister were thought to be sensitive about the implication.

In death, Saffron still had a hold. In life, he could get away with nearly anything he liked. And what he liked was taking advantage of other people.

THE young businessman on the make had already earned a reputation as a tough negotiator. He had started with one pub, was on his way to building a national hotel network and was keen to stake a bigger claim in the lucrative Sydney market.

He already owned four-star and three-star hotels in Kings Cross and had signed a contract to buy a tired-looking two-star accommodation lodge in the same area.

His reasoning was simple. It was a matter of arithmetic and economies of scale: televisions, jugs, toasters and linen would be handed down from the top-end hotels to the cheaper ones as the room rates and residents' expectations dropped. Less waste meant more profit, a formula he would follow for the next four decades.

The deal was done and he paid a deposit on the $2million contract. But three days before settlement, he received a call. It was the hotel vendor in Sydney, asking for a meeting to discuss the deal. He was polite but insistent.

The young businessman was blunt. There was no need for a meeting, he said: the bank cheque would be in the mail.

But the man with the charming voice kept insisting and an appointment was set: they would meet in a Sydney office the day before settlement.

When the man-on-the-make walked in, sitting behind an expensive desk was a small, dapper older man. And standing behind him was a bodyguard – only about 175 centimetres tall but built like a bodybuilder.

During the meeting the muscle man stood silently with his arms folded, glaring at the visitor. Subtlety was not his strong suit. Neither was the English language. Grunting was his go.

The older man began gently: 'Mr (name deleted), I am grateful for your time and I must apologise, as there has been a terrible mistake. The price for the hotel has been listed as $2 million when it should be $2.25 million.'

The younger man had already done many deals and understood a last minute try-on. 'A deal is a deal,' he said quietly. 'I will settle tomorrow as agreed.'

The older man responded. 'I mustn't have made myself clear: the price is $2.25 million.'

The younger man was getting restless, wondering how he could end the conversation and leave the building without offending the vendor or his bodyguard. 'It's $2 million and I'll settle as agreed,' he said.

The Sydney man pressed on relentlessly.

'Mister, I have done my homework on you and I know you are smart and I know you have a big future so it would be a tragedy if something went wrong.'

He paused then added: 'What if there was a fire? What if one of your hotels burnt down? Or more than one?

People could be hurt, businesses closed, insurance premiums could go through the roof. It would be a tragedy,' he said, shaking his head.

The young man looked down and on the desk he saw a name plaque – Abraham Saffron. Then it dawned on him. This was the Abe Saffron – known as 'Mr Sin' and 'The Boss of The Cross'. Suddenly, he saw that Saffron's offer was too good to refuse.

When the contract with the inflated price was pushed towards him he signed, stood up and walked out.

That was how Saffron did business: quietly and politely but with an unspoken threat.

Saffron could never have enough money and took shortcuts to make it. Making threats, exerting charm and extorting secret commissions were a way of life for him. And one of his main weapons was the threat of fire: what cynical and sometimes racist police privately called Jewish lightning'.

In the Saffron years where there was smoke there was fire and where there was fire there was Abe.

In the early 1970s fire regulations were not that strict and Abe seemed to be a victim of heat-related 'bad luck' more than most.

Lightning might not strike twice but 'torches' do.

In one case, his right hand man, James 'Big Jim' McCartney Anderson, was badly burned when Saffron's Staccato Club in Darlinghurst Road was set on fire. In another fire, an Adelaide club owned by a Saffron shelf company was also badly damaged.

A man was jailed for conspiracy to defraud an insurance company but Saffron was never charged. Six of Saffron's many properties, including gay bars, massage parlours and discos, were to catch fire between 1980 and 1982. All appeared to be deliberately lit.

Later, Anderson, who would become a star police witness against Saffron, alleged that in one case an insurance claim was made for 'sound equipment and lighting equipment that had been removed long beforehand.'

Saffron was the subject of interest in a coronial inquest into four fires and while the coroner found there was a good case against him on the grounds that the circumstances in each case were overwhelmingly similar, the Attorney General's department disagreed and once again Abe walked away, playing the part of the maligned businessman.

If there was one single event that changed the public perception of Saffron from colourful rogue to callous reptile it was a fire at Sydney's Luna Park.

In fact, Saffron gave reptiles a bad name. Snakes just eat rats. Abe employed them.

On 9 June 1979, the ghost train at the loved fun park was engulfed in flames, killing six children and the father of one of them.

It was widely held that Saffron had long wanted to own the property and had business interests in the fading beauty. One of his companies provided amusement machines to Luna Park and two company directors who leased the park were distant relatives to the gap-toothed crime boss.

The police investigation into the fires concentrated on the poor electrical standards and, some argued, energetically pushed the theory that the fire was just a terrible accident. But the inquest came back with an open finding – and pointedly rejected the electrical fault theory.

The fire started around 10.15pm, shortly before closing time, and took hold because of an inadequate fire hose system. Most felt that if the fire were deliberately lit, whoever organised it didn't want to cause death but to suggest that the owners were incompetent and should lose control of the complex.

'It was started with petrol. Whoever did it didn't know there was one (more) train to go through,' a source close to Saffron said.

Killed were John Godson and his two boys, Damien and Craig, along with four Waverley College students: Jonathon Billings, Richard Carroll, Michael Johnson, and Seamus Rahilly. Another young student was pulled to safety by staff.

Saffron always maintained he was not involved in the fire but in the absence of other evidence, the denial meant little. Abe was always economical with the truth. He spent his entire career denying he was any more than a misunderstood entrepreneur.

In May 2007 Saffron's niece, Anne Buckingham, implicated him in the fire but would not, or could not, provide facts to back up her assertions.

She dropped her bombshell in an interview with the *Sydney Morning Herald*, saying:

'The fire at Luna Park – very strange, that fire.' Then added: 'I don't think people were meant to be killed.'

While stopping short of saying her uncle organised the fire, she said she believed he wanted to buy the park and that he liked to collect things. She later tried to distance herself from her comments, but the controversy was well and truly reignited.

The National Crime Authority investigated Saffron and reviewed the arson investigations.

It found: 'Luna Park, it was alleged, had been coveted by Saffron for over 20 years and the fire in the ghost train had been lit as a trigger to evict the incumbent tenants and gain control of the park lease for himself.'

The Costigan Commission had conducted its own inquiry into other fires linked to the Saffron empire.

A New South Wales policeman gave evidence to the commission that one figure 'received a payment of money ... so that nobody could be found guilty of the committing of arson.'

But the fires had long gone cold, as had any leads in the cases. Yet again, Saffron would walk away as a suspect but nothing more.

IF one man built Kings Cross it was Abraham Gilbert Saffron. He promoted his nightclubs as glamorous, risqué, and with an 'international' flavour. They even served French onion soup. In fact, the food at Saffron clubs was notoriously bad but no one was there for the roast chicken. (In one club the chicken was just rubbery old rooster with feathers – that was Les Girls. But we digress).

Some clubs catered for film stars, politicians, senior police and gunmen. Abe didn't care who he ripped off. He instructed staff that when patrons were drunk on mixed drinks to just rub the rim of the glasses with spirits rather than provide a full nip in the mix – the Saffron version of a finger of scotch.

People liked the naughty feel. It seemed like a touch of Las Vegas where 'glamour' and girls were mixed with graft and gunnies.

Saffron opened the first of his many clubs – The Roosevelt – in 1947. It was later described as 'the city's most notorious and disreputable nightclub' and closed on court orders. He built Australia's first strip club – at Kings Cross, naturally – and promoted tours by stars such as Frank Sinatra and Tina Turner.

If you had a weakness for a good time or bad girls (or boys) Saffron could find you whatever you wanted – at a price. And that price could take a lifetime to repay. Because among Saffron's many business methods was one he found the most satisfying.

Abe had a prodigious and eclectic sexual appetite and he encouraged the worst in his clients and friends. He had one 'official' wife, Doreen, whom he had married in a synagogue, but he went home only three times a week. The other nights were shared amongst many mistresses and casual partners, mostly not of his faith.

While the arrangement may have saved on washing up at home it was not conducive to marital harmony. Doreen Saffron was so humiliated and depressed that she tried to commit suicide more than once.

Saffron was purported to be a sadomasochist who enjoyed inflicting and receiving pain. In one court case, it was alleged a 'completely depraved' Saffron had whipped a girl's naked buttocks at a private fetishist party. Abe later said the incident had been a 'joke' and the whip was a feather duster. No wonder he never suffered from hay fever.

He was also a notorious exhibitionist – building 'orgy rooms' where people could watch him do what he did best. As with everything he did, there was an angle: the two-way mirrors and peepholes in the rooms helped him build a form of insurance as lucrative as the fire policies he routinely cashed after each unexplained blaze.

Saffron took to photographing his more prominent clients with their pants down. Media barons, barristers, judges and state ministers were snapped in orgies with prostitutes, young boys and schoolgirls. Even in fast and loose Sydney such photos could be career-ending. No wonder that for decades Saffron was virtually untouchable.

Longtime Sydney journalist and Saffron watcher, Tony Reeves, in his book, *Mr Sin*, says that when Abe didn't have the appropriate picture he would organise fakes, once trying to compromise the state Attorney General by producing a photo of the politician horizontal with a notorious prostitute. Luckily for the prominent MP he had a prominent birthmark on his bottom. The lookalike used in the picture didn't have a birthmark – proving that on at least one occasion arse can beat lack of class.

One controversial police tape caught Saffron talking to his solicitor, Morgan Ryan, about High Court Judge Lionel Murphy and discussing how to arrange girls for Murphy.

According to Reeves, prostitute turned photographer Shirley Bega saw the dirt file as her way out of the Saffron sewer. He says the story – often repeated but never proved – was that she was shot dead by her estranged husband after she stole some of the photos. A corrupt detective, who kept the evidence for his own profit and protection, covered up the murder.

Certainly, it is still said that one prosecutor didn't try too hard in a Saffron-related case for fear his reputation as a family man would be slightly sullied if the pictures of him playing leapfrog with a schoolboy were made public.

Saffron, a belts and braces man, had another form of protection besides blackmail. Over the years, he paid millions of dollars in bribes. He paid off police from street coppers to the commissioners – and politicians all the way to longtime New South Wales Premier Sir Robert Askin, who was as rotten as a pork chop.

James Anderson would make a statement: 'In my capacity as manager for and partner of Saffron, I had first-hand knowledge of corruption of police to allow a blind eye approach to liquor law violations and other practices.'

He said there were weekly payments to police varying from $600 to $750 per club and larger payments of $5000 to senior officers. He said Saffron met the then Commissioner, former Olympic rower Mervyn Wood, on a P&O cruise ship 'for a conference on a new scale of bribe payments after Wood became Commissioner.'

Anderson revealed that Saffron's clubs worked with two sets of tills for 'black' and legitimate money and claimed millions went undeclared. This would come back to haunt Abe much later.

Anderson also alleged Saffron was involved in drugs although he couldn't prove it. Saffron routinely denied he was connected with drug trafficking but it was clear many of his prostitutes were users and dealers. And it is hard to believe that a man who spent a lifetime doing anything for money would stop short of selling the illicit powders that were rampant in the sex industry he dominated.

'Saffron is smart, always in the background, not dirtying his hands, but grabbing the dirty money,' Anderson said.

In October 1976 Saffron went public – claiming he was not involved in drugs and that the allegations against him were 'vile'.

Costigan was unimpressed and made a damning finding: 'Despite his protests of innocence, he is involved in drug trafficking. He imports. He distributes. He employs men who use violence to maintain his control and authority. His organization is a myriad of corporations. He uses people as agents and nominees, and shields himself from the criminal activity so that if it is detected, he will escape. Should this fail; he corrupts law enforcement officers to protect himself and his organization. The profits derived from these activities are protected from tax and if they were legitimate, making use of the latest fraudulent device as readily as the legitimate.'

ABRAHAM Gilbert Saffron was born just after World War I ended. His first years were spent with his family in a small flat above his father's drapery shop in inner-suburban Sydney.

By the time he turned eight, young Abe had already learned that vice paid more than tailoring: he made his pocket money selling cigarettes to his father's poker-playing friends. He left school at fifteen and joined the family business, Saffron & Son, in Pitt Street. His family wanted him to be a doctor. The closest he ever got was playing doctors and nurses with some of his broadminded prostitutes.

In 1938, Saffron was charged over a minor starting price bookmaking offence. In those days he lacked the police contacts to have the charge fixed – but he was a quick learner.

Two years later, in 1940, Saffron was convicted of receiving stolen car radios and received a suspended sentence. This apparent lenient treatment might have been connected with the fact that he almost immediately joined the army ... wartime courts encouraged young lawbreakers to avoid jail with a sudden display of patriotism. Regardless of the reasons why he joined up, young Saffron soon decided the army wasn't for him and transferred to the merchant navy, which had less front-line action than Tobruk or the Kokoda Trail.

It might have been a shrewd decision, for he survived the war when many of his contemporaries didn't. And he learned first hand there was more money in servicing servicemen than serving the nation.

In the Vietnam years, he was able to set up strip and vice businesses to cater for American and Australian soldiers on leave. He knew what had been known for thousands of years: sex sells.

In 1976, he was named in the South Australian Parliament as 'one of the principal characters in organised crime in Australia'. The South Australian Attorney-General, Peter Duncan, told Parliament some of Saffron's employees were linked to the disappearance and suspected murder of Sydney newspaper publisher Juanita Neilsen, who had led a crusade to clean up Kings Cross.

The Costigan Royal Commission into organised crime

subsequently subjected Saffron to intense investigations. The Commission gave him the code name Gomorrah – a none-too-subtle reference to his professional and personal obsession with sex.

A later hearing of the Licensing Commission was told he was known as 'Mr Sin', involved in pornography, connected with massage parlours and the underworld.

Despite an Australia-wide reputation as a crime boss, he was able to visit senior police in their Sydney offices as if he were a respected business figure making a donation to the Police Boys Club. His donations were always done in secret to the Old Boys Club. And they were cash.

In fact, in 1978, while under investigation for multiple offences he managed to have his fingerprints and photographs expunged from police records. Other official legal documents that should have been archived mysteriously disappeared. Nothing seemed out of reach of his corrupt network of police and public servants.

It was the start of an obsession to try to re-write his personal history that lasted until his death.

He was close to many senior police, including a deputy police commissioner, Bill Allen, meeting him at police headquarters seven times. It's a wonder he didn't have his own car space. Allen was later jailed for bribing the head of the Special Licensing Police on five occasions.

It was no surprise to anyone that Bill Allen was on the take. Victoria Police had information Allen was regularly paying a senior New South Wales minister $5000 from illegal gambling interests. When the information was passed to New South Wales police their response was to ask what it had to do with an outside law enforcement agency. They would deal with their own. And they did, usually with brown paper bags filled with used cash. Roger that.

Unsurprisingly, it was not the New South Wales police that broke Saffron's vice-like grip on vice.

Justice Stewart was a former New South Wales policeman who knew first hand how some elements of the force worked. He studied law later, becoming a judge and Royal Commissioner.

When he became Chairman of the National Crime Authority he was given 42 references from the Costigan Commission and while he didn't pursue all of them, he decided it was time Mr Sin was in the bin.

His plan was to do an Al Capone on the Teflon-coated crook and chase the black money, but it would not be easy.

'Saffron was notorious in Sydney as being untouchable. He was a corrupter of police and others. I took the view that this man had got away with so much for so long it was about time we tried to stop it,' Justice Stewart would later recall.

'I had some knowledge of him that I had come across in my Royal Commission and it was quite sickening.'

It took four years before the National Crime Authority was ready to move and Saffron seemed to think he would beat any investigation. 'He thought he was bulletproof. He knew the New South Wales police weren't going to do anything about him,' Stewart said.

Why wouldn't he be confident? He had beaten every previous attempt to stop him. His complex financial network involved 60 companies and a web of legal and illegal enterprises that had defeated the tax department and police around the country.

According to Abe's son, Alan, in his book, *Gentle Satan*, Saffron turned to his crooked network for help. 'One of Dad's New South Wales police friends was able to secure entry into the National Crime Authority headquarters in Melbourne and copy an entire file on my father.'

Stewart would recall that when the penny dropped with Saffron in November 1985 that he was in deep trouble he needed to spend one – urgently.

The former Royal Commissioner Stewart told *The Australian* newspaper. 'When the National Crime Authority team led by a seconded Victorian went to search the mobster's luxury home he came to the door clad in a pair of red boxer shorts and nothing else'.

According to Stewart, after the search police handed him his arrest warrant and Abe lost the plot – and control of his bowels.

'His red shorts turned yellow and they had to take him to the bathroom to clean him up,' Stewart remembered.

That's his story and he's sticking to it.

On the morning of Saffron's arrest police were not sure if he was at home or spending the night with one of his girlfriends. He had many phones but one number was reserved for a handful of his closest associates.

Chief Investigator Carl Mengler had managed to find the number and rang it that morning. When the telephone was answered, Mengler said, 'Abe, is that you Abe?'

The male voice at the other end asked: 'Who is that?'

Mengler responded, 'Abe, is that you?'

Again the voice asked 'Who is speaking, please?'

Mengler tried a third time and then muttered, 'Bloody phones,' to suggest he couldn't hear properly and hung up.

He had all he needed to know: Abe was home.

Not surprisingly, given his 'accident', Saffron was allowed to shower and change after his arrest. One investigator later said it was the first time he had escorted a man to court who was wearing Italian shoes, silk socks and a $5000 suit. Soon his designer clothes would be replaced by prison overalls.

As part of the probe, National Crime Authority investigators searched his huge strong room filled with documents.

'He stood in the door as we went in. He was just smiling as though to say, "If I shut the door they'd never find you".'

He was subsequently charged with tax frauds from 1969 until 1981. No wonder he needed a drycleaner.

Many of the Crown's claims, including bribing police, fell over but the big one stood. It was simple: as Jim Alexander had told authorities. Saffron's clubs ran two sets of books. One 'white' set, that were declared and taxed, and a second 'black' set, in which illicit profits were hidden and from which bribes were paid.

Saffron was convicted on the fourth attempt and sentenced to three years jail. He was released on 12 March 1990 after serving seventeen months with remissions for good behaviour.

Even in jail Abe tried to get others to do his dirty work.

Stewart would tell the ABC he was told Saffron plotted to kill him while behind bars. 'He was sharing a cell with another man who in fact was one of his employees. And the jail authorities told me and others in our organisation that they had put a listening device in the cell that was being shared by these two prisoners, and they heard that they were plotting that when the other man got out, which was going to be soon – he was getting out on parole or his sentence was over, one of the two – that he would put into effect a plan to kill me. And then I'm not sure one way or the other whether the man actually ever tried to do anything, but he certainly killed somebody when he got out. He killed a woman, murdered her, and was convicted of murder as I remember it, in one of Abe Saffron's sex parlours in Darlinghurst Road in some sort of a sadomasochistic affair.'

Many expected that, at 69, Saffron would withdraw to his luxury home, but he returned to business, concentrating on building an even more complex corporate structure so he would never again be caught with his red shorts down.

Old, rich and in relative good health, Saffron could have spent his autumn years in relative anonymity in his Vaucluse mansion but he remained unfulfilled.

Saffron was richer than he had ever been. There is no doubt he had a brilliant business brain and had invested soundly and legitimately in properties and companies.

But that was not enough. He was either so arrogant or deluded (or perhaps both) that he was obsessed with rewriting history. He wanted to be remembered as a businessman and benefactor rather than the glorified pimp and sly grog dealer he was.

Saffron had lost his circle of influence. The police he had bribed had retired, dropped dead or been locked up. The politicians he had duchessed were out of office or dead and the judges and lawyers he once could have blackmailed with his dirt file had passed away or had become irrelevant.

According to his son, Alan, in *Gentle Satan*, he even tried to contact the then Prime Minister, Bob Hawke. But the

'Prime Minister wouldn't take his call.' What a surprise.

Saffron boasted privately of having sent millions to Is-rael to 'buy tanks' and he donated heavily to Jewish chari-ties, but it could not buy him the respectability he belatedly craved. They would take his money and make soothing noises but they could not change (or privately forget) the fact that he had always been a crook and a deviate. No mat-ter how much cash he splashed on schools or Israeli arms, he was an embarrassment to his co-religionists.

But he still had money and no sense of shame. He embarked on a bizarre campaign using (or misusing) the courts he had spent a lifetime trying to avoid in a bid to rebuild his reputation.

But you can't buy integrity and you can't hold back the tide of public opinion.

He first was found not to be a 'fit and proper person' in Western Australia by the Gaming Commission. It's hard to declare a convicted tax cheat 'fit and proper', even in the freewheeling WA Inc. of Bond, Connell and Burke. He ap-pealed and fought a doomed case.

Next he was banned from holding a liquor licence in Perth. All his legal attempts to fight the rulings were doomed because the courts accepted he was a dirty rotten liar and his evidence could never be believed unless there were legitimate documents to back him up.

In his home state he applied for a liquor licence and was knocked back. When he filled out his application he failed to mention his prior convictions. Seventeen months jail had slipped his mind.

Oops.

Racing and gaming Minister Jack Face came off the long

run, describing Abe as 'everything that is evil.' He said Saffron would never get a licence in the industry he had 'disgraced and degraded over the years by his actions.'

Saffron spent a fortune appealing his tax convictions. He would have been better spending the money on a time machine if he wanted so badly to change the past.

When his appeal process was exhausted he said he would ask for a pardon, maintaining his innocence against overwhelming evidence.

Having discovered that he couldn't change the past he began to try and protect the present, issuing a series of defamation writs against anyone who dared bring up his past. No longer able to bully with muscle or 'torches', he took to issuing writs to anyone who referred to him as 'Mr Sin', the nickname that had dogged him for years.

He dropped a writ on the *Sydney Morning Herald* and was blown away. He issued another one against the *Gold Coast Bulletin* over a crossword.

The clue: Sydney underworld figure, nicknamed Mr Sin.

The answer: Abe Saffron.

He also issued against the authors of this book over a classic of its genre, *Tough: 101 Australian Gangsters*. His lawyers issued two years after the book was published. The writ claimed Saffron was defamed eight times – not bad value for money in just over two pages.

It listed the 'defamatory' claims as that:

He was an Australian gangster. (He was).

He offered bribes to police. (He did).

He whipped a girl. (He did).

He was described as completely depraved. (He was).

Had an Australia-wide reputation as a crime boss. (D'oh!)

Had caused six suspicious fires. (Pass the matches).

Was arrested by the NCA and charged with tax evasion. (Remember his shorts).

He was jailed for tax evasion. (It was technically conspiracy to defraud the Commonwealth of taxes. Same thing.)

We were confident of winning the case on two grounds. Saffron was a crook and his reputation could not be damaged as he didn't have one. After all, he had gone to jail, had been named in countless Royal Commissions as disreputable, had been refused licences in two states on the grounds he was not a fit and proper person and had been found to be a liar by more than one court.

But one of the serious limitations of the defamation laws is that they cater for the rich. It is well known in media circles that if you are to defame someone, make sure they aren't loaded.

Poor people can't afford the costs and solid workers can't afford the time.

But Saffron had time and millions of dollars on his hands. His plan was to fire off writs, not to clear his name but (it seems clear) to deter others from writing an unauthorised biography (He would have hated Reeves' warts-and-all book *Mr Sin* but didn't live to see it published.)

He wanted to be seen as a kind old man with a dickie heart rather than as the younger version, who was just a heartless dick.

A jury of four knocked back some grounds but accepted others. Strangely, the jurors said he was defamed by being described as a crime boss, that he had offered bribes to police and had been arrested by the NCA and jailed over tax evasion (What?).

Yet he was apparently not defamed by being referred to as 'Mr Sin', whipping a girl and setting up six arsons (Go figure).

This was not, as reported, a victory for Saffron. It was just round one. A full trial where the allegations would be tested was yet to come. Former police, authors, colourful racing identities and a few gangsters were prepared to make sure Abe would never win round two.

In the end, Saffron chose to withdraw on condition a small proportion of his legal fees were paid. The deal was done. No money went to Saffron. More importantly, the allegations were never withdrawn and the book remains in print. In fact, the Saffron writ increased sales.

As usual, when push came to shove Saffron backed down.

He knew if he went into open court the grimy past he was trying to bury would again become headline news.

Australia's colourful history is speckled with kind-hearted madams, likeable publicans who bent the rules and SP bookmakers who loved a punt.

Saffron was different. He didn't provide for people's secret desires – he exploited them. He funded an empire by finding individual and collective weaknesses and energetically enlarging them for his own profit. He was a maggot in an open wound.

He photographed prominent people in compromising sexual positions, forcing them to betray their duty in order to protect Saffron. He was not the first to offer bribes to officials but by catering to the base greed of many, he was able to erode the criminal justice system and the political process.

In his last few years he gave millions to charity but to most people in Australia he remained Mr Sin – the title he had spent a fortune trying to shed.

He suffered a heart attack in Israel in July 2006 but it wasn't fatal. He returned to Australia. While undergoing a relatively minor operation on his ankle he died in Sydney's St Vincent's Hospital on 15 September the same year. He was 86.

There were only 120 people at his funeral and none of them were politicians, police or TV stars. The cult of celebrity he had once pursued had moved on, leaving him where he belonged: a dirty old man in disgrace.

He left his legitimate and illegitimate families to squabble over his $25 million fortune.

The last words should be left to his son, Alan. 'My family could have been one of the great Australian business dynasties but, instead, my father was obsessed with greed and the dark side. Instead of using his brilliant talent for business to expand a legitimate empire he chose illegal activities, corruption and vice, combined with his own sinful needs. He was a man with no moral character who wanted everything for himself and anything he gave always came with consequences. I stood up to him and he repaid me by ignoring Jewish custom and giving the majority of his wealth to his long-time mistress and illegitimate daughter.'

14

BRUCE GALEA, GAMBLING MAN

He had spent more time in jail than police who trafficked drugs, took bribes, stole money, assaulted the public and 'fitted up' suspects with crimes they didn't commit.

GAMBLING boss Bruce Galea knew where he was going – so he came prepared. He brought his toothbrush.

It was a silent signal that he would be exactly that in the witness box – silent. There's nothing quite like bringing personal toiletries to court to show you are prepared to go to jail for contempt rather than answer questions. In Galea's case, some zingers from the Royal Commissioner about personal matters such as paying bribes to police and running illegal casinos.

Sharp punters are students of form and breeding and they were not surprised by Galea's reticence. They had him odds on to go to jail rather than reveal all he knew about decades as the Mr Big of Sydney gambling and the money he outlaid to stay in business.

And that is exactly how it turned out. Toothbrush in his pocket and tongue in cheek, he was stoic about what would happen – and what wouldn't happen.

'I won't be answering questions. I know you have to do what you have to do, but I have to do what I have to do,' he told Royal Commissioner Wood. 'We are only wasting time.'

Galea's forecast of his fate was as accurate as Supreme Court Judge David Hunt was astray in his predictions. Justice Hunt, the next judge to hear Galea's case after he was passed on by Commissioner Wood, said he could think of no better way to convince him to give evidence than sending him to jail.

'Coercive action against him (Galea) will eventually produce the information sought by the commissioner' and 'these are the only means by which such a result may be obtained,' Judge Hunt said.

The judge should have read the form guide on the Galea family before making his judgment. Had he been a punter, Judge Hunt would have been tearing up his losing ticket and hitch-hiking home.

Galea stayed silent in jail for more than two years until he was finally released when the Commission rose. At no stage did he ever consider asking to get out in exchange for telling what he knew about police corruption. At 58, he was of the old school and did not talk out of turn.

Galea's knowledge would have been considerable had it been exposed to the Royal Commission. It would have been detailed, accurate and drawn from personal experience – and from history handed down to him.

He was part of a royal family of colourful characters involved in Sydney's illegal gambling and an empathetic public loved them all, especially the family patriarch Perce, the Prince.

Perce Galea was a living legend who rose from a tough Sydney inner-suburb to bet in huge amounts, own champion racehorses, operate illegal casinos and pay whoever needed to be paid all the way up to the then New South Wales Premier Robert Askin to ensure his gambling halls stayed open and protected. He allegedly paid Askin an estimated $100,000 a year for protection, which was staggering money in those days. It sums up Sydney corruption – paying off the highest office in the state to turn a blind eye to illegal gaming and corruption.

Perce got his kick ahead while working as a young milkman. A two pints a day man on Perce's round, Rodney Dangar, tipped his horse Peter Pan in the 1934 Melbourne Cup. Perce threw ten pounds on it at 14-1 and picked up the sizeable amount of 150 pounds. Good cars and bad blocks of land changed hands for that sort of money in the Depression.

Perce went on to become a licensed bookmaker at the races but it was as an illegal SP bookmaker that he achieved his fortune.

Seizing the opportunity in the 1940s to create illegal gambling casinos, he did it all with style. His venues were plush, expensively decorated, sophisticated, stylish and offered patrons free drinks carried on trays by beautiful women in ball gowns.

His clubs drew what would now be called the 'A list'. On any given night you could find the movers and shakers of almost any section of society, including Premier Askin, the story goes, rubbing shoulders with anyone from politicians to sporting champions, managing directors to tycoons.

Security was assured by the heavyset men with broken noses discreetly positioned to interrupt troublemaking before it started. Big winners at the table were allowed to leave safely with a bodyguard to ensure they got to their car. Privacy from police was also guaranteed.

One night, a man in a dinner suit asked Perce in between bets how he could be so sure police would not raid the place.

'Why don't you ask those two police superintendants over there playing baccarat?' Perce replied.

He won the hearts of the racegoers and punters with his public affection for his great horse Eskimo Prince, which won the Golden Slipper in 1964 and dominated the two-year-old events. Perce won a fortune on that result alone and threw a wad of bank notes to the crowd to celebrate with him, earning the enduring nickname the 'Prince of Punters'.

Apart from being one of the most flamboyant punters Australia has ever known, he was also a pillar of the Catholic Church, a philanthropist and a fixture in society circles. One of his proudest moments was when he was photographed in a tuxedo at a charity function with then Prime Minister Sir Robert Menzies and the Catholic Archbishop of Sydney, Cardinal Norman Gilroy. He compared with Melbourne's notorious John Wren – a generation earlier –

with his mixture of religion, generosity and efficiently run illegal gambling activities.

One Galea story centred on the late media mogul Kerry Packer's younger days and his growing fondness for the punt despite a lack of knowledge and the financial resources to cope.

Sydney Morning Herald racing writer Max Presnell recalls that Packer was in the hole for around $10,000 and Perce was appointed as mediator between SP bookmakers and the Packer family. Galea had not risen to the top in the illegal activities caper without facing some tense moments with intimidating characters but he spoke in awe afterwards of his encounter with Kerry's father, Sir Frank Packer.

'What do you want, Galea?' Sir Frank had growled across a desk.

'Kerry owes ten grand to some hard and dangerous men, Sir Frank, and I suggest you pay,' Galea said.

Sir Frank then opened a drawer in his desk, took out a large book and wrote a cheque.

'I suggest you tell all parties concerned that they never let him on (for a bet) again, otherwise I will close them down and you'll find out what hard and dangerous men are all about,' Sir Frank said.

Years later Galea admitted: 'Unfortunately, we did (let him on)' as Kerry, freed from restraint after his father's death, cut loose with massive bets.

Unlike so many high-profile punters, and with the cash flow from his casino, Galea did not die broke and left a sizeable legacy for his well-liked sons Bruce and Clive. Clive graduated as a respected and respectable solicitor and became a prominent sporting media figure in later years.

Perce knew the value of well-placed sympathisers and paid handsomely to ensure his baccarat and roulette wheels kept turning behind closed doors. Bruce was said to be equally understanding about the need to pay for protection. This might be why he was regularly referred to as Sydney's 'king' of illegal gaming. A witness at an Independent Commission Against Corruption (ICAC) hearing said he was the biggest illegal gambling operator in New South Wales.

And a corrupt police witness admitted tipping off Bruce Galea's Chinatown gambling house about an impending raid. So it made for a tense appearance when he fronted the Royal Commission on 27 July 1995, to face questions.

Registered with the Australian Taxation Office as a professional gambler, Galea had police, whose co-operation he had bought with hard cash, trembling at the thought of the evidence he could give if he chose.

Former Liberal leader of the Opposition and eventual New South Wales premier Nick Greiner was replying to a push from Labor sports Minister Michael Cleary, a triple Australian representative in rugby union, rugby league and athletics, for a legal casino to be built, when he raised Bruce Galea's name.

'The honourable member for Coogee (Cleary) is an expert on casinos because his good mate Bruce Galea used to run and protect illegal casinos right round the city,' Greiner said in Parliament.

But, try as they might, official inquiries could not make Galea reveal his secrets. While police had postured in the public eye, stating their innocence before running off to roll over to the Royal Commission, Galea was like an oyster. He had already refused to answer questions at a closed hearing about whether he ran illegal gambling casinos and whether he had paid corrupt police. This was his last chance to escape jail.

But a Consorting Squad detective sergeant called John Swan, terrified of the consequences if he didn't, lost his nerve and broke ranks. He told the inquiry he regularly picked up $400 a week from Galea to distribute to other corrupt police. He named Galea as a bagman who not only paid bribes to protect his own operation but collected money from other casino operators for police.

Galea, sticking to his own rules, was pragmatic about the inevitable. As well as bringing his toothbrush to court he had also leased out his home and stored his furniture.

'He knew what was coming,' his brother Clive said later. 'He was never going to give anyone up. He never has. Why should he start now?'

Bruce said from the moment he got into the witness box that he would not be answering questions and urged Commissioner Wood to act swiftly to save everyone's time.

'Before we go any further, I'm not going to say anything further at all,' Bruce said in reply to a counsel for the Commission. 'Let's get out of here.

'I'm not running away from anything,' he told Justice Wood. 'I have respect for you. I have respect for this hearing and the Government that put the hearing in place. There's no disrespect for you or this Commission, but I won't be answering any questions today because I'm not in the mood to answer questions. Perhaps when I come back in twenty years. It's just not a go today.'

Commissioner Wood sent Galea to the Supreme Court where Judge Hunt sent him to jail.

Ironically, being jailed gave Galea a Ned Kelly image with the public. A lot of people liked the staunchness so lacking in so many of the bent police who squealed like stuck pigs when sprung with their snouts in the trough.

Maybe Galea had learnt his lesson from a previous appearance before a judiciary committee – ICAC in 1993. The hearing was told Galea had run a gambling club at Kings Cross known as the 77 Club. Later it would transfer to 31 Dixon Street in Chinatown.

Galea told ICAC it was a mah-jong and bridge centre and nothing illegal had ever taken place there. Asked how he was able to make a profit if all the games being played were legal and there was no percentage payment to him for expenses, Galea delighted the public galleries with his answer.

'I make my money from selling sandwiches for $7 and coffee for $5,' he said. 'And I charge people who bring food in from elsewhere.'

There was a pause. Then the Commissioner said: 'I simply do not believe you.'

Galea estimated that the Gaming Squad had visited his place 200 to 300 times for little result. The club had a classic illegal casino lay-out that gave gamblers ample protection from police raids by using lookouts – and being set up to get rid of gambling equipment swiftly.

Even the Commissioner was grudgingly complimentary about the security of the organisation, if not its activities.

'The general appearance was of premises which had been carefully arranged so that if police officers sought entry, there would be adequate opportunity to warn those engaged in illegal activity who could then remove various implements and monies giving the premises the appearance of lawful activity when the police entered the gambling room,' the Commissioner said.

Having the club on the third floor and accessible only by stairs made it more secure. So did half a dozen strategically-placed 'cockatoos' on nearby roofs and in the street. They were experts who could smell a raid before it happened. Especially if a rogue cop had warned them earlier.

The impact of any police raid would be considerably lessened by the approaching officers being spotted early; having to burst through the doors and climb three flights of stairs before breaking through a locked door. Behind which they would usually find people sitting around drinking coffee and playing bridge, chess or other legal games.

Visits to illegal casinos were almost a rite of passage for young males in Sydney from the 1960s to 1980s until gambling in legal casinos and licensed clubs made them obsolete. Two up was especially popular at illegal casinos and specialist two up schools that were well-known and equally well-protected.

One night a man came in to a game with his dog and, although this was frowned on, it was tolerated because the punter was a regular and was trying to end a brutal losing streak. For once, he had a good run and mid-way through the night was betting the maximum $1000 on every throw. Rolling in cash, he tried to get on for more and couldn't, so he bet his $1000 limit – and then bet another $1000.

'You can't do that,' said the boss of the game.

'It's not for me – it's the dog's bet,' came the reply.

Reluctantly, the boss allowed the bet and to his chagrin the punter and his dog both won.

'That's the dog's one and only bet,' said the boss. 'The dog's barred.'

Which is how that dog became the only one in the world ever to be barred from playing two-up.

BEING jailed for contempt made no difference to Bruce Galea's relationships with close friends. A steady stream of mates and associates visited regularly, including former New South Wales Sports Minister Cleary. He and Galea shared a lifelong friendship after meeting as schoolboys at Waverley College, Coogee.

Galea never speaks of his time in jail but it's known to have been incident-free because of his friendship with a couple of heavies he knew well from the gambling world. They made sure he was not a target.

'Bruce didn't get any favours from anyone while he was inside, just what he was entitled to,' a friend says. 'But he had a job in the jail post office and I think he had some sort of respect from the guards because he was doing his time quietly and had never given anyone up.'

Nudging 70 at the time of writing, Galea lives quietly in Sydney's eastern suburbs.

It was ironic that he had spent more time in jail than police who trafficked drugs, took bribes, stole money, assaulted the public and 'fitted up' suspects with crimes they didn't commit.

The public perception of gambling was that it was a traditional pastime and far less dangerous and socially destructive than drug dealing and the foulness of prostitution and pornography.

The man who had informed on Galea, Detective Sergeant Swan, had rolled over after first denying he was corrupt. He recanted to take advantage of an amnesty from prosecution and told the truth.

Swan said most of the consorting squad were corrupt and accepted shares of the money handed out by Galea. He said the police did virtually nothing for their money except that their presence in illegal gambling rooms was a deterrent for criminals hoping to intimidate winners and steal their money.

The only other witness at the hearings sent to jail for contempt was a former policeman named Charlie Staunton who was sacked from the service and became a private investigator with many friends who were still serving officers.

Staunton refused to answer seventeen questions including inquiries about his relationship with self-confessed corrupt officer Trevor Haken and his dealings with other police. Other witnesses described him as a right-hand man to Kings Cross drug peddler Billy Bayeh but refused to elaborate on their relationship.

Staunton cut an impressive figure but that did not help get his tongue moving. He gave selective testimony but shied away from the question of who was responsible for three forged letters of reference given to a judge who had then cut down the usual jail sentence to only 300 hours of community service for Bayeh.

'I take it that you would disagree with the suggestion

that (at least one of the documents was prepared by you,)' asked Commissioner Wood.

'Yes,' said Staunton.

He served nine months in jail before agreeing to talk to the Royal Commission and then only because the Commission went public to say Bayeh had secretly rolled over months earlier.

Staunton conceded that in his 30-month employment with Bayeh he had engaged in corrupt activities with New South Wales police officers, specifically acting as the middle man in payments between Bayeh and Haken that he knew would be passed on to other corrupt police.

As a finale the Commission played a tape of Staunton saying to Haken that the rumoured Royal Commission held no fears for him because being jailed would add to his status and boost the sales of his intended book and film rights.

'Wood can say "You're in contempt," he skited.

'I'll say "mate, fuckin' beauty ... because I'll get a million dollars for the book." I'll get two million for the fuckin' movie.'

The best laid plans ...

– WITH RAY CHESTERTON

15

WHO KILLED
REVELLE BALMAIN?

Police are used to young people
going 'missing' and turning
up within hours or days. The
trouble is, of course, that a
thousand happy endings for those
never really missing hide the
few who are.

NO ONE knew Revelle Balmain was missing, let alone
dead, until she didn't turn up at Newcastle that Sunday
morning.

Her mother had gone to the railway station to pick her
up from the 11am train as they'd arranged but Revelle
wasn't on it. Jan Balmain immediately felt uneasy. Beauty
of Revelle's sort attracts attention, not all of it good. And
it wasn't like her daughter simply to not turn up. She was
conscientious about family things.

At 22, Revelle was a striking girl, with a dancer's lithe figure combined with impeccable cheek bones and feline eyes. To look at, she could have been an actor or a pop star – or a Russian tennis pin-up of the sort admired for her face and figure as well as her forehand. Unlike Kim Hollingsworth, the policeman's daughter she'd met around the modelling and club scene, Revelle hadn't dabbled in cosmetic surgery.

As a model she had just been photographed for the cover of an edgy magazine called *Oyster*; as a dancer she had just signed a contract to perform in Japan for six months. She had trained in ballet as a teenager – including a scholarship year at boarding school in England – and had moved on to modern dance in the hope of breaking into showbiz. In this she was following her mother's own surefooted steps.

Jan, a country girl who had started Irish dancing as a child, had been a dancer on Channel Nine in the network's heyday as the home of variety and *Bandstand*. Now her showbusiness dreams were invested completely in her younger daughter.

But none of that mattered as the clock crawled past noon on Sunday 6 November 1994. All Jan Balmain knew was that Revelle had missed the train, that she wasn't on the next train either and that she didn't know why. It wasn't just a casual day trip: Revelle had specifically arranged to visit her parents for a farewell lunch; next day she was going to Brisbane to rehearse dance routines for two weeks before heading on the Japan tour.

Jan went home and called anyone she could think of who might know Revelle's movements, including her older daughter Suellen. No one knew anything. Then she called all the hospitals in Sydney. By late afternoon she could feel the panic rising. She went to the local police station at Nelson Bay around 6pm and insisted that a reluctant constable file a Missing Persons report.

Police are used to young people going 'missing' and turning up within hours or days, looking sheepish and ducking questions about a one-night stand, a party that got out of hand, a spontaneous trip to the beach or even just a forgotten appointment. The trouble is, of course, that a thousand happy endings for those who were never really missing hide the few who are.

This is the inbuilt advantage a random killer has: if nothing suspicious is witnessed, then the absence of a young adult is not taken seriously by the authorities for days. And, as any homicide detective can tell you, it means that in a handful of sinister cases, the 24-hour 'golden' period for an investigator is lost.

In those precious hours and days, the crime scene is destroyed or compromised, witnesses evaporate and their memories fade. Even relevant security footage can be lost. No one can tell which case is going to have a bad ending – but a mother's instincts run high. In this case, Jan Balmain insisted that the Missing Persons report be forwarded to Sydney. She was right.

Next day, Monday, a policeman called Grahame Mulherin called her from Rose Bay police station in Sydney, his first day there after transferring from the South Coast. What the family did not know then – but has been haunted by since – is that some of Revelle's personal property, apparently scattered from her handbag, had already been handed in to police on the previous day, Sunday.

287

A resident had found Revelle's gear scattered in Ainslie Street, Kingsford on Sunday and had done the right thing, turning it in to Maroubra police. A Constable Alderman handed the gear – a cork-heeled platform shoe, cane make-up bag, diary and keys – to Mulherin, along with some interesting information.

For the police, the fact Revelle's property had been scattered around Kingsford would soon take on some significance. But at first sight it might have seemed that the gear had been tossed away by a handbag thief. Not that any swifter action could have helped Revelle – but it might have led to her killer in time to make a case. Instead, the trail went cold.

What Constable Alderman had uncovered – and told Mulherin – was background about the missing girl that would shock her worried parents. Background that provided the best clue as to what had happened because it pinpointed the last person to see her alive.

Unbeknown to Jan and Revelle's father, Ivor Balmain, Revelle had taken up working for two escort agencies. In a story as old as showbusiness, the girl waiting for her big break was cashing in on her best asset, her looks, to bankroll her tilt at the glittering life that hung just out of reach.

There are always people on the shady side of the showbiz street waiting to exploit the girls (or boys) who choose the fake and desperate 'glamour' of escort work instead of facing the grind of lowly-paid jobs that would reveal the failure of their dreams. It is a way to make fast money to subsidise fast lifestyles. But it's a dangerous bargain, for all the justifications made for it.

What the efficient Constable Alderman had found out from Revelle's flatmate Geoff Spears (and relayed to Mulherin) was that Revelle not only worked for a model agency run by a Kathryn Margaret Hazel-Dawson (known as Lilli) but she worked under an alias for an escort agency called Select Companions, owned by Zoran and Jane Stanojevic. She had also worked for another agency, VIP, under a different alias.

On Monday 7 November, the investigation went off course. It was nobody's fault, really – more a case of misplaced confidence in an honest mistake. An acquaintance of Revelle's, a model called Sonya Lynch, assured the police that Revelle had called Lilli's apartment on Sunday morning and that she (Sonya) had answered the telephone and spoken to her.

Lynch admitted she had been half asleep at the time but insisted that she knew Revelle's voice well and that she was positive it was Revelle on the line. She was not the first witness to get a simple thing terribly wrong.

Faced with this 'evidence', Mulherin was understandably reluctant to assume the worst: that is, that Revelle had been murdered or was even a genuine missing person. The Balmains, and Revelle's older sister Suellen Simpson, were sick with fear but willing to grasp at the hope the supposed Sunday morning telephone call offered. It didn't last. The silence was too much. Every passing hour made it more sinister.

Later that Monday, Mulherin and a detective called Mick Gerondis spoke to local residents who had found Revelle's belongings in Kingsford. Meanwhile, there were other developments in that suburb. The police soon established that Revelle's last known movements were to meet an escort client at his house in McNair Avenue, Kingsford, on Saturday afternoon. The client's name was Gavin Owen Samer, and the police asked the escort agency to tell him to get in touch with them, which he did.

Mulherin asked Samer to come to Maroubra Police Station, which he did at 5.20pm on Monday, accompanied by his then girlfriend Michelle Oswald-Sealy. Samer, then aged 25, wore a zip-necked shirt, partially open. Mulherin noticed scratch marks on his neck, under his jaw and below his ear, and was curious about how he had got them. Asked about these, Samer said he didn't know, and his friend Michelle didn't know either. This wasn't surprising, as she had been away all weekend in Brisbane without Samer, who had celebrated his Saturday night home alone by pawning her clarinet for $250 to treat himself to some paid sex. He had called the Select escort agency and as bad luck had it, Revelle Balmain had taken the job.

The receptionist at Select, Lisa Mancini, knew Revelle had arrived at Samer's house at 3.50pm because, as part of the agency routine, Revelle had called in to say so. Around 6pm Revelle rang in again to say she was leaving Samer's house – but in fact she must have stayed until at least 7.15pm, when she called her friend Kate. The extra time she spent with Samer would suggest she had been offered extra money she didn't want to share with the agency. The call to Kate was the last time anyone had heard from her.

All of this made the police interested in Samer's demeanour, his alibi – and the scratches on his skin. Mulherin asked Samer to take off his shirt. There were more scratch marks on his ribs. He told the sceptical Mulherin he must have got them surfing. When Mulherin asked him about what appeared to be bite marks on his fingers, Samer said he'd hurt them surfing, too, or maybe cut them on string at work. Mulherin wasn't convinced and arranged to have forensic photographs taken of the scratches.

Mulherin had a look at Samer's car but did not find anything suspicious. It had been, of course, 48 hours since Revelle had been heard of, which was plenty of time for potential evidence to disappear. Mulherin took Samer back to his house to see the chequebook that Samer said he'd used to pay the girl. But when they got to the house Samer could not find the chequebook. He could not explain why it had disappeared. The garbage had already been emptied that Monday morning, which meant potential evidence might have been lost. It was becoming clear the investigation was a day behind – and a day is a long time in a suspected homicide. Which, by next day, it was.

Asked his version of events, Samer insisted that he had paid Revelle the agreed amount, plus a tip for staying extra time. Then, he said, he had driven her to a local pub, the Red Tomato Inn. He said that after she had gone into the hotel, he had gone into the bottle shop and bought some Strongbow cider and cigarettes.

Mulherin went to the Red Tomato Inn and showed a photograph of the missing girl to the manager, a Michael Eivers, who said something like: 'Have a look at the people that get in this place – if a girl like that walked in here, the whole joint would stop.' She had not been there, he said.

No member of staff or patron could recall seeing her. And no one could remember a man matching Samer's description buying Strongbow cider and cigarettes – a point that would be proven in the Coroners Court four years later when the bottle shop attendant went through every transaction on the cash register roll for that Saturday night. No one had bought Strongbow cider and cigarettes that night, which meant Samer was lying or suffering delusions.

Next day, Tuesday, detectives spoke to Revelle's close friend Kate Brentnall and took a statement from her about the fact Revelle had called her from Samer's at 7.15 on the Saturday night to arrange to meet Kate around 8pm ... but had never turned up. It was looking ominously likely that she had been killed soon after making the call – 22 hours before her mother raised the alarm with the police.

By now Revelle had been missing more than 60 hours and everyone was taking it seriously. When crime-scene police took photographs of Samer's scratches at the Sydney Police Centre, he knew he was a suspect. He took a lawyer with him.

Two homicide detectives joined the inquiry. They checked that Revelle's pre-booked air ticket from Sydney to Brisbane had not been collected. Any faint chance that she was 'hiding' was gone. The detectives' inquiries that week began the painstaking process of ruling out suspects to isolate the most likely candidate. Samer's girlfriend, Michelle, voted with her feet – moving out of his house with police present in case of any unpleasant scenes. It is not known whether she ever got back her pawned clarinet.

Detectives spoke to Revelle's boyfriend Piers Fisher-Pollard and another friend, Zoe Brock, and were satisfied they were hiding nothing. The same with her flatmate at Bellevue Hill, and so on through a list of friends and acquaintances.

By Friday 11 November, six days after the disappearance, four more homicide detectives were put on the case and the police force went public. They made a televised appeal for information and more people came forward with more of Revelle's belongings found in the streets near Samer's house, as if thrown from a car. A search and doorknock of two Kingsford streets that weekend produced more items – and some information.

One woman told police that she had been in her front garden a week earlier – on the Saturday night when Revelle had gone missing – and had noticed something odd. She had heard something metallic clink as it hit the bitumen near a dark-coloured station wagon which left the scene shortly afterwards. Curious, she had taken a look and found a set of keys, which she'd handed in. It turned out that they were Revelle's.

Why would someone in a car deliberately throw keys away? The detectives thought they knew the answer to that question.

They also knew what the family feared but could not yet admit: they were looking for a body. But they didn't know where to start. Fifteen years later, they still didn't.

ON DAY nine, Monday 14 November, it seemed that someone started running interference. Agnes Situe of 3D World Publishing answered a call from a woman who identified herself as 'Revelle Balmain' and asked to speak to Alex Smart – editor of *Oyster* magazine. Smart was unavailable and the so-called 'Revelle' said she would call back, but never did.

It was never established who the caller really was but police were sure it wasn't Revelle. If it wasn't a stray crank call made by a lunatic it was conceivably someone conniving with a killer or abductor. Oddly, it had to be someone who knew about the *Oyster* magazine shoot, as few would have. Someone still out there may be wondering if their information can be turned into $250,000 reward.

Meanwhile, another mystery was laid to rest – the real identity of the caller who'd sounded like Revelle when she had spoken to Sonya Lynch the first Sunday morning after the disappearance. It turned out to be Sarah Pussell, another model who worked for Revelle's boss and friend, Lilli, at the Satellite Modelling Agency. By accident, Sonya Lynch had skewed the investigation at the most vital stage, persuading the police that Revelle was not really missing and giving the killer an extra day to fudge his tracks.

As police and the Balmain family pieced together information from Revelle's circle of acquaintances, they found out more about her secret life. One model told them Revelle had spoken of meeting a fabulously wealthy Arab sheik, a prominent racehorse owner who had taken her out several times – once to an Arabian horse show – and had wanted her to visit the Middle East with him.

At first the family grasped at this: was it possible the sheik might have whisked Revelle overseas? But the police established the sheik had not been in Australia for months before the disappearance and ruled him out.

Another client was a wealthy Asian businessman called

'Michael' who had wanted Revelle to go to Thailand with him. But he and several other clients were all ruled out.

From day two, investigators had one prime suspect – and nothing would happen to change that. The family did not know what to think. It would take years, says Revelle's sister Suellen Simpson, to accept that she was not only gone – but dead. To accept her death was to give up hope, and in the absence of a body, or conclusive proof, they did not want to do that. Suellen and her parents were tortured by the possibility that people associated with escort agencies might have been involved.

'She had a lot of nasty people around her,' Suellen told the authors. She was unimpressed with Zoran Stanojevic, proprietor of Select Escorts. And she found out that Revelle had fallen out with the proprietor of VIP Escorts – the one who had introduced her to at least one super-rich Middle Eastern client – because he had demanded a bigger share of the fees she charged clients.

Early in the New Year, police spoke to Gavin Samer's relatives, who told them Gavin was argumentative and was known to have been involved in domestic violence. Around the same time, on 25 January 1995, listening devices were put into Samer's house until warrants expired on 10 February. There were no warrants to monitor anyone else.

IT took four years to get the Balmain case to the Coroners' Court, by which time the police, media and the family had exhausted every angle. Photographs and stories had been run on the anniversaries, and the family had distributed posters.

Gavin Samer's family, prosperous and respectable Jewish people in the 'rag trade' in Surry Hills, had done their best to look after their prodigal son's legal interests. The surf-chasing, hard-drinking and marijuana-smoking Gavin was a black sheep compared with his hard-working brother and sister, and the parents had employed him in the family business transporting fabric around in the Holden Commodore station wagon that doubled as his surf wagon.

The family invested in the best lawyers they could afford to represent Gavin. And, according to Sydney police sources, they got what they paid for: a skilled advocate who – four years after the event – was able to suggest enough alternative scenarios to win the main suspect the benefit of the doubt.

The lawyer was able to point to the proprietors of both escort agencies, hint at the possible guilt of other escort clients, and throw a little mud at a circle of friends that Revelle's own mother described in the witness box as 'evil' people who had led her daughter astray.

The main alternative scenario put to the inquiry was that Revelle might have fallen foul of the owner of Select Companions. The agency owner, Zoran Stanojevic, provided contradictory evidence about his whereabouts on the day Revelle disappeared, but consistently denied he had anything to do with it.

He would technically remain as the second suspect. But, to be fair, given that police did not seek evidence of his alibi until years after the event, it was little wonder he was unsure of his movements on a given day. The fact that detectives had not checked the alibis of Stanojevic or another escort agency proprietor in 1994 was not so much due to laziness as their belief that they already had a better suspect.

The coroner heard a claim that a former client of Revelle Balmain, a wealthy commodities trader called Mark Coulton, had told a friend she had been murdered by the agency for 'moonlighting' – doing extra sex work for cash on the side.

'She's ten-foot under and no-one will find her body,' Coulton was alleged to have told a friend but he strongly denied under oath ever making the statement. It was all grist to the mill for the lawyer that Gavin Samer's parents reputedly spent their life savings to hire. A little bit of mud clouds a lot of water.

Jan Balmain's evidence was the outpouring of a twice-broken heart. She told how her daughter, born at Manly in 1972, had been cherished. She had gone to Locket Valley, an Anglican primary school at Bayview, then to St Lukes at Dee Why before taking up the ballet scholarship in England at sixteen.

And she revealed another family tragedy – a far more private one – that could have had a bearing on the behaviour of her doomed and beautiful daughter. When Revelle was four, she had found her fifteen-month old brother Matthew drowned in the family swimming pool.

'And I don't think she ever really fully recovered from that,' Jan Balmain said to a hushed court room. 'It was a very big impact on her life and I know it took us many years to deal with it and we never really knew with Revelle how she dealt with that.'

In court, says Revelle's sister Suellen, Gavin Samer cut a strange figure 'frozen in his seat, glaring at a fixed spot at the back of the room' as if he didn't trust himself to make eye contact with the Balmain family. Or had been instructed not to.

After several sitting days, the deputy state coroner John Abernathy identified Samer as the main person of interest but fell short of recommending charges.

'While Mr Samer certainly had the opportunity to kill Ms Balmain, and rightly in my view is the main person of interest to police, there is no plausible motive proved,' he said.

Samer's evidence could be summed up in a line. He stuck to what he had told the police from the start: that he had dropped Revelle at the pub and then gone home, watched television and fallen asleep.

After the inquest, he was hardly seen in Sydney again.

IN the decade since the inquest, new detectives have come and gone without making any impression on the Balmain file. It was as if the coroner's finding had ruled a line under the investigation. Nothing new turned up to spur fresh efforts and apart from occasional anniversary coverage, the disappearance became just another cold case – one of a list of heartbreaking mysteries filed away at police headquarters.

The families of the disappeared endure a special sort of hell. Their torment is even worse than for relatives of unsolved murder victims because they do not get to lay their dead to rest and then to grieve. When people vanish, it takes years for those left behind to accept that their loved one is dead and never coming home. Some never accept it.

Suellen wrote to the authors in 2009: 'Mum is still having nightmares about what may have happened to her. I am fairly matter of fact to get the information I need but I can tell you it is the saddest story, it rips the heart out of your chest – the shock, the disbelief, the anger, the pain and the not knowing. Except the fact that the murderer is still wandering our streets. Still free.'

The family took years to accept that Revelle was gone forever. But they have never given up hope that her killer will be found and justice done.

In July 2008 the authorities offered a $250,000 reward for any information that would help convict Revelle's killer. The announcement was linked to a statement by the homicide squad that they had used advanced forensic testing to gather new evidence from Samer's former house in Mc-Nair Avenue, Kingsford.

Homicide Squad commander Detective Superintendent Geoff Beresford nominated the house as the crime scene. A 'full forensic search was carried out of the crime scene at Kingsford' and exhibits from the original investigation had been re-tested to establish links with either of two suspects, he said.

'We have fresh evidence as a result of those examinations', he said. 'Following that evidence, coupled with the announcement of today's reward, we are hopeful that we will get additional information that will bring this investigation to a successful conclusion.'

Translated, the police-speak meant they had run DNA tests on Revelle's diary, keys, her make-up bag and one shoe – and were trying to rattle the prime suspect and maybe even lure a witness who no longer felt bound to keep an old and awful secret. The $250,000 reward – up from $100,000 – looked as if it was meant as bait for someone. Or perhaps it was just an attempt at public relations for a struggling Government. Rewards make cheap headlines because they are rarely, if ever, paid out.

One line in the police media release stated that 'both suspects' still lived in Australia. One of the two, however, could hardly get any further away. When five detectives went looking for Gavin Samer to ask him some questions, they found him nearly as far south as he could go – a long way from his Sydney life in every way.

FOR a middle-class Sydney boy who once had expensive tastes, Gavin Samer is slumming it these days.

He first came to Cygnet in southern Tasmania some time in 2005, washed up after the apple-picking season along with other drifters. There are – or were – a million apple trees in the Huon Valley and the annual influx of pickers is part of the rise and fall of the seasons in those parts.

Cygnet is a one-horse town with three pubs – known inevitably as the top, middle and bottom pubs, a description that relates to geographic position rather than their respective quality.

It was to the middle pub that Samer turned up after one apple harvest. The pub needed a cook and the stranger with the dark hair, Roman nose and cheesy grin said he was one. He pulled on the check pants and started knocking out counter lunches – but it didn't last. In a week or so, he came into the bar along the street at the bottom pub, the Commercial, where the proprietor noticed the check cook's pants and promptly offered him a job. This time he stayed.

He eventually acquired a local girlfriend – a big woman who also got a job in the pub. When not working, Samer drank a lot and gambled more, mostly on Keno. One week he won $3500 but kept gambling until it was all gone.

Samer didn't endear himself to anyone but no one took much notice of him until the five Sydney detectives came to town in the winter of 2008. As soon as they hit town, Samer bolted. But after his boss appealed to his girlfriend, he came back to be interviewed voluntarily. First he went to see local 'bush lawyer' Michael Munday, well-known for brushes with authority over alleged abalone poaching, a profession in which he is acknowledged as an expert.

The police interviewed Samer and his girlfriend separately. They made it clear they were there to re-interview him about the night Revelle Balmain disappeared – and to get a DNA sample from him to check against new tests done on her property in Sydney. Samer refused to hand over a DNA sample.

The secret was out. Within hours everyone in the district knew the pub cook was a suspect in a murder in Sydney. People started to watch him more closely – and to recall incidents and look at them in a fresh light. Those who worked with him noticed his colourful turn of phrase. When the cook mislaid his boning knife in the kitchen he would say: 'Where's me fuckin' stabber?'

This was, by all accounts, regarded as the height of good humour by his workmates and girlfriend, a robust former taxi-driver more respected around Cygnet than Samer ever has been. The locals know her pedigree and her form and it impresses them: some among her extended family were known as hard cases and she was considered the equal of any of them in a disagreement. Girls grow up tough in rural Tassie's closeknit families. They can also be broadminded and loyal. Samer's consort does not cramp his style when it comes to drinking his daily quota of VB stubbies and a regular 'choof' of the local green product.

After a big day on the knives and hotplates, slinging parmas and mixed grills, Samer liked nothing better than to retire to the two-storey house they rented from the publican in Solley Court to have a drink and a smoke and play music so loudly it annoyed some of the neighbours. But it wasn't always a happy home.

One night, staff from the pub went to the house after a 'domestic' in which a bench top was damaged by a knife. Another time, after an argument, the woman's Maltese cross terrier was cut in the head and had to be taken to the vet to be stitched up. Samer said later a knife had 'fallen off the bench' and hit the dog's head.

The publican treated the couple well, renting them the house at less than market rate. But since one day in late October 2009, the house in Solley Court has been quiet. Because that was the day Samer and his woman left suddenly. They gave the pub exactly nine minutes notice, threw their belongings into a borrowed van and headed down the road to Huonville. They stayed there in a sort of shed – a former panel beaters' – but not for long. Within two weeks they had gone again. Why is hard to know.

Samer's former workmates wonder if it's anything to do with a black joke the publican had made at his expense. One day in mid-September she saw on the television news that human remains had been found in bushland in Sydney. Later, walking past the kitchen, she yelled something like: 'Hey, Gavin. You want to be careful – they've found a body in Sydney.'

Her attempt at humour backfired. From that day he was agitated, she said later – and once he called her 'a pig'. A month later, he was gone. The last they heard of him he was somewhere around the old penal colony at Port Arthur.

At the time of writing, there was insufficient evidence to charge Samer and in the eyes of the law he remains entitled to the presumption of innocence. And Revelle Balmain's family remains entitled to answers. The case remains open.

Anyone with information on the murder of Revelle Balmain should call Crime Stoppers on 1800 333 000. If they do not wish to claim all or part of the $250,000 reward they can remain anonymous.

16

MURPHY'S LORE

The Cross was Chris Murphy's
patch because so many of his
clients did business there.

THESE days Chris Murphy is in the news again because
he's reportedly dropped more than $100 million into the
financial black hole at the centre of the Opes Prime crash.
Win or lose, Murphy does things in a big way. His way.

Although he has been a millionaire stockmarket player,
a huge punter who rubbed shoulders with the likes of Kerry
Packer and John Singleton in betting rings and casinos, he
made his name and his first fortune as a tough criminal
lawyer.

From the 1970s to the 1990s, the Cross was Chris Murphy's patch because so many of his clients did business
there. One of them, a power lifter, bouncer, prizefighter
and bodyguard known as 'The White Rhino' killed a drug

addict there one night with one punch. Murphy got the
big man off the murder charge because he's good at it and
that's what they pay him for. But he didn't have any illusions: his client might have beaten the rap but that didn't
mean he was innocent. Not much at the Cross is.

Once, in the mid-1980s, Murphy took a respectable
brother-in-law to the Venus Room in the Cross, on a recon-
naissance mission to show the in-law how the other half
lived.

'On stage a naked girl's spraying a sailor with cream and
licking it off,' he recalls. 'My brother-in-law said, "This is
Sodom and Gomorrah – when does the fire start?"' One
club, he says, was closed down after a man was kicked to
death there. Another had bouncers wearing tee shirts with
the slogan We don't call the police. In that place and time,
the cops were just another gang, 'the big blue gang', taking
their whack of the wages of sin. Or maybe more than their
whack.

Murphy knows how the Cross chewed people up. But
like a lot of Sydneysiders, he has affection for the strip.
When the Wood Royal Commission was on in the mid-
1990s, he used to have coffee most mornings at the legendary Bar Coluzzi in Victoria Street, Darlinghurst, alias
Goldenhurst, and once known as Razorhurst in the days
when razor gangs roamed East Sydney between the wars.
In recent times Murphy switched allegiances to another
nearby café, but the scenery is the same: people on the
make in a city on the take.

At the height of the Cross's reputation as Sin City central, Murphy was Sydney's crime lawyer of choice: the

playboy, punter, scourge of crooked cops, friend of people in high and low places, incorrigible performer, self-publicist and patron saint of (almost) lost causes, and champion of the downtrodden.

He still has the shingle and works the odd case. When actor Matthew Newton (subsequently *Underbelly II* star) struck trouble over allegations that he struck his then soapie-starlet girlfriend Murphy agreed to handle it.

His office has a frosted glass door that says 'Christopher Murphy Lawyers Inc' that looks to be straight from a Raymond Chandler novel. When the author came knocking, Australia's most colourful legal identity was talking tactics.

The gravel voice sounds like the prize fighter he once wanted to be, but the tongue's as silver as his hair.

The slightly predatory good looks – part-Romeo, part-rogue – once made him a fixture on most-eligible-bachelor lists in women's magazines. They are no longer as chiselled as they once were. But for a long time the silver hair, dark eyebrows and piercing grey eyes made him a natural to play the part of, say, the handsome lawyer hero in a television show.

Which, in a way, he is: star of his own real-life serial, and writer and director as well. When the author came calling while the police corruption Royal Commission was sitting, Murphy was coaching a thin teenage girl for her supporting role in this week's episode of Murphy's Law.

Behind her sunglasses, her eyes were hollow and red-rimmed, as if she'd been crying or sleepless, or both. Her face was drawn, lip trembling.

Across the street at the Downing Centre local court, news cameras were waiting. Murphy said how shocking it was that the media can hound people like this. He didn't look shocked. He borrowed a jacket from the girl's brother to hide her face, warns her to keep it covered.

It's 9.40am: show time. Murphy flanks one side. The girl's Vietnam veteran uncle takes the other. In the lift, Murphy applies the finishing touches. 'I'm not sure the sunglasses are a good look in court,' he says smoothly. 'Maybe a bit sinister.' She obediently whips them off.

Downstairs, he checks the jacket is rigged over his client's head, takes her arm and steers her expertly across the street and through the media scrum. A photographer brushes briefly with the clerk.

Cut to crowded lift, then a crowded courtroom. Murphy goes through the mob like a kelpie through sheep, herding the girl to a chair. He prowls back and forth, like a pro boxer set to step into the ring. He's not nervous, but she is. A muscle flutters in her jaw.

When the magistrate appears, Murphy sits and studies his papers, polishing his lines for the performance ahead. It's just after 10am. After disposing of some minor matters, the magistrate gives his cue. 'Now, Mr Murphy,' he says, with a meaningful glance at the crowded press seats.

There's an expectant hush. The sort that other Sydney larrikin, Paul Keating, commanded when standing to speak in Parliament.

The pair share more than black Irish looks and growing up near each other in poor Catholic families in Sydney's west. They have a devastating ability to use Australian vernacular the way streetfighters use knuckledusters. Watching them is almost a blood sport.

Murphy rises, managing to be somehow dignified and indignant at the same time. 'The defendant is an 18-year-old person,' he says quietly. 'Outside the court this morning news cameramen were less than a metre from her, sticking cameras in her face.'

He throws the switch to outrage. 'A few minutes ago my young clerk had a rabid, frothing photographer scream at him, "Get out of the way, you f ... idiot!" This is a tragic case involving the death of a young girl but the defendant had nothing to do with that death. She is just outside the jurisdiction of the children's court. She is sitting the Higher School Certificate. She has been terrorised in the press ... terrorised by a newspaper rattling tins asking pensioners to hand over their coins to 'fight drugs'.

'Meanwhile, there are kids up and down the coast comatose from alcohol abuse and the alcohol is supplied to them by someone. But in this case we have rabid, redneck terrorism.

'The incident this morning was within the court confines.

'You must, Your Worship, be getting close to examining this contempt of court.'

Angry Murphy pauses, switches into character as concerned Murphy.

Shooting a worried glance at the girl, he confides to the magistrate and the entire press corps, scribbling furiously: 'She's under the care of a psychiatrist for stress, and is unable to stay at her own home.'

Then the question. 'I am asking Your Worship to adjourn the matter.'

Bingo. Not only does the magistrate adjourn until February, he criticises media coverage of the case in general, and of the girl in particular.

'Clearly, she is distraught,' he says. 'The lines of sadness are etched across her face. It would not serve the public interest for the media to hound and harass her or we may have two tragedies on our hands. This is not a hunting ground. It is a place for justice.'

Murphy couldn't have scripted it better himself. His client still has a long way to go, but in ten minutes he has done what he's best at: changing perceptions, twisting opinion.

The headline in next morning's *Sydney Morning Herald* reads: 'Ecstasy Case: Magistrate Warns Media'. It's the first step in a classic Murphy defence. Another chapter of Murphy's lore.

The first case Chris Murphy did, in 1971, made the newspapers, too. But it was the 'Milperra Massacre' of 1984 that made his name outside the closed world of prostitutes, thieves and drug dealers.

A CRIME reporter, Lindsay Simpson, who co-wrote a best-selling book on the bikie gang war that ended with seven dead in a shoot-out at a hotel car park in Sydney's wild west, quickly noticed that Murphy was no ordinary lawyer.

In a long and tedious case, Murphy 'always kept everyone in court awake', Simpson recalls. It prompted her to write a profile on him early in the marathon trial. She tipped well: Murphy eventually beat murder charges against the 31 Bandido gang members he defended.

Says Simpson: 'He's a genius at telling the story behind

the story, at presenting the human face of crime. He bridges the gap between the law and ordinary people.'

John Slee, a legal correspondent (and qualified lawyer) who has watched courts for 30 years, says Melbourne's Frank Galbally in his heyday in the 1960s is the best comparison with Murphy 'in his aggressive approach to the law and success in the law'. But Murphy, he says, is 'quintessentially Sydney'.

There are other ruthless courtroom tacticians, shameless grandstanders, punishing cross-examiners. But none apart from the late Galbally were loved, hated or feted like Murphy, whose reputation outstrips what he does for a living, and how well he does it.

The highlights of a brilliant career in crime are carefully preserved in scrap-books in his office. How he represented the rugby star Johnny Raper, charged with receiving stolen goods. And Virginia Perger, the prostitute at the centre of the 'Love Boat' sex scandal. When Perger didn't appear at court one day, Murphy told the judge: 'She's been up all night working, Your Honor!'

Another time, representing a Melbourne man with many Victorian convictions but few in New South Wales, he told the magistrate: 'Your Worship, he's a state-of-origin thief.'

When ten South Sydney players were charged with drug offences in 1990, Murphy took the brief. When then Australian heavyweight boxing champion Dean Waters and his father were charged with murder in 1989, Murphy beat the rap.

When Rod Stewart allegedly assaulted a Sydney photographer, Murphy got him out of it for a song. When Jeff

MURPHY'S LORE

Fenech broke a greengrocer's nose, Murphy talked it down
to a $300 fine.

He beat the cannabis charges against soap-opera lead
Dieter Brummer. He's worked for the Rolling Stones and
Joe Cocker.

The New South Wales police don't like Murphy, and he
doesn't like them. But it's true to say they understand each
other perfectly.

One of his personal bests was extracting a massive settlement for a youth called Darren Brennan, shot in the face
in a bungled police raid. The settlement can't be divulged,
but is believed to be at least $500,000. Murphy denounced
the Tactical Response Group, which did the raid, as having
'a fire station mentality'.

The group was later disbanded.

POLICE and Murphy go back a way. Never one to bother with fancy cars, for years he drove a red Honda Civic
with the number plates VERBAL, an audacious swipe at
the once-common police practice of getting convictions by
swearing falsely that an accused had verbally confessed to a
crime but wouldn't sign a written statement.

The car was often vandalised outside courts and police
stations, a good reason not to drive a Ferrari to 'work', even
if he could be bothered with conspicuous success symbols.

He had death threats from corrupt police. They were
just getting back at him, really.

As a teenager and young lawyer, Murphy bred and raced
greyhounds. He named one dog 'Constable Plod' and another 'Oink Oink' – a story he tells, ironically, walking from
his office to the Royal Commission on police corruption.

He laughs gleefully at the memory of punters in the betting ring 'all calling out "Oink Oink!" '

Minutes later, in the huge Royal Commission hearing room, Murphy gets bored and slips outside for coffee. His client, private detective Michael Oliver, won't be on until later in the week, and the evidence is dull.

It wasn't dull last January when Murphy was hauled before the Commission and grilled over his sources for a sensational front-page story he wrote for the Sun-Herald newspaper, for which he has written a racy 'law' column since 1990, mainly poking fun at the police and judiciary.

Murphy's exclusive revealed that the notorious criminal and star informant 'Neddy' Smith had been secretly taped, in his protection cell in Long Bay, boasting to another prisoner that he'd committed six unsolved gangland murders.

Ordered to reveal his sources for the tape transcripts, Murphy played his inquisitors like a matador taunting a bull, prompting the journalist Evan Whitton to reach for the dictionary to define 'bravura'. The words he found were: 'a florid passage or piece requiring great skill and spirit; a display of daring; a brilliant performance'.

Not your average family solicitor.

SO who is Chris Murphy? And what makes him run? Trying to answer that is like trying to trap a bubble of quicksilver: touch it, and it shoots away. The truth is he's not too sure himself.

During a lunch break at the Royal Commission, he sat at his usual corner table in his then favourite restaurant, Tre Scalini, eating his usual snapper with mineral water and pondering the question. Meanwhile, he talks about a dozen other things.

Back then, the fashionable setting fitted Murphy's reputation as one of the Sydney social A-list, a heavy-duty party boy on the prowl with a succession of models and actresses twenty years his junior. Since a heart scare a few years before, he rarely drank, and tried to get more than three hours sleep a night, but he was still a workaholic who played hard. Since then, he has married and had small children.

Some days he used to sit at this table with the then top jockey Shane Dye, whose brashness and success mirrored Murphy's own, and irritated some people the same way. Other days, it might be James Packer, then heir to Australia's greatest fortune he would inherit on the death of his father Kerry. Or ocker advertising guru John Singleton, a mate Murphy once defended on an assault charge. Or television executives negotiating for him to host the pilot of a new show – something he says Clive James told him he should try.

Murphy appeared on one of Geoffrey Robertson's hypotheticals, on drug use. And he defended the villain of the piece, naturally, when *60 Minutes* put the domestic cat 'on trial'.

Like one of Runyon's Broadway wise guys, Murphy knows nearly everybody worth knowing, and many who aren't, in a city where colourful racing identities have rubbed shoulders with colourful advertising, police, media, business, union and political identities ever since the Rum Corps.

His boon companion in the 1980s was David Water-house, brother of Robbie, the bookmaker once warned off every racecourse in the world over the Fine Cotton ring-in.

Another friend, who once shared Murphy's bachelor apartment in the fashionable Connaught Building, was a professional punter who accompanied Murphy on legendary betting expeditions.

Murphy dubbed the pair 'the odds couple'.

Neighbours at the Connaught have included missing hit man Christopher Dale Flannery, media star Richard Wilkins and the late singer Michael Hutchence. It's that sort of place.

Murphy admits being a 'mad punter' since childhood. He won't comment on rumours he used to go high-rolling in Las Vegas with Kerry Packer, but reckons he used to be second only to Packer punting on horses during a purple patch in the 1980s. In one month in 1987 he spun $400 into $3 million at the track – including a win of $365,000 on one horse. He reputedly gave away $300,000 to friends and lost the rest, plus a beach house and other property, on Elders-IXL shares.

That would worry some people. Murphy laughs about it. Boom and bust has been his life cycle, and still is.

His grandfather, Samuel Murphy, was born in the Rocks under the Harbour Bridge, blinded at Gallipoli, and returned to rear eight children. Six of Samuel's sons fought in the next world war.

One, Vincent Birdwood Murphy, brought home a pregnant Welsh bride of gypsy blood, Christine Evans, to a life almost as poverty-stricken as she had left behind in the valleys. Christine, cursed with brains, was determined to give her children the education she had missed.

Chris was the second of six children raised in a two-bedroom war service house in Lakemba, shared with his grandparents. So a total eleven people were thrust together by poverty and fierce family loyalty into a two-bedroom house.

How the knockabout kid from the wrong side of town came to be a sometime millionaire, consort of beautiful women and playmate of the rich and powerful, is a very Australian story.

It's the story of a poor policeman's son who became a cop-baiting lawyer who boasted he 'never did deals' with police.

Murphy doesn't criticise his father, but is ambivalent about him compared with his admiration for his mother. He describes her slaving heroically in factory jobs to keep the family together and educate her kids.

The lawyer in him sees a mile off the inference that he's spent his life getting back at police because of some grudge against his late father. He shrugs it off.

'People look for some Freudian thing,' he says. 'Dad had that violent Irish temper when he was drunk, but so did a lot of other people.' End of subject.

One old friend says she suspects the teenage Murphy once took up boxing so he could 'stand up to' his father. Another tells the story differently. Sure, Chris wanted to be a fighter when he left school, but his furious mother had told him, 'I haven't worked in a factory all this time so you can be a boxer.' Then she burnt his boxing gear.

This seems in character with the feisty woman Murphy describes so fondly years after her death. If there's one reason he didn't end up either behind bars like some of his mates or merely the smartest truck driver in the street, it was his mother's belief in her children.

He worked his way through law at university, digging ditches, driving trucks, doing anything he could to 'make a quid'.

This taught him things law lectures didn't. Then he worked for a veteran criminal lawyer, Mark Murray, who taught him some tricks.

He learned his trade around the courts. The Milperra case won him contacts and a profile and a street reputation as a guy who got results, and the rest is history.

So much for the public Murphy. Privately, he's complex: the tough guy who's a soft touch, a good hater but impulsively generous, the workaholic hooked on adrenalin and deadline pressure, hungering for the applause that comes from making it look easy when everyone knows it's not.

'If there's one thing that motivates me,' he said, 'it's injustice.' He still gets angry when he talks about how, 30 years ago, a sadistic teacher used to hurt boys who wouldn't fight back until the day Murphy, then 16, jacked up.

Then there's loyalty. 'One of my earliest memories is when I was four, coming home on the bus with my sister, who was five. A big girl, about 15, hit her. We went home crying.

Next day Mum got on the bus with us and knocked the big girl out of her seat.'

It's 5.15pm. Murphy watches Channel 10 news to see how his client has been treated. He yells to his secretary to call the station's chief of staff, and grabs the telephone. 'Listen,' he barks, 'about ...'

Five minutes later, he's still talking.

CHRIS MURPHY'S idea of justice is illustrated by an incident involving his youngest sister, Anne. Born with Down's syndrome, she was in her late 30s and travelling daily on a school bus to a workshop for the handicapped when she started to get upset about using the bus.

Murphy found out an 18-year-old schoolboy had been taunting her. He armed himself with a camera, got on the bus, sat next to the culprit and began taking photographs of him.

The youth demanded to know what he was up to.

'Welcome to the worst day of your life,' Murphy said, then told him who he was. 'I'm going to school with you all day, to see what sort of a system turns out people like you.'

In the schoolyard Murphy gave the boy a choice: he would follow him into class or they could go straight to the principal. He chose to go to the principal.

Then it was the principal's turn to make a choice. Either the photographs and the story went in the newspapers or he could arrange a program for pupils to visit the sheltered workshop to learn that handicapped people should be treated decently.

The principal saw things Murphy's way.

17

GEORGE BROWN'S BODY

```
They drove him to the airport
 after the races. They never
       saw him again.
```

IT'S not easy to break a man's arms and legs. It must have taken two men – big, powerful men – to do what they did to George Brown before they killed him.

It was impossible to tell, afterwards, in which order the killers broke his bones. Impossible to tell how long it took, or why they did it that way. Were they trying to get information from him, or sending a warning to others? Or, most barbaric of all, were they inflicting pain for its own sake?

This much is known. Whoever killed George Brown systematically tortured him first. They twisted his left arm until it was wrenched from its socket and the bone snapped. His right arm was shattered above the elbow. 'Like a green stick,' recalls a policeman whose thoughts still often turn to the far-off night he was called to a nightmare.

They used a blunt instrument – probably an iron bar – to do the rest. Both legs were broken above the knee. Death, when it came, was from two savage blows that fractured the skull.

They put Brown's broken body in his old green Ford, and drove into the country for nearly an hour, followed by a getaway car.

There, on a deserted freeway, late at night, they rolled the Ford down a gentle slope about 50 metres off the bitumen.

They doused it and the body in the front seat with what police call 'an accelerant', probably petrol, and set fire to it. Then they drove away – and vanished.

This was not a gangland slaying in Chicago or a drug war in Miami. George Brown was not some Mafia hitman being repaid in kind. He was an Australian horseman.

It happened on an autumn evening in Sydney, in the hours before midnight on 2 April 1984. In the long years since, no one has been charged with the murder. And in the racing world Brown belonged to, where he was liked and is still mourned, the betting is that no one ever will be.

But few talk about who killed him, or why the case remains unsolved. They're too frightened. The sort of 'muscle' reputedly hired to do the job still roams Kings Cross: human pit bulls that attack on command but don't always stop.

THE long road that led a bush boy who loved horses to the big city and violent death starts in the outback. George Charles Brown was born at the bush hospital in the tiny

Queensland town of Miles on 6 December 1945, the last of his parents' four children.

His father, Alan Brown, had fought on the front line in the Middle East, then New Guinea. During the war, his wife, Margaret, and three older children had lived in Brisbane.

Alan Brown was a bushman, and when he was discharged he used a war-service loan to buy a property called Warramoo, 3500 hectares of lonely country twenty kilometres from Miles.

The baby was eleven years younger than the youngest daughter, Jean. Next was Alan junior, known as 'Manny', then Lesley, the oldest.

When George was fifteen months old, his mother died. Jean, then thirteen, became mother, teacher and playmate to the infant with the fair curls and blue eyes. She taught him his first words and, later, to read and write.

She didn't have to teach him to ride. Like his big brother, one of the best horsemen in the district, George loved horses. He sat on a pony before he could talk, rode all over the property behind his sister's saddle at three, and struck out on his own soon after.

There was no telephone, no radio, no television, and no school for Jean and George. Their father and brother often rode off for up to a fortnight, droving cattle, leaving the two home alone.

A lifetime later, Jean's voice would quaver as she described the bond between them. At night, if she was frightened, the little boy would sleep with her. By day, they weren't bored or lonely.

'George rode a pony called Nellie,' she told the author.

'If he fell off he'd get straight back on. He'd always catch her himself. He was so small he'd climb up on a gate to bridle and saddle her. He never had toys or any other children to play with. He had animals.'

The motherless boy's favourite was a motherless foal he reared. He also had a dog, a cat and a calf, and talked to them the way other children talked to each other.

The Browns rarely saw outsiders. George, like Jean, grew up painfully shy with people outside the family.

In 1952, when George was seven, his father died. The property was sold, Jean went to work in Toowoomba, and George went to live with his married sister, Lesley, in the nearby district of Drillham.

He missed Jean. Like many a lonely child, he survived by nursing a dream. He wanted to train horses.

Meanwhile, his brother Manny, a top rodeo rider, had gone to England and become a minor celebrity by training as a bullfighter, an ambition that ended when he was gored at his debut in Spain.

Manny returned to England to breed and break in racehorses. In 1962 he married. George, seventeen, sailed to England to be best man. He stayed five years.

MANNY Brown got his little brother jobs with good horse trainers. He graduated to the stables of Major Peter Cazalet, where he strapped a horse called Different Class, owned by Gregory Peck, and schooled the Queen Mother's horses over jumps. Soon, he was riding in steeplechases.

After 30 rides, and a broken collar bone, he gave up race riding to concentrate on training. He was, he decided, getting too big to be a jockey, anyway. In late 1966, he decided to come home.

Brown became foreman for the then prominent trainer Brian Courtney at Mentone and, later, Caulfield. He met a country girl, Rose Effting, at a dance in 1969. He was polite, barely drank and didn't smoke, a rarity in racing stables. They married at Cheltenham in 1970; the first of their three children was born the next year.

At Courtney's that year, Brown was pictured in a turf magazine holding two of the stable's best gallopers. One, ironically, was the crack sprinter Regal Vista – later the medium of one of Australia's most celebrated ring-in scandals, when he was substituted for the plodder Royal School at Casterton in a scam masterminded by a dodgy car dealer called Rick Renzella.

Soon after, Brown went to Brisbane to work for the trainer Fred Best at Hendra. He worked with another Queenslander with the same surname, Graham 'Chunky' Brown, who remembered him as 'one of the kindest men with a horse you've ever seen.'

When George Brown left to try his luck with a trainer's licence back in Victoria, his mate wasn't to see him again for nearly thirteen years – until the day they met before a race at Doomben that was probably George's death sentence. But that was later.

Brown's first winner was an old horse called Mark's Kingdom, at Nowra, trained from stables behind a house his father-in-law owned at Darlington Point in the Riverina. He worked a few cast-off gallopers, broke in young horses for other people, dreamed of being a city trainer.

The chance came when he landed a job as a private trainer for a retired bookmaker and wealthy owner, Jack Mandel, who had stables next to Randwick racecourse. The boy from the bush was now a bit-player in racing's Hollywood, training alongside the biggest names in the game: T. J. Smith, Cummings and Begg.

A couple of years later he took the plunge as a public trainer, working from rented stables around Randwick. It wasn't easy. Skill and dedication aren't enough to win success in the toughest business outside the boxing ring.

For all his experience, the shy horseman didn't have the flair for self-promotion, the head for figures or the ruthlessness shared by the big names. He landed more than his share of wins with a small team, but winners weren't as regular as the rent and fodder bills.

Brown's dream of making it as a trainer didn't wilt, but his wife did. Rose Brown said later she knew he loved the children, but if it came to spending his last ten dollars on a bag of chaff instead of groceries, the horses would get the chaff. Rose hated racing's uncertainty.

They parted amicably. Rose, her daughter and two sons went back to Darlington Point. They kept in touch, and when he could he'd send money. 'I couldn't fault him, only that for him the horses came before everything else,' she was to recall. 'I still wanted him to be successful.'

SUCCESS came, but slowly. Despite getting a few city winners, Brown struggled to balance the books. Two of his owners, Geoff Newcombe and Dick Keats, arranged a bank loan so he could pay fodder, float and farrier's bills.

'He'd eat bread and jam three times a day to feed his horses properly,' recalls Keats. 'He'd ride work himself. I remember him riding a rogue horse he had. He'd wrap his legs in newspapers for padding to stop the blistering, because he didn't want to spend money on long boots.'

Yet it looked as if Brown was making it. He was getting bigger owners, and had some boxes on the course as well as rented stables in Tweedmouth Avenue, Rosebery. He had been earmarked for a 20-box complex 'on the hill' on the racecourse, a sign of recognition.

Photographs don't do George Brown justice, say those who knew him. For all his travels and his craggy face, he had a naive quality that prompts the Brisbane trainer Laurie Mayfield-Smith to say of him: 'He struck me as somebody out of The Sullivans. He wasn't the gangster type. He never bragged about betting, or anything else.'

But Dick Keats noticed changes in Brown in 1983. One was that he started to wear better clothes, giving up the fusty suits he'd stuck to in the tough times. Keats guessed the trainer was spending cash he hadn't had before. He couldn't guess where it came from.

And it was clear Brown was worried. By the end of that year Keats and Newcombe had trouble talking to him, and he looked haggard. 'His weight dropped right away. He wasn't happy,' he recalls.

BY late 1983 Queensland racing stunk. The smell hadn't yet hit the public, but interstate bookmakers were nervous about bizarre form reversals in Brisbane.

The once-fearless Mark Read and several other big Sydney bookies cut Brisbane bets to a quarter. They knew that when certain people plunged large amounts on Brisbane races, they always won.

The first public whiff of scandal came in early 1984, when two horses, Wishane Myth and Aquitane, were scratched after being nobbled.

Meanwhile, George Brown was more quiet and moody than ever. He wasn't the type to pour out his heart, but relatives caught hints of inner turmoil in telephone calls.

He told his sister Jean and his brother Manny he was getting threatening calls. Specifically, he had been told that his horse McGlinchey 'won't win' on at least two occasions. He told Jean he didn't know 'who would want to do this to me'.

Some time in the two weeks before his death, he told his estranged wife he was worried because he'd been approached to ring-in a horse in Brisbane. He'd been offered 'big money', but didn't want to do it. She asked him who'd made the offer. He said he 'couldn't say'.

Rose Brown was uneasy. On an earlier trip to Sydney for the children to see their father, she had taken 'a couple of funny phone calls' at his flat.

When she had told him about the calls, he passed it off as a former lover of Pat Goodwin, the woman described as his de facto. He blamed the same man for attempting to burn his car in the street a few months before. In light of later events, Rose doubts this.

KAREN Godfrey was only eighteen but in the year she'd worked with Brown – 'he was more like a workmate than a boss' – she'd proved herself. So when he sent three horses to the Brisbane autumn carnival in late March 1984, she got the job, with a veteran stablehand called Jackie Paull.

Star of the trio was Different Class, a city winner named after the horse Brown had strapped for Gregory Peck in England. The others were a promising maiden called Young Cavalier, and a bay filly called Risley.

Risley had won two weak races in Sydney the previous year but was not, on form, any better than 14-1 quoted against her winning the last race at Doomben on 31 March, a Saturday.

Brown flew from Sydney for the races. He met his old workmate 'Chunky' Brown. They had a drink 'for old times' sake'.

If George Brown was surprised – or worried – that Risley's registration papers hadn't been checked early that day or at trackwork during the week, he didn't show it. When stewards called for the papers just before the race, he said they were at the stables nearby. He went to get them, and was fined $50 for being late.

As he saddled Risley he told Godfrey there was 'a bit of money' for the filly, but that he didn't like her chances. It was some understatement. Risley was backed from 12-1 to 8-1 in Brisbane and Sydney – and, curiously, from 14-1 to 4-1 at Wollongong. Someone down south liked her chances. Someone who wouldn't be happy when she ran second last.

When Brown checked the filly after the race, 'he was really quiet,' the strapper recalls.

Brown's sister, Jean, and her husband were there that day. They later recalled he was concerned by Risley's poor run, and had criticised the jockey. They drove him to the airport after the races. They never saw him again.

ARTHUR Harris was in that era an odd man out in Sydney racing. Known for mathematical skill and a phenomenal memory, he is no ordinary racecourse tout, in character or style.

A psychology graduate, philosophy expert and prize-winning classics scholar, Harris turned to setting race markets instead of bridge or chess. For a decade he was a form analyst for the bookmakers Bill Waterhouse and his son Robbie. Until 1985, that is, shortly after they were warned off every racecourse in the world over the Fine Cotton scandal.

David Hickie, a Sydney investigative journalist and racing expert, says of Harris, 'Arthur carries the history of the last 30 years of New South Wales racing in his head.' Harris is also a trenchant critic of his former employers.

This goes back to early 1978, when Robbie Waterhouse was accused of involvement in allegedly trying to nobble a greyhound at Wentworth Park greyhound races, and subsequently attempted to implicate Harris to deflect blame.

Harris never forgave him, although he later worked for the Waterhouses again. In 1986 he appeared on the ABC program *Four Corners*, accusing Robbie Waterhouse of trying to cover up the botched race-fixing.

Both Hickie and former AJC chief steward John 'The Sheriff' Schreck describe Harris as honest, and with racing's interests at heart. That assessment, combined with his passion for keeping records, makes his recollections of some events very interesting.

By the time Risley went to the barrier at Doomben, the Sydney races at Rosehill were over. Harris was amazed at the amount of money being bet on the unknown filly. He was also surprised to see first-hand how much a well-known bookmaker bet on her.

In a statutory declaration he later swore for the New South Wales Thoroughbred Racing Board hearing he stated several intriguing things. One was that he had considered backing Risley himself because of the confidence of a bookmaker he knew, but decided not to, 'as I formed the opinion that on its ratings it would be hard pressed to win ... I did, however, watch the horse closely on the closed-circuit TV. After the race I went to (the bookmaker) and said: "It did absolutely nothing".'

GEORGE Brown was rattled. On the Sunday morning after the Doomben race, the small daughter of a friend walked into a loose box where Brown was treating a horse. He screamed at the child. Her father was shocked; they had never seen him behave that way.

Next morning, Brown met another trainer, Les Bridge, at the track to return a borrowed saddle. Years later, Bridge chooses words carefully as he recalls it. 'He was concerned about some race in Brisbane. He said he was disappointed with the way the horse ran.'

Bridge talks of how much he liked Brown, then adds suddenly: 'I know he was unhappy with what happened in Brisbane.' He pauses. 'I hope they dig up something.' Another pause. 'You hear different things ... but you hear a lot of things in racing.' End of interview.

That Monday night, Brown was due for dinner at his partner Pat Goodwin's house, a few streets from his Rosebery stables. He didn't make it.

Goodwin later told police she had called him about 6.50pm to say there'd been a call from Brisbane. She said he told her: 'It's been a quiet night ... I will leave here at 8 o'clock. I have to drop in on – '

Then he had paused and said: 'I'll be there at ten past eight.' Goodwin claimed not to know who he intended to see.

An owner, Ted Hendry, rang him twice, at about 7.20 and 7.40, and spoke briefly. Rose Brown rang either just before or just after Hendry's second call. She needed money to take their son Wayne, then eleven, to Sydney to see a specialist. It was a request he would never usually deny, no matter how broke.

But this time, she says, he 'wasn't himself'. He curtly accused Wayne of 'bunging on' the illness. They were staggered. He had never acted like that before.

'It didn't sound like him,' she says. 'I wonder now if he was with whoever killed him.'

TRAFFIC was light on the F6 freeway at Bulli Tops, near Wollongong, in the hour before midnight. But one driver noticed a car on fire about 50 metres off the northbound lane, and reported it at the toll booth, 23 kilometres away.

A freeway patrol came, but reported the fire was no threat to traffic. Later, someone called the Fire Brigade, which relayed the call to the Bulli volunteer brigade. It was 28 minutes past midnight.

After putting out the fire, the volunteers saw something in the passenger seat of the blistered green Ford. It was a body. Or what was left of it.

When Senior Constable Peter Strik, of the crime scene unit, arrived the body was lit up by flood lights, but barely recognisable. The hands, feet and forearms had been burned away.

'It was just a lump of charcoal,' Strik was to say. 'There was no way it could be identified by sight.' Although he didn't know about the broken bones until the post mortem was done, he could see the stump of the left arm twisted from its socket. He automatically treated it as murder.

'It just didn't look right. I've always wondered why we never got anywhere with that one,' he muses.

ARTHUR Harris was asleep in the unit he used as an office on Tuesday 3 April, when the telephone woke him at 6am. It was Joe Amphlett, who worked for the Australian Jockey Club. He sounded alarmed. He said police believed a body found in a burned-out car overnight was George Brown, and that he'd been murdered.

Bad news spreads fast. About 7am, Harris declares, 'I had occasion to ring (a racing identity) at his home ... towards the end of this discussion I said to him: "Incidentally, there is a scandal at Randwick. The police are everywhere. They think trainer George Brown may have been murdered." (The identity) said he'd already heard.'

At Randwick races later that week Harris approached a punter well known at the time for landing huge plunges on Brisbane races.

In his statement Harris swears: 'I asked him what he knew of the George Brown murder. He said: "He was supposed to do a ring-in ... He got cold feet and did not switch horses. The money went on SP and they lost heavily. They sent a couple of men around to teach him a lesson. The men were high on drugs and went too far".'

Two years later, in the homicide squad offices, Harris says a detective called Jim Counsel told him the same story, of 'two men who flew from Brisbane on the Sunday before George Brown was murdered and flew back the morning after he was murdered with plenty of cash. They purchased a new sports car.'

RARELY had so many police worked so long on a murder and produced so little. From the start the case was clouded by two flimsy theories that attracted headlines and fed rumours.

One, easily discredited, was that Brown owed SP bookmakers $500,000. Friends and relatives told police he'd always been a small bettor, rarely betting more than $50 for himself. Experts said Brown's financial affairs showed no sign of big punting.

Then there was the theory – pushed hard by certain racing and media people within hours of the killing – that it was a 'crime of passion', a brutal variant on the staple homicide police call a 'domestic'.

In fact, the cold-blooded abduction, torture, murder and public display of the broken body had the hallmarks of an underworld execution by two or more killers, with the intention of creating fear. Some domestic.

A detective who worked on the case claims his inquiries showed only $3000 was bet on Risley nationwide. Therefore, he says, the murder was probably not connected with a ring-in gone wrong, and was more likely a 'crime of passion'. Intriguingly, though, the head of the New South Wales homicide unit in the mid-1990s disagreed, saying the cause was still being investigated.

David Hickie, who checked with bookmakers at the time, says tens of thousands would have been bet on Risley to force interstate odds from 14-1 to 4-1.

John Schreck, later in charge of cleaning up racing in Macau, dismissed the chances of Brown's murder being a domestic as 'a million to one and drifting'.

A MONTH after the murder a journalist, Errol Simper, interviewed many racing people, then wrote a story that included these telling paragraphs:

'Besides sadness, there is a considerable amount of silence among those who knew the trainer. They prefer not to discuss his death and, if they do discuss it, many refuse to be identified.

'Some are seemingly – and understandably – very nervous. If nerves aren't the explanation, then the matter may be even more strange. Taut, blanket silence is hardly a typical reaction from people who have just seen an innocent and respected friend and colleague outrageously murdered.'

A quarter century later, the silence lingers. Racing people once close to Brown stayed nervous, tight-lipped and anonymous all that time.

'Money got a bit short for George,' explains a former Sydney trainer cryptically, 'but he got cold feet. Honest people find it hard to do dishonest things.

'Nothing will ever be opened up. It's too big. I think you're better off letting sleeping dogs lie. Karma will get the bloke behind it. He's stewing in his own juice.'

Another friend of Brown's says he is angry at what happened, but scared. 'What you are doing is terrifying. I have made phone calls and been told to drop it. It's too dangerous for me and my family ... It's too big, too political, for the police.'

But they all agree on one thing. That George Brown died because he did not substitute another horse for Risley.

WAYNE Brown, blond and blue-eyed, is hauntingly similar to his father, George. For years, at the races, people would stare at him, then introduce themselves as 'friends of your father's'.

They feel sorry for him. Some, he senses, are even ashamed that racing somehow led to the terrible thing that happened when he was a kid. Back then, his mother says, he would sometimes ask her: 'Mum, how come they can find all these murderers, but not Dad's?'

Wayne, as his father did, had an ambition to be a horse trainer. Like his father, he worked with horses since before he left school: strapping, riding work, the lot. Later he drove a horse float to save the money to help set up. He even married an accountant who was working for the Bart Cummings stable.

Some day, he once told the author, he'd train at Randwick. Some day he'd get stables on the course the way his father was going to. Meanwhile, George Brown's boy has a friendly word for everyone in the racing game.

Almost everyone, that is.

The New South Wales homicide unit suggests that any information about George Brown's death can be supplied anonymously.

18

FINE COTTON
UNRAVELLED

'It was stupid and the blokes
who did it were so foolish
they made the Three Stooges
look like High Court judges.'

MONEY talks. In racing, sometimes it shouts, which is why bookmakers around Australia were alarmed about Brisbane racing well before George Brown was tortured and killed in April 1984.

Something stunk in Queensland, and the stench reached Sydney. Money poured onto Brisbane horses that showed fantastic form reversals. Among the 'smarties' in on the racket were some who plotted their moves in the pubs, clubs and coffee joints in the Kings Cross strip. People whispered that Sydney gangsters and racing identities like Mick Sayers and George Freeman had inside knowledge about the Brisbane connection.

'The same guys keep backing the right ones – and they always won,' said swashbuckling bookie (and betting plunge specialist) Mark Read about the strange events north of the border.

Then came the Fine Cotton debacle. The 'ring-in' (secret switch of a quality racehorse for the battling bush horse Fine Cotton) might have won a fortune for those in on the rort, if the original plan had been followed. But by the time the race was run in the Spring of 1984, the plot had turned into a farce that disgraced not only the obvious perpetrators but two of Sydney's biggest racing identities – father and son bookies 'Big Bill' and Robbie Waterhouse.

The Waterhouses never got jailed – as two of the hands-on organisers did – but they (and others) were disqualified from racing for life for 'prior knowledge' of the ring-in, a penalty later reduced on appeal. Speculation about the two Waterhouses' alleged role in the rort has never faded despite their claim they were just 'following the money' by backing the horse.

This is how it happened, though some details – and some players' identities – remain cloudy.

ON Saturday 18 August 1984, local apprentice jockey Gus Philpott was legged on a runner in the Second Commerce Novice at Eagle Farm. It was an ordinary race and, as far as Philpott knew, he was on a very ordinary horse: an eight-year-old plugger from the backblocks that should have been around 40-1 in a city race. But for reasons Philpott couldn't fathom, the horse with no form had been backed off the map. As he cantered to the start the cash flooded in for Fine Cotton all over Australia – and in betting shops in

Vanuatu, Fiji and Papua New Guinea. The coast to coast plunge was worth pay-outs of around $2 million – enough to buy a street of houses in 1984.

The dogs were barking that something dodgy was on and so even the sleepy Queensland stewards were watching hard, aware that their already-tattered reputations were under the microscope. Philpott rode the now hot favourite (backed from 33-1 to 6-4) perfectly, winning in a photo finish. What he didn't know yet – but the world was soon to find out – was that his mount was really a multiple city winner called Bold Personality, crudely dyed and painted to look more like the country cousin, Fine Cotton. It was a lousy disguise, even if the lunatic betting hadn't raised suspicion.

Even before the horse got back to the winner's stall, the crowd was jeering 'Ring in!' and the dye was starting to run down the imposter's legs. By then a worried steward was asking the trainer, shifty small timer Hayden Haitana, for the horse's registration papers. Haitana, as much a con man as a trainer, went through the motions of searching for the papers then expressed surprise that they were 'missing'. The steward obligingly suggested checking with the owners for the papers and reporting back to the stewards' room. Haitana knew a chance when he was given it: he gulped down a beer at the bar then walked off the course – and vanished.

To the embarrassment of police in several states, he wasn't seen again until he came out of hiding to appear on *60 Minutes* many days later to plead he had acted under duress.

It was an obvious line of defence and the chatty Haitana was no stranger to telling lies – but that didn't mean he wasn't genuinely frightened. Even if he hadn't raised the spectre of George Brown's torture and death five months before, it loomed large. And he did raise it – claiming a standover man had threatened him and his family: 'He showed me his gun and then he said "Look at this here – do you want to end up like the trainer Brown?" '

The case made headlines right up until Fine Cotton finally died in early 2009 in suburban Brisbane, aged 32. It was a notorious debacle. As an anonymous 'insider' told a Coffs Harbour reporter many years later: 'It was stupid and the blokes who did it were so foolish they made the Three Stooges look like High Court judges.'

But the funny thing is that the plotters might have got away with it but for a stray kangaroo.

Maybe.

AS HORSES go, Fine Cotton was an unlikely celebrity. A plodding bush galloper with neither flash pedigree nor performance, he was only one step ahead of the knacker's van most of his career.

So when a stranger offered to buy the eight-year-old at a country meeting in early 1984, his owners jumped at it. They couldn't have guessed the gelding would be at the centre of a scandal that would haunt racing and bemuse Australians for a quarter century.

Key aspects of the Fine Cotton affair are still a mystery – a fact that galls some authorities. Most intriguing is the question of who masterminded the nation-wide plunge on the horse that raced as Fine Cotton at Eagle Farm that day.

It is almost certain the same people were connected with the previous series of 'form reversals' that made Brisbane racing stink of corruption in the early 1980s.

The generally-agreed facts of the case are these: in early 1984, a smart Sydney galloper, Dashing Soltaire, was bought for $10,000 and sent to Queensland, where two men began combing country tracks for a cheap, slow horse that resembled him. They found Fine Cotton. Like Dashing Soltaire, he was a brown, had similar white markings and was foaled the same year (1976) so would have at least a partly correct brand on his shoulder. He had won a few bush races but was well past his limited best.

The two horses were kept in training and, in August, Fine Cotton was given several starts within a few days to ensure Brisbane stewards were used to seeing him race and so would make only a cursory check at a later date.

Meanwhile, both horses were transferred to Hayden Haitana, a transient Coffs Harbour trainer. Why him? It appears that his brother, jockey Pat Haitana, had met an inveterate hustler and horse dealer called John 'The Phantom' Gillespie while having a 'holiday' in Boggo Road jail in Brisbane some months before. Inevitably, Gillespie spruiked a 'foolproof' way to make money by substituting a high-quality horse for a poorly performed one in a weak race, then betting up big.

Pat Haitana suggested his brother Hayden – then training a small string in Coffs Harbour – as the man to prepare the plunge horse. Within weeks, the jailhouse scheme was turning into reality, with the purchase of Dashing Soltaire and Fine Cotton.

Fine Cotton was entered for the Second Commerce Novice at Eagle Farm on 18 August. So far, for the bad guys, so good. But in racing, disaster is only ever a hoofbeat away, and the scheme was derailed not only by the lunatic leaking of the 'mail' about the sting, but by the sort of accident that makes racing the ultimate game of chance.

With only days to go, the horses were being trained from a paddock on an isolated property near some bush, and a kangaroo startled Dashing Soltaire, which galloped away and hurt itself. Had Fine Cotton been hurt, it wouldn't have mattered. But, as usual in racing, good horses get hurt and slow ones don't.

Haitana knew the plan was now a disaster in the making but when he tried to pull out he was told it was too late – and he was assured that stewards, police and even racing writers had been 'fixed'. Haitana would later say he would rather risk being caught than anger those he said were acting for the scheme's backers. Already the tip had been leaked to far too many people, which would mean an avalanche of money on race day.

It meant he and his helpers had to find another substitute – quickly. Apparently desperate to appease 'heavy' people involved, they bought Bold Personality, a city winner with ability – but the wrong colour and markings. He was a bay, not a brown, and did not have white on his legs in the same places as Fine Cotton. He was also foaled in 1977, not 1976, which meant every identifying brand on him was different from Fine Cotton's. Added to which was the fact that too many people were by this time a party to the plot, not only because Haitana talked too much when he was drinking, which was most of the time. An anonymous racing source told a reporter years later: 'Hayden was notorious for being a bullshit artist, particularly when he'd been drinking, which was pretty frequent. He could have sat around the bar and described the plan down to the tiniest detail and not a single person would have believed a word.'

The black comedy just got worse, according to the same source. Stand-in strapper Tommaso Di Luzio was despatched to Coffs Harbour to pick up Bold Personality. But Di Luzio reportedly left the horse sweltering in a heavy rug for the hot six-hour float trip north, ensuring it arrived in Queensland distressed, severely dehydrated and in no condition to race.

Panicky, Haitana decided to drench the horse to overcome the dehydration but while he went to find the necessary gear, some 'helper' stupidly forced a tube down the horse's nostrils, causing it to bleed.

In a scene a sitcom writer could hardly make up, the bumbling crew attempted to dye Bold Personality's coat to make it look more like Fine Cotton. Clairol hair colouring failed and whitewash wouldn't stick to the horse hair.

In desperation, they spray painted white socks on him. In the end, the horse was such a mess that Haitana bandaged its legs to cover them and hoped for the best. It was ridiculous, and doomed to failure, but he didn't fancy the alternative. Even after he and con man John Gillespie were jailed over the scam, and other associates were warned off racing for life, they never blew the whistle on the masterminds they tacitly implied were behind it.

Persistent allegations that Robbie and Bill Waterhouse were behind the Fine Cotton ring-in surfaced within days. Both Waterhouses denied planning the sting but could not deny heavy betting on Fine Cotton and were subsequently outed for life. Fingers were pointed at racing and public officials, politicians and police – even a Catholic priest, Father Edward O'Dwyer, who was sprung leading a plunge on Fine Cotton at Kempsey dog races.

Stripped of his licence when warned off after the Fine Cotton scandal, in 1989 Robbie Waterhouse informed the Australian Jockey Club he 'did not seek to dispute' its findings about his involvement and expressed 'remorse'. In 1992, he was sentenced to eight months of weekend detention for lying to the Racing Appeals Tribunal over the ring-in.

In 1998 he was allowed back onto racecourses and in 2001, after an orchestrated lobbying campaign, he was handed back his bookmaker's licence, a move cheered by boosters and jeered by those with long memories. But it came at a cost: in the meantime his family had publicly torn itself apart in a feud that began over the Fine Cotton debacle.

THE Waterhouses are bold personalities, but not brave ones.

One advantage of the best private-school education money can buy is that since the days when their forebears ran cockfights, sly-grog and waterfront rackets, they've rarely got blood on their own manicured hands.

So, on the morning Robbie Waterhouse dealt his brother David the blow that has plunged the family into the vendetta now threatening to destroy it, he used a telephone, not a dagger.

But the wound went deep, and the public airing of the feud made sure it would not heal for years. Perhaps ever.

The call from Robbie came early on 21 September, 1992, from the house with the million-dollar harbour view in Clifton Gardens that he shares with his wife, the fashionable horse trainer Gai Waterhouse, sometime actor and only daughter of the late champion trainer T.J. Smith.

What his elder brother said that morning devastated David. Just how much was revealed three years later, on the fourth day of the Australian Jockey Club hearing into Robbie Waterhouse's application to be allowed back onto racecourses, when the tall man let slip his deadpan mask for a few minutes after hours of tough questioning by Robbie's counsel, Frank McAlary QC.

David's unblinking croupier's eyes, which had gazed without expression somewhere above the committeemen's heads all day as the barrister blustered and bullied, flashed as he recalled a conversation that seems to be seared into what his associates describe as a photographic memory. The soft voice, so often hard to hear, was painfully clear to everyone in the room.

'Robbie said, 'You have no redeeming features. Get out of our lives and get on with your own life.'

'I said to him, 'What about the money I've loaned you?' He then said to me: 'We have just used you'.'

The hearing was hushed. Either this was a painful insight into a man's heart and a family feud, or David Waterhouse is a brilliant dramatic actor. A profession for which, some might say, his family has both the looks and natural aptitude.

343

Earlier, the lean man with the patrician profile and tortoise-shell glasses had told the hearing he'd lent Robbie $220,000 and their father, Bill Waterhouse, similarly large sums to cover betting debts and legal costs between the Fine Cotton scandal of 1984 and a marathon court case in 1989-1990 (when another branch of the family sued for a share of the multi-million dollar Waterhouse estate).

David, odd-man-out of the three children of 'Big Bill' Waterhouse and Suzanne, the former dental nurse he married twice, was never quite the colourful racing identity his father and brother became.

He once tried bookmaking, was a successful professional punter for a while, sharing the Waterhouse taste for gambling, but he turned also to art collecting and the world outside the race track.

When Robbie and his parents turned their backs on David – apparently dismissing him as an accident-prone nuisance – it seems they under-estimated the bitterness of his reaction.

For once, in a family that for generations had done much for gain something meant more than money. Here, among the skyscrapers of tinsel town, was the ancient story of betrayal of brother by brother.

Cain and Abel in Zegna suits.

ACCORDING to a close friend, David Waterhouse was 'in shock' after his brother's rebuff. The friend (afraid of being identified 'because the family are very spiteful people') says David had to fly to a country race meeting later on the day he took Robbie's call. He rang his wife, Jeanette, from

Bankstown airport, and said, close to tears: 'This is it. I'm finished with them. I'm so glad I've got you.'

At that point, the relationship with his father and brother could have been patched up, Jeanette later told friends. But, to David's disappointment, no member of his family contacted him – not even his mother, whom he'd taken on a long trip to Europe some time before, and supported in her strange, fractured marriage to his father. She had famously tolerated the fact that after re-marrying her following a lengthy separation, Bill had maintained his Thai 'mistress'.

The story is that David has seen Robbie only twice since the telephone call and was fobbed off both times when he asked for payment of the debt. He hasn't spoken to his father since 1992.

Meanwhile, David was concerned because he suspected his father and brother were selling off assets that were part of a family trust set up in 1962, in which he has an equal third share with Robbie and their sister, Louise Raedler Waterhouse.

The reasons for the family feud spilling into the AJC committee room at Randwick in the mid-1990s go back to the ring-in scandal of 1984. After Fine Cotton, the Water-houses' intriguing web of finances and business interests – from Fijian betting shops to Swiss bank accounts and suburban pubs – started to unravel. And so did the family loyalty they'd once prized.

They had problems. Warned off every racecourse in the world, Bill and Robbie weren't able to operate as licensed bookmakers, choking off a cash supply. Their assets were frozen for several years pending the court case brought in 1989 by Martin Waterhouse, the son of Bill's brother, Charles, who died in 1954. Then, after paying huge legal fees, Bill and his former bookmaker brother Jack had to settle assets worth millions on Martin, his two brothers, sister and their mother.

The result: Bill and Robbie Waterhouse were two-time losers and, by millionaire standards, short of ready money. They had (and still have) the trappings of wealth: harbourside homes, luxury cars and overseas trips. But when David asked for his money, they brushed him off.

It may well have been their biggest mistake since Fine Cotton.

THE festering dispute was brought to a head, according to David's version of events, after publication in 1990 of a book called *The Gambling Man*, nominally written by Kevin Perkins but allegedly produced by Bill Waterhouse, who in 2009 would produce another questionable piece of biography.

The Perkins book led to defamation actions, and David was incensed when his father and brother implicated him in these by alleging he was a co-author.

It was this, David claims, that prompted him to swear affidavits about the alleged extent of Robbie's involvement in the Fine Cotton case, an action which made him star witness at the Australian Jockey Club hearing into whether Robbie should be re-licensed.

In the affidavits, and in the AJC hearing, David painted a vivid picture of his brother detailing his part in the ring-in as the pair walked the streets outside Robbie's house in September, 1984.

'There were just the two of us,' David told the hearing.

He said Robbie had told him: 'I paid all the expenses except for the horse. Gary Clarke (an associate) has been the front for me at the Brisbane end. I have nothing to fear if everyone stays solid.' Robbie had allegedly added he'd 'planned the ring-in before he went to England for the Derby' in June that year.

David said he had lent his father $300,000 soon after the ring-in, money he says was needed to help pay punting debts of almost $1 million plunged on the Fine Cotton ring-in. He said Bill told him two days after the race: 'We could have made millions if it had come off.'

David, to use his brother's alleged phrase, 'stayed solid' for ten years. The first sign that the estranged brother and son would turn against his family came when his solicitor arrived at the Waterhouses' North Sydney office in mid-1995 with a message that David had 'a hot affidavit' naming Robbie as organiser of the Fine Cotton affair.

The deal was that David would sign and file the affidavits unless certain conditions were met.

But what were they?

Louise Raedler Waterhouse, an elegant, fine-boned woman with a sleek bob of dark hair, sat at her brother Robbie's side throughout the hearing, and clearly supported him. She testified that the solicitor relayed a demand for $1.5 million – and the message that if it wasn't paid David would present the affidavit to the authorities.

But David swore that he asked only to be taken out of the defamation proceedings. Asked earlier about his sister's testimony, he dismissed it as 'creative accounting'. He confirmed seeking $3 million through the courts from the family trust, but denied the affidavit was an attempt to 'blackmail' his family into paying up early.

Either way, Bill Waterhouse's reported response to the offer was blunt. Asked what her father had said, Louise answered delicately: 'He said David could go and get something-ed. He used a rude word. My father is old-fashioned in some ways. It is the first time I have heard him say that word.'

If Bill Waterhouse thought he could bluff his youngest son, he was wrong. David had found the nerve to get blood on his hands.

THE younger Waterhouses are Sydney's Kennedys. Handsome, clever, well-educated and well-dressed – but unable to shake off the shadow of bootlegging forebears and the suggestion that under the glossy exteriors are people who take shortcuts to get what they want.

To see Robbie Waterhouse squirm around the Fine Cotton accusation reminded a watcher of another pretty boy who once had the world at his feet: the late Teddy Kennedy, skewered by Chappaquiddick. In both cases, neither man could allow himself a straight answer.

The truth is, there is an element of voyeurism in the spectacle of a wealthy, well-known family destroying itself. It's like watching a car crash in slow motion. A sense of grim satisfaction filtered from many onlookers in the AJC hearing room where the drama unfolded at the end of 1995.

If he sensed any antipathy, Robbie didn't let it show.

His charm is legendary, his voice smooth, his smile quick. One of his in-laws says he studies books on how to project the right body language – to come across as plausible and frank without making any damning admissions.

He drew well in the genetic lottery; at 41 his boyish good looks and dark hair made him look years younger. In 2009, the hair was grey but he still had the looks inherited by son Tom (also a brash young bookie) and daughter Kate, one of racing's best-known public faces.

The diminutive nickname 'Robbie' indicates a parental favourite, and hints misleadingly at a softness that few detect in the character of the eldest son of the most ruthless bookmaker in Australian racing's chequered history.

If there is a fault, he looks slightly effete, far more like his small, fine-boned and once-beautiful mother than his stout and imperious father. But Robbie inherited his father's calculating mind, the mind that took a shady publican and small-time bookie's son through law in the 1940s – when other young men were fighting a war – then from the bar table to the betting ring, fame and fortune.

THE Waterhouse history would make a television serial, a sweeping saga of a family on the make, rolling on from the Rum Corps for six generations.

In fact, part of the family history has already become fiction. There is a story – so often repeated in newspapers and at least two books since the 1950s, that it passes as fact – that the Waterhouses are descended from an officer and gentleman, a Lieutenant or Captain Henry Waterhouse, who arrived with the First Fleet in 1788, and later helped John Macarthur import the first merino sheep.

There was an officer called Henry Waterhouse in the First Fleet, who went home and later returned with the Third Fleet. But a genealogy expert commissioned by Bill Waterhouse in the 1960s to track down this socially-desirable connection wrote a 12-page report stating that after 'rather exhaustive research ... my conclusion is that no legitimate relationship exists to Captain Waterhouse'.

The captain fathered one daughter, Maria, who died childless in England in 1875. The expert stated the racing Waterhouses' real ancestor was one Thomas Waterhouse, an apprentice carpenter at Darling Harbour in 1828, and son of a Windsor farmer of obscure origins.

This must have disappointed the king of bookmakers, because he allegedly ignored the research he'd asked for – instead citing Captain Henry Waterhouse as a forebear whenever something was being written about the family.

Regardless of pedigree, or lack of it, for almost 200 years Waterhouses have made fortunes as bookmakers, hotel keepers and builders. Those are the official occupations. Stories also abound of smuggling, cock fighting, black marketeering and sly-grogging.

'Lights were put under the wharves to try to stop them smuggling stuff off the ships at night,' asserts one longtime observer who has been on first name terms with three generations of the family. 'They were in everything.'

The taste for fighting cocks goes back to Bill and Jack's great-grandfather, Thomas Waterhouse, a famed streetfighter who had thirteen children, ran the Greengate Hotel at Killara and most of Sydney's cockfighting. The blood sport, illegal but still strong in the 1950s, was run for betting, and where there was betting, there were Waterhouses. Preferably with the odds in their favour.

At his peak in the 1960s and 1970s, Bill Waterhouse was one of the biggest and, it seemed, most fearless bookmakers in the world. He took on and beat huge punters like Frank (later Sir Frank) Duval, known as the 'Hong Kong Tiger', and Felipe 'Babe' Ysmael.

Robbie's meteoric rise from country racetracks to the rails at Randwick in just seven years, something that took others 25 years, raised eyebrows. His father's view ('He's a genius') didn't cut ice with those who pointed to the family's wealth and influence as a more likely explanation.

Although the Waterhouses' potent political 'pull' in Sydney has waned since Sir Robert Askin was the state's premier, their name for decades drew a nervous reaction among most who know them and many who don't. On the record, associates and relatives are tight-lipped about 'Big Bill' and Robbie. Off it, they have more to say, little of it complimentary.

Racing people tell black jokes about the family. Says one former bookmaker: 'They say if Jesus Christ had been a Waterhouse, Pontius Pilate would have been crucified.'

When Robbie married the legendary trainer T. J. Smith's daughter Gai in 1980 it was hailed in the social pages, rather cloyingly, as a 'fairytale wedding' between the 'prince and princess' of racing.

Wherein lies a sub-plot to the Waterhouse family war – the falling out between Tommy Smith and his brother, Ernie, over the Waterhouse connection. Ernie Smith's thinly-veiled distaste for his niece's choice of husband exploded into acrimony when Gai took over from him as stable foreman – cutting out the prospect of Ernie's son, Sterling, taking over the Tulloch Lodge empire when Tommy retired.

Once asked his reaction to the Waterhouses' troubles, Ernie Smith's retort was short and sharp: 'I've never had anything to do with them. I've never mixed with them, and never will.'

19

McMILLAN THE VILLAIN

> Working on the theory that
> desperate prison escapees do
> not use umbrellas, he opened
> the brolly, held it close
> to his face and strolled
> off to find a taxi.

WHEN the police came for David McMillan, they used a sledgehammer on the door. They found him in bed with the doomed and beautiful Clelia Vigano, the society restaurateur's daughter who would later die in a prison fire.

McMillan was 25 then, already an accomplished drug trafficker who had parlayed a polished line of patter, a photographic memory and multiple passports into so much money he had trouble spending it. Sometimes he would fill a plastic bag with cash and wander Melbourne, buying beautiful things he didn't need: sports cars, clothes, the latest electronic gadgetry. He was the most charming of villains: a 'conman cum commodity dealer,' one investigator called him, in grudging admiration.

The charm meant a lot of Melbourne people got to like him while he was spending money. The villainy meant many tried to forget him once the law caught up. Late one night, one of his brother's girlfriends — young, beautiful, innocent and 'a little tipsy'— came knocking at McMillan's elegant South Yarra apartment, seeking counsel for a broken heart.

McMillan recalls that he must have cut an outrageously theatrical figure that night: part Mikado, part mobster, part agony aunt. 'I was hospitable — if that is accurate for someone who answers his door at 1am wearing a $4000 Japanese bridegroom's kimono with matching pistols (silenced, of course) holstered under each arm,' he recalls, lampooning his younger self.

The guns were as much an affectation as the silk kimono. Part of a heist of several hundred weapons stolen from a South Melbourne warehouse by a robber friend, the pistols did not last long. He gave up carrying them after accidentally putting an armour-piercing round through the floorboards of a first-floor bedroom – straight through the ceiling of his father-in-law Ferdi Vigano's Brighton bar. Luckily it was a few minutes after closing time, when the place was empty.

'Guns were boys' toys for sure and not as much use as we'd hoped at that age. After Danny Mac [the late armed robber Danny MacIntosh] took down Guthrie Trading [a firearm warehouse] we all looked like cowboys. The robbery left us with repro Lugers, .357 magnums, countless .22 target pistols (those that so well went on a lathe for silencer fitting) and .38s to spare. The police were not happy and complained, in fact begged, that we be responsible as to who was allowed to purchase. They feared nutters tooled up and drunk.

'I bought a .357 Automag, a fine and expensive automatic with no gas leak so that with sub-sonic ammo, it was muted if not whisper quiet. Unfortunately my experience of the damn things was not promising. One night at dinner in Acland Street, St. Kilda, I excused myself to fetch some papers from my car. Nearby I came across five louts laying into some poor kid who was toothless and in the gutter. I took one of the pistols from my Fiat (they have a little stash glove-box), screwed on the fat silencer for effect and walked to the group and waved the thing about.

'To my surprise, it was the kid in the gutter who spoke first: "Mind yer own fucking business," he spat out, struggling to his knees. "What's it to you!"'

I went back to my meal.

'I realised bang-bangs were more trouble than they were worth. Hung up and buried, reserved only for special occasions.'

But giving up guns did not mean giving up 'the life', despite discreet warnings from a network of well-connected friends, some of them lawyers.

Looking back, the message was clear, he admits: quit before the police get serious. Even when warned of a taskforce, Operation Aries, set up to snare him and his accomplice Michael Sullivan, he ignored it. He knew they were tapping telephones but he wanted to play the game.

Drugs and money gave him false confidence. The result: after a marathon trial in 1983, a tough prison sentence imposed to send a message to intelligent, educated young people who should know better than to flout the law. Inside, he wrote a fluent inside account of prison life published by the *Australian Financial Review* but any remorse was strictly for show. Apart, he says, from his guilt over Clelia's death. If it hadn't been for him, she would never have been jailed at Fairlea, where a fire killed her – along with the South American girlfriend of his friend and partner-in-crime, Sullivan, a former world-class pole vaulter who had turned to drugs after injury crippled his athletic career.

When he was paroled in 1993, McMillan pretended to go straight but in secret plotted to beat the system. The trouble was, the system had changed, so that when he went back to his old false passport trick, the police were watching. They'd been tipped off by a former jailmate who said McMillan was 'the smartest crook he'd ever met'. But apparently not smart enough to quit.

McMillan's charm, cultured accent and intelligence grated on police. A retired detective who worked on the case told the authors: 'We let him go to Thailand and get picked up there because we thought he might get hanged.'

It was a harsh call but they almost got their wish. When Thai police, tipped off by their Australian counterparts, grabbed McMillan in possession of drugs just before Christmas in 1993, the best he could hope for would be to have the mandatory death sentence commuted to 99 years – if he survived a couple of years in irons, which many didn't.

He didn't intend to stay long enough to find out.

AS jailbreaks go, it was pure Bollywood. When McMillan checked out of the 'Bangkok Hilton' one August night in 1996, it was thought no European had successfully escaped from Klong Prem in living memory, although some inmates had been caught – or died – trying.

McMillan, then 40, had first bribed his way into a cell with four prisoners on the first floor of a two-storey block. Then began an elaborately nonchalant period of preparation. They built a bookshelf in the cell with a heavy plank that would be vital to the plan. In a craft workshop elsewhere in the prison they made robust wooden frames for pictures that would never be framed. And through a network of discreet friends – including a loyal girlfriend, a jazz singer, and an outwardly respectable Melbourne accountant – he organised various items that would be vital when the day came. Among them were the smuggled hacksaw blades he and a strong helper would use to weaken the window bars on the night of the escape. After breaking a couple of bars, they wedged the plank between two others to form an overhanging beam. Then they looped his 'rope' – a coil of webbing used for craft – over the plank well away from the outside wall, so McMillan could let himself down silently, without touching the loose tiles on the wall and creating a racket that would alarm the guards – or nosy inmates. First, of course, he had to squeeze his lean, oiled torso through the gap. His Scandinavian accomplice stayed behind, preferring to face punishment for assisting than take the risk of being killed or captured in the escape attempt.

McMillan slipped past sleeping guards to the hobby room, retrieved tools and other 'props', including a roll of heavy gaffer tape that he used to rig a ladder by taping the picture frames to bamboo poles — and scaled the inner five-metre wall. Then he cut barbed wire, crawled under razor wire, carried his ladder across open ground and used it to cross the stinking open sewer inside the outer wall. Finally, he scaled the outer wall, praying as he climbed over electrified cables that rubber gloves and rubber soles would save him. He lowered himself the final nine-metre drop with the rope just as the sun rose.

So far, so lucky. But as a Westerner he risked challenge from guards arriving for work. The fake, black-painted balsa-wood 'handgun' he'd carried as a bluff was little use in daylight. It was time for his other secret weapon — a compact umbrella.

Working on the theory that desperate escapees do not use umbrellas, he opened the brolly, held it close to his face and strolled off to find a taxi. It worked – but there were plenty of barriers ahead.

'It was astonishing to feel how quickly I divorced myself from the prison standing across the road that morning, looking at the building,' he later told the authors. 'I knew that it was over, in the past, and in some odd way that all along I'd been a volunteer.'

After picking up a doctored passport from a safe house, he went to the airport, using two taxis to confuse the trail.

He directed the taxi to the arrivals area, suspecting the departure door would be watched, then prayed that the cash card he was carrying would deliver enough currency from an ATM to buy a ticket. The first machine he tried didn't work. With seconds to spare he got the cash, bought a ticket and at 10.20am was on a Lufthansa flight to Singapore, boarding as prison guards arrived at the airport to look for him. Then he vanished.

Back at Klong Prem, cellmates were beaten for collusion; warders faced disciplinary action. Eight remaining Australian prisoners got leg chains.

The risk had been enormous – but he'd always thought it was worth it. 'In Bangkok I would have received a death penalty which would have been reduced to life (or 99 years) after about two years on death row,' he told the authors. 'That meant being chained to a wall for the duration wearing welded leg irons.'

In the Australian Parliament seven months later, the future Australian Attorney-General, Robert McClelland, was praising the good work of Australia's Embassy in Thailand when he said something that still amuses McMillan: '... a prisoner ... escaped from the Thai jail in quite exceptional and athletic circumstances. In terms of mere escape, it was really quite an achievement. He took the opportunity after his escape of dropping a note to the Australian embassy to thank them for all their tremendous work and said that he hoped he had not caused them any embarrassment by his escape.'

By then, the only westerner ever to break out of Klong Prem and into Hansard had reached London via a rendezvous with his lover in France after hiding with powerful friends in the remote Baluchistan province of Pakistan, near the Afghani border. And he was plotting his next move from the city in which he had been born.

CAULFIELD Grammar has produced its share of the worthy and the notable – lord mayors, captains of industry, leaders in business and bureaucracy, politics and the professions, respected members of rowing clubs, racing clubs and Rotary clubs. But even the best schools have their wayward sons.

In Caulfield's case, there was Christopher Skase, who flew high, dreamed of being a film mogul, then fell to Earth – exposed as a flim-flam man, disgraced before dying in exile. And there is Nick Cave, the Lou Reed of Wangaratta, whose musical and lyrical brilliance survived the dark influence of drugs to make his mark in the wider world.

Then there is David McMillan a.k.a. Westlake, Dearing, Poulter, Magilton, Rayner, Elton, Knox, Hunter and many more aliases.

Like the young Skase, McMillan was a dreamer and schemer with an eye for the main chance, an ear for information and a head for figures. Like Cave, he was a restless, creative spirit drawn to the dark side. He succumbed to the worst of both impulses — the desire for fast money, the weakness for drugs.

Bright, ambitious and a drug user, McMillan was barely 20 when he took on a growth industry. Instead of trying computers or honing talents as a photographer, cameraman and writer, he became a drug trafficker. At least, that's the prosecution case; when McMillan was arrested in the early 1980s, his defence argued he was a harmless user who subsidised his habit with gold and gem smuggling. A jury acquitted on all but one charge of conspiracy to import heroin — but the judge didn't buy it, sentencing him and two accomplices to 17 years.

That was in 1983. The trial of McMillan and his associates — the former elite athlete Michael Sullivan and Thai national Supahaus Chowdury — had run almost six months, and it took the jury a record eight days to reach its verdict. The result disappointed McMillan but didn't surprise him. Before the trial, he orchestrated an audacious scheme to escape from Pentridge Prison in a hijacked helicopter, part of a plan involving disguises, an interstate truck ride hidden in cargo, a sea-going boat and a light plane.

A tip to police foiled what would have been another James Bond episode for a man who lived life as if it were an action screenplay, him playing the sort of rogue who's supposed to get the girl, the money and the last laugh. The real story is a little bleaker.

HIS mother is old and a little vague now, dozing away her days in a Brighton unit after being the life of the party for decades. He still calls her 'Rosie'. When she married his father John in the 1950s, she turned heads. In 1950s photographs she looks like Princess Grace of Monaco. They were Australians transplanted to London. John McMillan, after distinguished war service, managed Rediffusion Television and went on to receive a CBE. By the time David was two, the marriage was unravelling and the raffish Rosie had met an Italian film producer who sent her (with David and his sister Debbie) to Australia to have his baby, promising he'd send for them. He never did.

Rosie and her brood did the best they could.

'I suppose I had about five stepfathers,' McMillan recalls. 'Surely, the most understanding would have to have been George Arnaud — French George — who, until he met my mother, was a quite contented bachelor with a successful fashion business in Flinders Lane.'

Arnaud looked after the two older children in his big Kooyong Road house while Rosie and baby Simon 'decamped to Lake Eyre to play cook for the land-speed record trials for Donald Campbell' in 1964.

'She went for the strong, silent types,' McMillan says drily. One of Rosie's consorts was the infamous abortionist, Dr Jim Troup, and she finally ended up with George Tsindos, long time proprietor of Florentino's restaurant. A regular at social events with the millionaire set, Rosie had no money of her own. McMillan suspects that childhood anxiety about money and his mother made him fixated on providing lavishly — regardless of how he did it. While sister Debbie worked hard and half-brother Simon would become a respected journalist and television producer, David was always willing to take short cuts.

At 12, he earned a weekly wage – and schoolyard fame – presenting the 'Peters Junior News' on television. After switching from Prahran High to Caulfield Grammar he directed and starred in an action movie spoof his classmates still laugh about. In it, he escapes 'jail' with a replica pistol, foretelling what would happen in real life 25 years later.

It's as if, says a lawyer who once represented him and became his friend, he was unable to separate real life from the reel unspooling in his mind.

For someone who impressed most people he met as charming, clever and generous, the young McMillan developed – or affected – some bad habits early in life.

When he arrived at Caulfield Grammar in fourth form in 1971 – the form above Nick Cave – he seemed, one former classmate recalls, 'from another world'.

The teenage McMillan didn't blend in. Or he didn't want to. By an accident of birth – he was born overseas and his parents were divorced – he was different in ways he didn't try to hide, from his smart accent to his subversive attitude. It struck some of his classmates later that his cultivation of differences between himself and the herd was an affectation that came to define his character and behaviour. Hard work and obeying rules was for others. He was too cool.

While most families lived ordinary lives in conventional suburban homes, McMillan lived by then in an apartment in Alma Road, St Kilda, with his mother and the two other children. This whiff of bohemia fascinated schoolmates who caught a glimpse of life with Rosie. She seemed, as one put it later, 'a bit more glamorous than our mothers, with a cheeky sense of humour'.

Meanwhile, at school, McMillan fanned his own notoriety and showed an early taste for the best things money could buy.

'He was a dodgy bugger,' recalls one classmate. 'He gave the impression of living life on the edge,' recalls another. From scamming free canteen lunches to using credit cards he said he'd 'found', he made his mark in ways that teachers and parents frowned on. 'He wasn't a good influence,' judges one classmate, 'but he was ever interesting.'

McMillan helped publish the student newspaper. In the one photograph of him in *The Grammarian* he sits at the centre of a group, dark hair curling around his lean face, holding a copy of MAD magazine as he looks coolly at the camera.

Not everyone fell for McMillan's winning ways. A veteran housemaster, 'Kanga' Corden, took a classmate called Paul Tankard aside one day and warned 'that I wasn't doing myself any favours hanging around with the likes of McMillan,' Tankard told the authors. 'Kanga had McMillan's number, all right.'

It was a timely warning. When year 11 finished, McMillan vanished from the school. His classmates didn't know exactly why at the time but it turned out he had been forging prescriptions — and cheques. The following year, like many another wayward youngster, he found himself studying (or not studying) his final year at Taylor's College.

Taylor's was, and is, a Melbourne institution in both senses of the word. For years, it has offered an alternative route to tertiary education for those prepared to pay – and who, for various reasons, are not enrolled elsewhere.

Among Taylor's annual intakes of hardworking students was a sprinkling of more colourful characters, rebels against mainstream education. Some of these were failures having another try; others had been expelled or had left elsewhere under a cloud. In the class of 1973, David McMillan fell into this category. The following year it was a tough kid from Marcellin College called Alphonse Gangitano, later to become a notorious gangster and, later still, dead famous, shot by an underworld associate in what would become a great career move. In death, he became the 'star' he always wanted to be in life, albeit played by local hero Vince Colosimo rather than the Hollywood heart throbs Alphonse fantasised about.

Unlike Gangitano, McMillan was never going to be a gunman or a bash artist. It wasn't his style. But, for all his intelligence, he wasn't destined for an academic career, either. He skipped classes, forged passes, and that was the end of his formal education. At 17, he was picked up for passing dud cheques and was already on a road leading to what a media lawyer friend later wryly described as 'his Midnight Express life'.

An eclectic and voracious reader, McMillan devoured information he thought he could use. The boy who'd regularly duped the school tuckshop was graduating to the big time, still by trying to beat the system.

He was later to try the more cerebral criminal arts – forgery, disguise, fraud and smuggling – but, at bottom, he was a confidence man. Everything else he did was based on his ability to befriend and to deceive. But, like all con artists, he had to convince himself before he could convince others. If he imagined himself as a character from *The Day of the Jackal*, there was also some Walter Mitty in his readiness to lace reality with fantasy. It was hard to know where one starts and the other ends.

There are people in Melbourne – otherwise sensible people at the top of their professions – who firmly believe that McMillan was a misguided genius who was, however briefly, a whiz kid in the advertising industry in his early 20s. Proof of this, they claim, is that he was the creative force behind several well-known television advertisements in the mid-to-late 1970s.

Whether McMillan even worked in advertising at all is a moot point – and, if he did, he was never prominent. People in the industry don't remember him, and yet he told friends he'd been responsible for successful Mars Bar and RC Cola commercials, among others. A close relative also remembers things differently, saying he had never held down a job for long, even if his knowledge of photography and film might have won him enough work on the fringes of advertising to weave a believable tale from a thread of truth. The truth, says the relative grimly, is that his greatest talent was using deception to avoid work.

'He was very kind in some ways, but cruel in others – and always a shocking liar. He was always trying to con other people and very lazy.' An example: as a primary school student he was offered pocket money to weed the garden, but he immediately tried to persuade a neighbour's child to do the chore for him – at a reduced rate. He didn't want the work, only the profit. 'And he got caught doing it,' says the relative. 'That sums him up.'

Ask him now, and he says that after a year at Taylor's, he dabbled in working as a film projectionist. And that a part-time job at a dodgy city cinema – which catered to 'the raincoat' brigade – put him in touch with the fringes of the underworld. He worked with girlfriends of safe-crackers and thieves who had turned to selling drugs when police surveillance cramped their style. His connections with student pro-marijuana activists bridged two worlds: hippie culture and hard core crime.

McMillan's first serious crime was to smuggle hashish from India in a 1950s Grundig radio. 'A fairly avuncular customs guy pulled the radio out of the case. You could smell the hash. He looked at the passport and then at me and said, "Take your radio, get going and never let me see you again". I didn't realise he was letting me go because he didn't want to wreck my life. (At the time) I thought I was wonderful. So suddenly I was in charge of international hanky panky.' It wasn't until much later he realised he'd been too arrogant to understand he'd been given a second chance. Perhaps it would have saved him many years in jail had he been arrested that day. Instead, he turned to importing heroin, using multiple passports and a friendly travel agent.

'I came back to rose petals and red carpet,' he jokes. First alone, then with Sullivan, he made obscene amounts of money — but never enough to quit. His own belief is that authorities started watching after he imported a wildly expensive car ('a reproduction 1930s Bugatti', he says derisively) from the US, using a false name and passport. But it might be that he came under notice in more ways than one. You could not make – and spend – the sort of money he was without attracting some attention. Especially if you happened to live near a wily veteran policeman.

LONG after the old copper had retired from 'the job' and taken up bowls, the force still used him as an example to recruits of how curiosity and alertness can crack a case wide open.

The lesson went like this. Back in 1980, like neighbours everywhere, the policeman was curious about the new people in the house next door. They were young, good-looking, smart – and conspicuous spenders. The woman drove a Porsche and her boyfriend a Fiat. They had friends with a late-model Rover, an Alfa Romeo and a big American car, and they came and went at all times of day and night. Glance through a window and you'd glimpse the latest in electrical gear and cameras.

Then there was the landscaping and the renovations – even in an affluent Melbourne bayside suburb like this, it seemed like over-capitalising. A sign, perhaps, like the 'grass castles' in the vineyards of Mildura and Griffith, of black money with nowhere else to go.

But the really suspicious thing about the people next door, it seemed to the old cop, was that they didn't seem to work. They would disappear for days or weeks at a time, but when they returned they lived the indolent lives of spoiled teenagers with bottomless allowances. Late to bed, late to rise, eating out most nights. Their main past-time was to amuse themselves, it seemed to him.

The policeman started jotting down car registration numbers, and running the usual checks on the names that came up. He passed his suspicions on, up the chain of command.

First came the surveillance and the intelligence gathering. The policeman's nomadic neighbours were near enough to 'cleanskins' but if they lacked criminal records, they were on the way to getting them. For a start, they were using heroin – and dealing in it to support not only their habits, but their affluence. It was soon clear they had more than cars and cameras – they had properties everywhere.

Heroin brought them into contact with people for whom treachery was a way to survive. It was only a matter of time before a word was dropped discreetly in an interview room in return for bail or a blind eye. And the word was that the private school crew with the European cars did more than use the stuff and sell it to others. They were importing it.

It wasn't as if McMillan and his crew didn't get some warning. His lawyer called him in one day to say 'big people' had warned him they couldn't overlook it any more. A taskforce was being formed. McMillan arrogantly insisted the police had suspicions but no evidence. He said he had not yet invested enough to retire. Besides, he had 'business partners' who wanted enough for their retirement. The temptation for 'easy money' was too great.

It couldn't last. After a cat and mouse game with investigators culminating in a James Bond car chase, he and Sullivan lost ten years in jail and the women they loved. Then, instead of going straight, came the Thailand debacle in 1993, followed by the great escape of 1996.

After that — the missing years.

CUT to 2009. The location is Chislehurst, a village turned suburb south of London in Kent. It's outer commuter belt, where collars are white, lanes leafy and mortgages hefty. Richmal Crompton, who wrote the William books, lived here. Now David McMillan does, too, in a two-storey brick house with a Porsche in the drive, Asian antiques in the hall, French champagne in the refrigerator, a pair of pedigree dogs on the couch.

It all, he says, belongs to his partner — a Londoner called Jeanette who fell for him while visiting her husband in prison in Pakistan ten years ago, where McMillan had been locked up during his border hopping years. Her husband, accused of smuggling tonnes of hashish, lost both the case and his wife. Her two teenage daughters now regard McMillan as a father figure.

For years, old friends and family members in Australia grew suddenly vague when McMillan's name was raised, but now his 'retirement' means he can drop the secret life he led after going over the wall at Klong Prem. Luckily, he says poker-faced, he faces a death sentence in Thailand, where they lash condemned men before machine-gunning them. It means Britain will not breach its anti-capital punishment policy by extraditing him. And although he 'owes' Victoria a few months of parole, it is not enough to trigger extradition. He is safe if he stays quietly in Britain.

At 53, he says, he has given up his wicked ways 'to turn my hand to trade'. It's almost honest. He tinkers in a shed, restoring furniture. Well, not so much restoring, he admits, as transforming wooden dining room sets bought from local charity shops into gleaming 'French' artefacts. Easy work for someone who has built so many containers with hidden smuggling compartments.

'A spray of antique white eggshell, a layer of matt finish and hand-brushed gold lines topped by that distressed effect made to imitate 100 years of family living,' he purrs.

The profit margin is good, he says: £200 ($A390) purchase, £150 of materials and a sticker saying 'WAS £1750

— NOW £1100.' It's not the Sopranos but it's a living. Proof that it's hard to keep a bad man down.

In 2008, he wrote a book: a self-mocking journey through the violence and despair of prison, climaxing with the jailbreak. As for what happened between Bangkok and the present — being harboured by a Baluchistan warlord, arrested in Pakistan and banged up in Sweden — he says he's saving that for his next book.

BIBLIOGRAPHY

Apart from original research of newspaper files and interviews with sources too numerous to mention on both sides of the law, the authors have drawn on the assistance of Sydney journalist Ray Chesterton for those chapters relating to the Wood Royal Commission. As acknowledged in the text, we have relied heavily on the work of Deborah Locke and Trevor Haken with Sean Padraic where appropriate.

For their generous guidance we are grateful to Mick Kennedy, David Waterhouse, Chris Murphy, Stephen Gibb, Scott Paillas and Dylan Welch. We thank Harry Rekas and Danie Sprague for nailing the right images.

Chenoweth, Neil: *Packer's Lunch* (Allen & Unwin)

Dale, John: *Huckstepp: A dangerous life* (Allen & Unwin)

Drane, Robert: *Fighters by Trade* (ABC Books).

Goodsir, Darren: *In the Line of Fire* (Allen & Unwin)

Haken, Trevor with Sean Padraic: *Sympathy for the Devil* (ABC Books).

Lennox, Gina and Rush, Frances: *People of the Cross* (Simon & Schuster).

Locke, Deborah: *Watching the Detectives* (HarperCollins).

McMillan, David: *Escape* (Monsoon Books).

Noble, Tom and Smith, Neddy: *Neddy* (Kerr Publishing).

Reeves, Tony: *Mr Sin* (Allen & Unwin).

Reeves, Tony: *Mr Big* (Allen & Unwin).

Saffron, Alan: *Gentle Satan* (Penguin).

Silvester, John and Rule, Andrew: *Tough: 101 Australian Gangsters* and the *Underbelly* series of books (Floradale & Sly Ink).

THE CAST

ROLE	ARTIST
John Ibrahim	Firass Dirani
Kim Hollingsworth	Emma Booth
'Eddie Gould'	Diarmid Heidenreich
'Chook' Fowler	Damian Garvey
'Joe Dooley'	Will Traval
George Freeman	Peter O'Brien
Georgina Freeman	Georgina Haig
Jayne Haken	Natalie Bassingthwaighte
Trevor Haken	Dieter Brummer
Lennie McPherson	John McNeil
Louie Bayeh	Steve Bastoni
Bill Bayeh	Hazem Shammas
Deb Webb (Locke)	Cheree Cassidy